W9-AMA-964

# Living
# with
# Nuclear
# Weapons

# THE HARVARD UNIVERSITY NUCLEAR STUDY GROUP, AUTHORS OF *LIVING WITH NUCLEAR WEAPONS*

ALBERT CARNESALE: Professor of Public Policy and Academic Dean of Harvard's John F. Kennedy School of Government. Dr. Carnesale served on the U.S. delegation to the Strategic Arms Limitation Talks (1970–72) and as the head of the U.S. delegation to the International Nuclear Fuel Cycle Evaluation (1978–80).

PAUL DOTY: Director of the Center for Science and International Affairs and Mallinckrodt Professor of Biochemistry, Harvard University. Dr. Doty was involved in the Manhattan Project and was a member of the President's Science Advisory Committee in the Kennedy and Johnson Administrations.

STANLEY HOFFMANN: Chairman of the Center for European Studies and Douglas Dillon Professor of the Civilization of France, Harvard University. Dr. Hoffmann's recent books include *Duties Beyond Borders* (Syracuse Press, 1981) and *Primacy or World Order: American Foreign Policy Since the Cold War* (McGraw-Hill, 1978).

SAMUEL P. HUNTINGTON: Director of the Center for International Affairs and Clarence Dillon Professor of International Affairs, Harvard University. Dr. Huntington was the Coordinator of Security Planning for the National Security Council (1977–78). His most recent book is *American Politics: The Promise of Disharmony* (Harvard University Press, 1981).

JOSEPH S. NYE, JR.: Professor of Government, Harvard University. Dr. Nye was Deputy to the Under Secretary of State for Security Assistance from 1977–79 and is the author of, among other works, *Power and Interdependence* (co-authored with Robert Keohane, Little Brown, 1977) and *Energy and Security* (co-edited with David Deese, Ballinger, 1980).

SCOTT D. SAGAN: Staff Director of the project. Mr. Sagan is a Ph.D. candidate in the Department of Government, Harvard University.

DEREK BOK: Author of the Foreword. Mr. Bok is the President of Harvard University.

# Living with Nuclear Weapons

The Harvard Nuclear
Study Group:

**Albert Carnesale**
**Paul Doty**
**Stanley Hoffmann**
**Samuel P. Huntington**
**Joseph S. Nye, Jr.**
**Scott D. Sagan**

With a Foreword by Derek Bok

HARVARD UNIVERSITY PRESS
CAMBRIDGE, MASSACHUSETTS
AND LONDON, ENGLAND
1983

*Copyright © 1983 by The Harvard Nuclear Study Group*
*All rights reserved*
*Printed in the United States of America*
*10 9 8 7 6 5 4 3 2 1*

*This book is printed on acid-free paper, and its*
*binding materials have been chosen for strength and durability.*

ISBN 0-674-53665-7

# Contents

# Preface

As scholars we spend much of our professional time at Harvard University teaching and writing about nuclear weapons and world politics. Some of us have been thinking about nuclear weapons for three decades; others are more recent recruits. Some have dealt with these problems in government service and consulting; others have kept more of an academic distance. Some have lived in a world without nuclear weapons; others have not. But we all share the same concern: Can humanity continue living with nuclear weapons? And we have each spent many hours discussing that concern with our students, our friends, and our families.

As Derek Bok remarks in his Foreword, educators often treat transcendent social issues through such temporary devices as "teach-ins" or by professional writings aimed at other specialists. Rarely do scholars try to write about nuclear issues in the same way as they discuss these concerns with neighbors and families. But nuclear weapons are too important to be left just to classrooms and specialized journals. We all need both to ask and to understand the following important questions: First, what is the nature of our nuclear predicament? Second, what nuclear weaponry currently exists and why? Third, what can be done?

The answers to each of these questions could easily fill separate books, but that was never our aim. Nor is this book a treatise on the horrifying effects of nuclear weapons, or on all the complexities of international politics and foreign policy. It does not present an extensive analysis of

ix

the economic costs of arms programs, the bureaucratic processes of the American government, or politics within the Soviet Union. Rather, it is an honest effort to provide both the necessary information and an overall approach to aid concerned citizens in addressing the central problem of our time. The book focuses particularly upon nuclear problems facing the United States, but we hope the discussion can be helpful to people in other countries as well.

Sometimes our discussion necessarily touches on technical issues. When this happens, we have tried to make them readily comprehensible to the average reader. We have also used only unclassified information. Though concerned citizens sometimes assume that nuclear issues are too top secret to be understood by the public, in our experience this is simply not true. In a society as open as ours, classified information is not only rarely essential in order to comprehend an issue, but in the past, top secret information has sometimes turned out to be incorrect.

As specialists and as citizens, we each have our own views on the various issues we discuss. This book is a collective effort and does not represent the full views of any single author. Indeed, we do not always agree among ourselves, but since our purpose is less to convince the reader of the correctness of a single point of view than to help him or her think through nuclear problems, we have treated such issues by explaining why we disagree. Many readers may not share our beliefs or accept our conclusions. But we hope we have been fair when presenting alternative views and clear when explaining how we came to our conclusions.

Although this book is an endeavor equally shared among its authors, the reader might be interested to know the process that we used. In May 1982 President Bok approached five scholars at the Center for International Affairs and the Center for Science and International Affairs, who were actively teaching and writing about nuclear weapons. This group developed an overall outline, discussed it, and then each member developed detailed chapter outlines for further discussion. At that point, Scott D. Sagan, a Ph.D. candidate in Harvard's Department of Government, joined the group and directed a staff consisting of William Durch and Daniel Poneman. They have ably assisted Mr. Sagan in the critical task of fleshing out first drafts of the chapters. The entire group met regularly to discuss these drafts and subsequently shared the responsibility of writing second, third, and sometimes fourth drafts. The importance of Mr. Sagan's role is indicated by the decision to list him as a full co-author.

We also wish to acknowledge a number of debts. Most important is the one we owe to Derek Bok as the stimulus and catalyst for this book. Barbara Eyman and Mary Ann Wells typed and retyped the numerous drafts; and James Goldgeier and Larry Alberts served the project as research assistants. We are also grateful to the following people for reading and commenting upon, though not necessarily agreeing with, an earlier draft of the manuscript: Richard Betts, Robert Bowie, McGeorge Bundy, Abram Chayes, the Reverend Bryan Hehir, William Kincade, Josef Joffe, Richard Pipes, George Rathjens, Henry Rowen, Thomas Schelling, Helmut Sonnenfeldt, and Jeremy Stone.

We also wish to add in fairness to our colleagues at Harvard University that this book does not represent the opinions of the entire university on nuclear weapons issues. It is our book. We do not pretend to speak for our colleagues, many of whom are expert in and have strong views on the subjects addressed herein. All shortcomings of the book are, of course, our own.

The Harvard Nuclear Study Group

Albert Carnesale
Paul Doty
Stanley Hoffmann
Samuel P. Huntington
Joseph S. Nye, Jr.
Scott D. Sagan

March 1983

# Foreword

The origins of this book date back to a spring morning in 1982 when I discovered that James Reston had devoted his Sunday column to the growing nuclear arms debate. As he put it, "One of the many questions about the future of nuclear weapons is whether the people of the United States will get enough facts on this immensely complicated military and moral issue for the searching inquiry the subject requires. In short, will it be decided by government decision, by public education, or by political demonstration? . . . So far, the demonstrators have outnumbered the educators. . . ."

After mulling over the possibilities for improving on this record, Mr. Reston speculated on the role that universities might play and ended with a quotation from the president of the Rockefeller Foundation, Richard Lyman. In Dr. Lyman's words, "Almost the worst thing the universities could do would be to opt for a few easy and dramatic gestures, satisfying outlets for our frustrations that might make us all feel a nice warm glow of self-righteousness, but would do nothing to advance our basic understanding of the problem."

Mr. Reston's concerns can be traced to a dilemma raised in the 1920s by his mentor, Walter Lippmann. It was Lippmann who first grappled seriously with the problem of how democracy could function when the general public was so poorly informed about important national issues. Although he spent his life in journalism, he had little faith that newspapers could give the citizenry an adequate understanding of public issues. In his mind, newspapers presented a disjointed picture of the world, offering bits of arresting information about crises, colorful events, and matters of human interest, but rarely combining these fragments into a clear and comprehensive whole.

The more Walter Lippmann pondered the problem, the more pessimistic he became. Having despaired of achieving an informed electorate, he initially pinned his hopes on the expert and the experienced public servant, but eventually gave up on them as well. In the end, he could only observe that "the problems that vex democracy seem unmanageable by democratic methods."

Few Americans have been quite so pessimistic. Most of us simply ignore the problem or muse about the prospects for the popular media to do a better job of informing the public. What James Reston introduces is the thought that *universities* can have a role in helping educate the body politic to think more effectively about important issues facing the country.

This suggestion may not seem particularly new. After all, individual professors write books and articles on national issues. And faculties give courses for their students that touch on questions of current public concern. But universities have hardly conceived of taking on an institutional responsibility to educate the public as a whole. This is a task that they have traditionally left to newspapers, television, magazines, and other media with the experience and the capacity to reach huge audiences.

And yet perhaps this division of responsibility is a bit too neat. In fact, universities have been expanding their audience in recent years by reaching out to groups quite different from their traditional student bodies. At Harvard, for example, in addition to our 15,000 regular students, more than 40,000 other people come to receive some kind of formal instruction ranging from a few days to a few years in duration. Many of them come seeking help in preparing for new and difficult challenges: newly elected congressmen, rising business executives, government officials, lawyers, judges, practicing physicians. Most come to Cambridge for instruction, but some study in facilities abroad or travel the high seas to distant points of interest in the company of our professors.

Although this growing audience is still composed of

groups of students of one kind or another, in at least one instance we have gone beyond any reasonable definition of student and have attempted as an institution to educate the public as a whole. The example to which I refer is the *Harvard Health Letter*—a publication of the medical school which currently enjoys a circulation of more than 300,000. This letter is not a scholarly publication. It announces no new discoveries and advocates no controversial theses. It simply sets forth what is well established and what is still in dispute about issues of health that concern ordinary people—whether to have an annual checkup, whether to avoid foods that contain cholesterol, whether chemotherapy or radical surgery or X-ray treatment is most suitable for various kinds of cancer. The point of the enterprise is to help readers make sense of what can often seem a confusing and contradictory jumble of reports and assertions about matters vital to their well-being.

If one takes account of these new audiences and new educational responsibilities, Mr. Reston's question does not seem so revolutionary after all. We decided to take it seriously and to do our best to define what functions we might perform in order to contribute to the public debate over nuclear arms. We concluded that we could do at least three things.

First of all, we could inform our own community through courses, lectures, and public meetings so that discussions of these important matters could proceed on a basis of careful analysis and informed judgment. This is an obvious goal for a university, but it has not always been achieved in the case of controversial issues of deep concern to college students.

In addition, we could reach out to reporters who have the task of informing the public on issues of national security and arms control. Already, nuclear debates have sprung up in cities and towns and even regions of the country that have previously shown little interest in such issues. In such localities, newsmen have often found themselves reporting on an extraordinarily complicated set of issues for which they had little preparation. If we were willing to offer courses for congressmen, for local officials, for hospital trustees, and school principals, then surely we could find room to invite journalists to a program where we could offer them something of the history, the technical background, the issues and arguments that underlie the current arms debate while also giving them material and reading lists to help them learn more about the subject after leaving Cambridge. To date, we have offered three such programs and will offer more if the demand for them continues.

Our most ambitious thought was to try to supply the public as a whole with an objective account of the basic facts about nuclear arms control that sorted out the various issues and proposals and presented the arguments for and against each position. Properly done, such material might be useful, just as our medical letter has been useful in the field of health. In both cases, the public is confronted with a confusing barrage of news stories, speeches, and proposals of every kind. In both instances, the public has grown distrustful of conventional sources of information. What concerned citizens lack above all is a credible body of knowledge and analysis with which to evaluate each partisan statement and eventually arrive at a thoughtful, informed opinion. What we might try to do, therefore, is not tell people *what* to think but give them the facts and ideas that will help them think more effectively for themselves.

This book is the product of these deliberations, and I am enormously grateful to my colleagues—Al Carnesale, Paul Doty, Stanley Hoffmann, Sam Huntington, Joe Nye, and Scott Sagan—for agreeing to write it. As one would expect of such a novel venture, the final product is not exactly what I envisaged at the outset. At an early stage, the authors concluded that they could not refrain entirely from expressing their own opinions without making the book too bland and undiscriminating in its treatment of arguments and ideas. Even so, the authors have attempted to be true to the primary purpose of the volume: to help interested people learn *how* to think for themselves about issues of nuclear arms rather than to promote the views of the authors. Thus they have tried to include all the essential information that lay readers need in order to understand the subject, and to present fairly all the significant arguments on all sides of every important issue. When they express an opinion, they are careful to label it as such and to point out views in conflict with their own.

Readers may ask whether the final product is a "Harvard book" with some sort of official endorsement from the university. The answer is clear. Harvard is a collection of many individuals possessing many different opinions. There is no way in which a single book can adequately represent their views. I can, however, express my personal belief that Harvard has a role in helping people think about important public issues. In seeking to carry out this purpose, the book has my strong personal endorsement. The opinions of the authors, of course, are theirs alone and do not have any official status within the university.

In the end, I recognize, any effort to discuss the problem of nuclear arms is bound to be controversial. Those who have strong views on one side or the other are likely to claim, however hard the authors try, that the presentation is biased and unfair, that important facts are omitted, and that telling arguments have been ignored. With the prospect of such criticism, cynics will ask why anyone could be foolish enough to attempt such a book, for cynics have always taken a dim view of educating the public. Nevertheless, we should not forget that it was an informed public opinion that pressed for an end to slavery; it was an informed public opinion that sought an end to child labor; it was an informed public opinion that helped persuade politicians to protect the environment, to integrate schools and lunch counters, and even to place a limited ban on the testing of nuclear weapons. If we believe in democracy, it is surely a worthy enterprise for universities to do their best to inform the people. And if they do, there is surely no more important subject with which to begin than an issue that bears so directly on our very survival on this planet.

Derek Bok
January 1983

# PART I

## The Nuclear Predicament

# 1

# The Nuclear Debate: What Are the Problems?

In the Greek myth, Prometheus stole fire from the gods and gave it as a gift to mankind. His punishment was a life of recurrent fear: he was chained to a pillar high in the mountains where every morning, day after day, year after year, the vultures descended. Still, every night his wounds would heal. Thus, for his entire life, Prometheus faced each dawn with the memory of fire and the fear of pain.

Modern man has been like Prometheus in the night, ever since we stole the fire of the atom on July 16, 1945. At five thirty in the morning, in the desert near Alamogordo, New Mexico, the first atomic bomb was detonated. Witnesses said the blast lit the sky like "several suns at midday," a flash of fire so intense that a blind woman saw the light. An immense fireball rose ten thousand feet before it dimmed. Soon came a hot blast of air and then, an observer wrote, a "strong, sustained, awesome roar which warned of doomsday and made us feel that we puny things were blasphemous to dare tamper with the forces heretofore reserved to the Almighty." The atomic age had begun.

In early August, the fire was rekindled over the Japanese cities of Hiroshima and Nagasaki, engulfing both in flames and changing forever the nature of all-out warfare.

3

Within a generation leading industrial nations could build still larger weapons and could deliver them anywhere on earth. All the cities of any nation could be turned to ash by the ultimate military weapon. There was no defense against the atomic fire.

Today, two nations have built tens of thousands of nuclear weapons. Three others have accumulated hundreds. No nation has used its atomic arsenal since 1945; many could do so in the future.

The consequences of using just a single nuclear weapon are difficult to comprehend today. Even the fates of Hiroshima and Nagasaki can no longer serve as a guide, for most modern nuclear weapons are 3 to 50 times as powerful as the bombs of 1945. It has been estimated that a 1-megaton bomb exploded a mile above the center of Detroit would kill approximately 500,000 people and injure some 600,000 others. A similar blast over Leningrad could cause 900,000 deaths and over 1 million injuries. The use of a few hundred such weapons on urban targets could destroy even the largest nation as a functioning society. Recovery would be highly problematic; at best, it could take generations.

The human race has never faced such a danger. Because of the horror of it each individual necessarily resists thoroughly incorporating these nightmare visions into the way he or she looks at the world. Since the nuclear age began in 1945, this resistance has been apparent: people have alternated between political arousal against the terrible possibility of war and apathy or denial of it so that they could pursue their daily lives and for a time be oblivious to the shadow that is always with them.

Now, in many Western industrialized countries, the public is in a state of political arousal, due to a heightened sense of fear. Inevitably, a search for an escape or relief will follow. This search can take three directions: first, a return to denying that nuclear dangers exist; second, finding refuge in simplistic, unexamined solutions; third, a commitment to finding ways to more secure grounds that take into account the complexities of the situation, yet promise a less threatening future. The aim of this book is to examine what is involved in the last alternative.

## FEAR AND FIRE

Why doesn't mankind simply return the fire to the gods?

Why not abolish nuclear weapons? Why not cleanse this small planet of these deadly poisons? Because we cannot. Mankind's nuclear innocence, once lost, cannot be regained. The discovery of nuclear weapons, like the discovery of fire itself, lies behind us on the trajectory of history: it cannot be undone. Even if all nuclear arsenals were destroyed, the knowledge of how to reinvent them would remain and could be put to use in any of a dozen or more nations. The atomic fire cannot be extinguished. The fear of its use will remain a part of the human psyche for the rest of human history.

This fear is realistic and must not be forgotten. It can prevent complacency and produce prudence. It is almost certain that such fears have served as the major restraint against the use of nuclear weapons since 1945. American and Soviet leaders, even in the midst of confrontations, have been most careful not to use the weapons at their command. Indeed, they have seen to it that American and Soviet troops have not met in direct combat for fear that fighting might escalate to nuclear war. The longer this situation continues, the more firmly the tradition of non-use is established.

But even this positive effect of fear must not obscure the fact that fear is never the substitute for policy. In a sufficiently severe crisis, fear might be forgotten, prudence put aside, and drastic actions taken. Nuclear war could begin through accident, misunderstanding, or miscalculation in ways that fear could not negate. Therefore, nuclear nations, individually and collectively, need to develop policies and practices which address all the conceivable routes through which nuclear war might develop even though the basis for these routes is built on fear.

Atomic fire has become an inescapable part of the human heritage. Wisely controlled, it will remain unused in war and can prevent the reoccurrence of large-scale conventional conflict. Unwisely attended, it will break forth at some unpredictable time and consume much of humanity.

All governments and all individuals, experts and the public alike, have the obligation to strive together in order to succeed in the task of preventing nuclear war. This is surely the most demanding challenge that humanity has ever had to face. The obligation falls particularly hard on the citizens of the United States, for it was here that the fire was brought forth.

## THE GROWING PUBLIC ROLE

The growth of public concern with nuclear weapons issues in the early 1980s, especially in Western Europe and the United States, has been unprecedented in scope and endurance. Previous arousals of public interest seemed to relate to specific issues: the early protests of the Committee on Nuclear Disarmament in Britain centered on the deployment of Britain's own nuclear force; in the late 1960s, protest in the United States centered on the placement of anti-ballistic missiles in suburban areas. The present revival likely had its origins in the prolonged negotiations of SALT II and the anticlimax of its not being ratified. In addition, people felt the steady Soviet military buildup for two decades had been excessive, and the invasion of Afghanistan underlined their fears. Then the arrival of the Reagan administration heralded a further deterioration of U.S.-Soviet relations. An accelerated U.S. military buildup was accompanied by unfortunate rhetoric that emphasized the war-fighting capabilities of our nuclear forces.

The collective effect has been to direct many Americans' attention to nuclear war, often for the first time. Public interest groups expanded this concern by emphasizing, for example, the total inadequacy of medical care after a nuclear attack. A nuclear freeze movement gathered momentum in the grass roots, and in the 1982 elections various forms of a nuclear freeze were endorsed by referenda in eight states and many cities. In short, large sections of the public have given notice that they want to play a part in determining the broad outlines of future nuclear policy. As in the case of human rights and the environment, many individuals are determined as never before to have a voice in determining America's goals in nuclear policy and arms control.

Deciding what policies to support and what actions to take is, however, difficult and complex. For many, the heart tells of the need to do something, but the mind has not decided what that something should be. The public calls for both military strength and nuclear peace. But when assessing how much strength is required to maintain peace, the public's voice is uncertain. For example, should the U.S. nuclear arsenal be as large as the Soviet arsenal? In April 1982, 83% of those polled said that "it doesn't matter if the U.S. or the Soviet Union is ahead in nuclear weapons." Yet at the same time, 78% believed it was "somewhat important" or "very important" that the U.S. produce "as many nuclear weapons as the Soviets." (See box.)

What is very clear, however, is that the public wants its government to follow policies to reduce the likelihood of war. What might such policies look like? What choices exist?

## ADVOCACY vs. ANALYSIS

The choice the United States faces is not, and has never been, "Better Red than Dead." Most Americans reject both alternatives. It is better to be "Armed than Harmed," and if the nation pursues intelligent policies it need never choose between surrender or death. Where people who have studied these issues disagree is over what kind of arms policy the United States should follow.

The debates over national security policy are often extremely confusing. One source of confusion is that advocates of different policies focus on different threats in their public presentations. The "layman" hears one "expert" outline how horrible a nuclear war between the superpowers would be, and on that basis argue for a policy of disarmament. Then another "expert" concentrates on the Soviet Union's massive arms buildup, its treatment of its own people, and its ideology, and argues that the United States must therefore build up its nuclear arsenal.

## Do You Care Who Is Ahead?

Question: I'm going to read a few statements that deal with a nuclear freeze. For each, I'd like you to tell me whether you agree with it, or disagree, or if, perhaps, you have no opinion on that statement. . . . It doesn't matter if the United States or the Soviet Union is ahead in nuclear weapons because both sides have more than enough to destroy each other no matter who attacks first.

Question: In thinking about the United States's national defense, how important is it to you that the United States produce as many nuclear weapons as the Soviet Union does . . . very important, somewhat important, or not important?

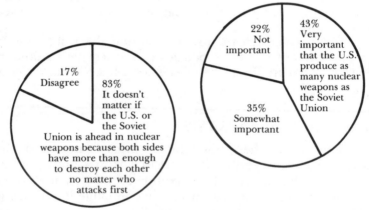

Note: In a *Los Angeles Times* March 1982 question, "Do you think the United States needs more nuclear weapons for its defense, or do you think the U.S. now possesses enough nuclear weapons to destroy its enemies?" 50% of those surveyed said the U.S. now has enough, 31% said we need more, 18% were not sure, and 1% refused to answer.

SOURCE: Survey by ABC News/ *Washington Post*, April 21-25, 1982; reported by *Public Opinion*, August/ September 1982, p. 37.

SOURCE: Survey by NBC News/ Associated Press, May 10-11, 1982; reported by *Public Opinion*, August/ September 1982, p. 37.

Common sense, however, tells most people that these two problems—the threat of nuclear war and the threat of the Soviet Union—should not be treated separately. They are two sides of the same coin: how to best preserve American security in the nuclear age. What the interested citizen lacks is not the arguments supporting a particular position, but rather an analysis of the pertinent information as well as the full range of nuclear issues. Before hearing another debate on whether to build the MX missile or whether to ratify SALT II, what's necessary is to know how to put all these issues into perspective. And they are seldom well served by merely hearing two incompatible extremes.

What is the nuclear debate all about? How did we get here? What should our strategy be? What policy options does the United States and its allies have? What can be done about the nuclear predicament?

This is the niche that this book seeks to fill. For the most part, it does not advocate any single position, nor does it offer any single solution to the problems of nuclear policy. Although we will suggest some policy directions and argue against others, our primary concern is education. What we do advocate is that interested citizens learn more about nuclear weapons policy. If the concerned public is to fill an enlarged role in policymaking, to move beyond the present focus on fear of nuclear war and search for ways to avoid it, it has to examine numerous opinions, take in a good dose of history, absorb a number of facts, and explore the full range of issues involved.

## THE CITIZEN AND NUCLEAR WEAPONS

Many citizens who are concerned about nuclear weapons policy, however, are deterred from learning more about it for two basic reasons. First, they think their opinion doesn't matter. Many Americans seem to think: Why bother to learn about these issues if no one in Washington listens to what I say, anyway? Second, some people, even if they want to learn more about nuclear weapons policy, strategy, and arms control, hesitate because they think these issues are too complex for them to understand.

Both attitudes are wrong.

Individual opinions do matter. Each citizen is not just a target of nuclear weapons; each is also an actor in the nuclear drama. The opinions of the American public play an important, though not always determinant, role in maintaining American security. This is true in two ways.

American public opinion influences American policy. How the individual votes, what policies elected officials believe the public supports and the vigor of such demands, all can influence decisions in Washington. In 1972 broad public support paved the way for the SALT I treaty and in 1981 and 1982 public pressure in the United States and among European allies hastened the Reagan administration's pursuit of arms control with the Soviets. Public action has also influenced American policy in the other direction in the past. In 1976, for example, President Ford chose not to attempt to finish negotiations for a SALT II agreement with the Soviet Union because he was afraid that an agreement would damage his chances of winning the Republican nomination.

Thus, to a certain degree, the recent vacillation of American policy toward nuclear weapons has reflected the inconsistent messages politicians have received from the public on these issues. What the voter thinks matters. Whatever the mixture of arms control and defense spending incorporated into our future security policy, public support for the decisions made will be an important factor in determining whether the government's policies can be fully implemented.

Second, what the individual thinks can even influence Soviet policy. For example, public opinion in the West affects, to some unknown degree, Soviet perceptions of the NATO alliance's willingness to defend itself. A sound security policy ultimately depends on the spirit of a nation's people, their capacity for sacrifice, as much as on the skill of our generals or the leadership of our politicians. A national security policy which lacks a broad public consensus as its foundation is more likely to be seen as irresolute by potential adversaries.

Another reason some individuals are reluctant to learn about national security issues is that the whole subject appears to be too complex, too dependent on professional training or classified information. Indeed, in May 1982, a poll reported that 63% of the American people believed that the "question of a nuclear freeze is too complicated for the public to decide."[1] The complexity of the subject is not, of course, made any clearer by the jargon of the field. An interested citizen hears about "circular error probable," "escalation ladder," and "fratricide" and thinks the issues behind this jargon cannot be readily understood. Even the most determined reader can get lost in a jungle of mysterious acronyms: ALCMs, GLCMs, and SLCMs seem to block one's understanding; NORADs and NATOs, SALTs and STARTs confound and confuse.

It is true that the problems of nuclear strategy and arms control are complex: hence, the difficulty in coping with them. But it is not true that interested individuals, if they devote the time and energy to learn, cannot understand the essence of the issues involved. And in the process they may identify experts on whom they believe they can depend in matters of detail.

After all, elected officials, who in this country make the final decisions about American security policy, are usually laymen in this field as well. They have not spent years learning the details of various weapons systems or the intricacies of arms control negotiations. They have not concentrated on the differences between ICBMs, IRBMs, and MRBMs. In the United States, the people who control these complicated weapons are politicians, interested in guns and butter, usually as much butter as possible and only as many guns as necessary.

The elected official has to listen to various opinions on the alternative policies for American security and then, to the best of his or her ability, decide what is best for the nation. The citizen's task is no more and no less. Of course, the individual's responsibility for national security policy is not as great as that of the nation's leaders. But the individual's concern that the best decisions be made is, however, exactly the same.

## FIVE PERPLEXITIES

The complex world of nuclear weapons policy poses five problems to all who enter it, the policymaker and the concerned citizen alike. These nuclear quandaries are intertwined and arise on a personal plane as well as on the political level. They are not difficult to understand; they are only difficult to live with. They are even more difficult to do away with.

## THE TEMPTATION OF DENIAL

Perhaps part of what makes the existence of nuclear weapons relatively easy to live with is that one doesn't have to think about them very much. Nuclear weaponry, as long as it is never used, does not greatly influence our daily life. We spend part of our tax dollar on nuclear arms, but we eat and sleep, love and hate, live and die, without being affected by the nuclear arsenals the United States or the Soviet Union have built. We want to keep it this way.

Because we are human and want to make sure that nuclear war does not occur, we need to think seriously about the problem, to see nuclear war as it really could be. But because we are human, a dilemma of denial presents itself when we stare at the horrors of war. There is a temptation to "tune out" the problem, to think that if one does not want war to occur, it cannot occur. We know that ignoring the danger of war will not make the danger go away. But when we think about the terrible possibilities, it is only human to recoil from the vision.

This denial of what nuclear war is like takes two dominant forms. The first is most prevalent among defense analysts; the second more common among laymen. Denial of the horrors of war can be witnessed among civilian strategists, military men, and policymakers in the penchant for euphemisms, the use of innocuous language to mask the ugly reality of war. The term "counter-value targeting" replaces the disturbing reality of aiming nuclear weapons at the enemy's population. In strategists' jargon, a missile base is not destroyed, burned up, or annihilated; it is "taken out," a term suggesting, one academic writes, "the relative good humor of a clean body-block in a football game."[2] Even the everyday phrase "nuclear exchange," a psychiatrist notes, "sounds like something pretty good—almost like gift-giving."[3]

Ironically, the use of apparently cold, detached language in strategic debates may arise precisely because those who use such phrases are neither cold nor detached, but are human, expressing their denial in a different way with emotions. This phenomenon is not unique to the nuclear era, but it is probably more common now. Can it be avoided? Should it be avoided?

Black humor is not the same kind of denial, but treating the subject lightly so as to release the tension is a common way of coping with fear. Nuclear war would be so horrible that individuals are tempted to laugh at its disturbing absurdity. Reverting to humor is an age-old way of reducing anxiety; it is not the response human beings want to have, but they have it anyway. Tom Lehrer's songs created this response. Even that classic film of the 1960s Stanley Kubrick's *Dr. Strangelove* was based on a serious book about how a nuclear war might begin. Instead of portraying dangerous possible paths to nuclear conflict, *Dr. Strangelove* became an absurd fantasy. It was subtitled "Or How I Learned to Stop Worrying and Love the Bomb." One way to stop worrying was black humor.

Both these forms of denial are human, but it is also human to search for a better understanding of the vast problems nuclear weaponry creates. If we are to manage these problems successfully, we have to treat the problems seriously and minimize our natural tendency to deny the horrors. Facing the reality of nuclear war, however, does not mean that coping with the problems is any less difficult. All the pictures of Hiroshima and the visions of future disaster can tell one is what to avoid—not how to avoid it. Still, acknowledging the potential horrors of war in the nuclear age should serve as a constant reminder of the necessity of keeping those horrors in the realm of "the potential."

The goal then is to be realistic without being fatalistic; to treat the dangers soberly without being inhumane. This is a difficult challenge for every concerned individual. It is, nonetheless, a prerequisite for progress.

## THE PRESENCE OF UNCERTAINTY

Long before nuclear weapons were invented, strategists noted that all military decisions are made in a kind of twilight. There is never adequate knowledge of what is to come in any war. A general cannot see what lies over the next hill, cannot know the content of his enemy's plans, cannot even be sure of how his own forces will react under the pressures of battle. All military decisions are made with an imperfect vision of future events. Uncertainty is ubiquitous.

In the nuclear age, all strategic decisions, in peacetime and in war, must still be made in a kind of twilight. With modern satellite photography we can count an adversary's missile launchers, but we cannot see inside his mind. We have highly sophisticated weapons, but they have not been tested in a nuclear war. Indeed, strategic decisions today must be made in even more darkness than was often the case in the past, for at least two reasons. First, the Soviet Union is a closed society which protects its secrecy as an asset in its international competition with the United States. Second, and most important, there is profound uncertainty on both sides due to lack of experience. Since 1945 no one has fought in a nuclear war. As long as there is continued nuclear peace, we can *fortunately* never truly know, to give only two examples, whether nuclear war can be limited in any meaningful way or whether missiles are as accurate in warfare as they are in testing.

The dilemma of uncertainty is that decisions must be made despite this lack of perfect knowledge. Defense planners and politicians try to take uncertainty into account, but can never eliminate it. They must plan and choose among alternative policies in the inevitable twilight of international politics.

Uncertainty exists throughout the spectrum of strategic analysis, from decisions of the most general sort to extremely technical issues. At the most general level, for example, it is often said that as long as nuclear war does not occur, deterrence is invisible: if a potential adversary does not attack, one can never *know* whether a deterrent strategy succeeded or whether it was unnecessary in the first place. Perhaps the enemy never wanted to attack at all. As long as we cannot know Soviet intentions and calculations, a deterrent policy will be invisible even as it fulfills its task. As long as it works we will never have known how much nuclear weaponry was enough.

At the other extreme, the more technical level of individual weapons systems, uncertainty abounds as well. For example, both the U.S. and the USSR compute the accuracy of their missiles from tests made on an east-west trajectory, but would use them in war over the north pole. How that would influence accuracy is uncertain. The Soviets have built an anti-ballistic missile system around Moscow and an elaborate air defense system around the country's borders. How well they would work in war is uncertain. Both superpowers have built expensive command structures for nuclear conflict. Whether they would survive the first attack is uncertain.

Thus uncertainty clouds most issues in nuclear weapons policy. It makes the answers to problems we face speculative at best. But uncertainty does not absolve the strategists, the government, and the citizens from the responsibility of making the wisest possible choices. It only makes the choices more difficult.

## THE PERSISTENCE OF RISK

Is there anything worth the risk of nuclear war? There is a widely held belief that a thermonuclear war between the United States and the Soviet Union would be so horrible that absolutely nothing is worth the risk of such a calamity. This argument is half true and half misleading: that such a war would be horrible beyond belief is absolutely true, but this does not necessarily mean that there are no objectives worth the risk of nuclear war. Indeed, it would be difficult to argue that taking a *small risk* of nuclear war would not be justified for the goal of preventing an even *larger risk* of nuclear war.

This statement sounds contradictory, but it is not. In a world of sovereign states, there is a persistence of risk, and a potential cost associated with every action. Of course, responsible statesmen in the nuclear age should be prudent: they should never take any unnecessary risks when the costs of miscalculation are so great. But the statesman who runs no risks incurs many. Consider an important example from recent history.

In October 1962 the Soviet Union secretly placed nuclear missiles on the island of Cuba, some ninety miles from the United States. Soviet leaders had repeatedly, in public announcements and private assurances, denied that they were taking such actions. The government of the United States, again both publicly and privately, had repeatedly warned that it would not tolerate Soviet missiles emplaced so close to American shores.

When President John F. Kennedy was shown irrefutable evidence of the Soviet missile emplacement—U-2 photographs of the missile bases in Cuba—he and his advisers discussed the matter for six days before deciding on an American response to the challenge. The decision, to place a naval blockade around the island, was not a risk-free response. This, Kennedy honestly admitted to the nation on the night of October 22, 1962:

> My fellow citizens, let no one doubt that this is a difficult and dangerous effort on which we have set out. No one can foresee precisely what course it will take. . . . But the greatest danger of all would be to do nothing.

Why did the president believe that "to do nothing" about the missiles in Cuba would be an even greater danger than accepting the "difficult and dangerous" course of the blockade? He accepted some risk of war in the short run, because he believed his actions would reduce the risk of war in the long run, by discouraging future Soviet aggressive behavior. Inaction might have led to an even more dangerous future. This the president also explained that night in his address to the nation:

> [This] sudden, clandestine decision to station weapons for the first time outside Soviet soil—is a deliberately provocative and unjustified change in the status quo which cannot be accepted by this country if our courage and our commitments are ever to be trusted by either friend or foe.

The 1930's taught us a clear lesson: Aggressive conduct, if allowed to grow unchecked and unchallenged, ultimately leads to war.[4]

The American government managed the 1962 crisis with skill and restraint—offering a compromise to the Soviets and giving them sufficient time to call back their missile-laden ships, for example—and the missiles were withdrawn from Cuba. The president carefully supervised American military actions to ensure that his orders were not misunderstood. He did not push his success too far or ignore the real risks of war.

The point here is not, however, to make the blockade a model for American action in the future: different circumstances may call for different policies. Rather, the point is to underline *the persistence of risk* in international affairs. *Every* proposed response to the Soviet action—doing nothing, enforcing a blockade, or invading Cuba—entailed some risk of nuclear war. Kennedy's task—and we think his success—was to weigh accurately the risks entailed in each course and decide on policy accordingly.

This is also the task of the concerned citizen today. There are no risk-free "solutions" to the nuclear dilemmas faced by the United States in the 1980s. Increasing American commitments to allies or reducing such commitments, accepting certain arms control agreements or rejecting them, building certain kinds of weaponry or not producing them, all are decisions that entail some risks. The goal is to weigh, as accurately as possible, the risks of each course.

## THE PROBLEMS OF COORDINATION

In the modern world, there are many important differences between the United States and the Soviet Union as well as one major shared objective. The shared objective is to keep the nuclear peace; neither superpower wants to fight a nuclear war. The differences between the world's two most powerful nations are, however, both relentless and stark. Policy prescriptions which ignore these differences—antagonistic ideologies, divergent nuclear strategies, dissimilar domestic political systems, and conflicting interests in some areas of the world—are unlikely to be productive.

Indeed, because of this combination of genuine rivalry and genuine common interest, both superpowers are cautious even when pursuing policies designed to minimize the likelihood of war between them. Neither superpower can completely trust the other; neither can control the other's actions. Both must, however, strive to reduce the risks of war.

American policymakers must make their own decisions, but must always base them on what they believe Soviet policy will be. Some policy options can be useful if tried alone. But many can only succeed if both superpowers act together. And doing one's best is still important. For even if one cannot control the dangers alone, one's own actions can help. Even if one cannot "solve" the problem, one can reduce the risks of catastrophe.

## THE DANGER OF DISCOURAGEMENT

In the nuclear age, the dangers the United States faces are both numerous and enormous. It would be best if all these dangers could be eliminated, but in international relations as in all of politics, the goal is to relate the desirable to the possible. The impossibility of achieving perfect solutions should not, however, breed discouragement. It should only strengthen determination to persevere.

When facing enormous problems, there is a special attraction to the assumption that only radical answers can suffice. Hence, the strong pull of utopian visions of both the extreme left and the extreme right: the ideas that only a world government can solve all our problems or that sheer military muscle is all that America needs. Both prescribe all-purpose solutions, but each ignores the real world. In the real world, packed with huge nuclear arsenals, mere military muscle, unless built and exercised with restraint and skill, will not ensure American security. In the real world of sovereign states, a world government is a dream for the distant future, not a practical goal for current policymakers.

The danger of focusing on utopian objectives is that they can take attention away from practical and positive

steps that can be taken now. Such actions may only produce incremental progress toward the goal of national
security. But incremental steps matter.

It would be a tragedy if opportunities for practical
progress toward nuclear peace were missed because our
goals were set too high, beyond the reach of what is
possible. In his book *The Fate of the Earth,* Jonathan Schell
has reminded people of the dangers of nuclear war, but
his "solution" is precisely such an impossible goal. "The
task," he wrote, "is nothing less than to reinvent politics:
to reinvent the world."[5]

In reality, however, neither politics nor the world
were invented by men, nor can either politics or the world
be reinvented. Rather, these arrangements evolved through
trial and error, through sacrifice and occasional gifted
leadership, to an organization of life on earth that has
reached unprecedented attainments. The nature of humanity, the complex mosaic of civilizations, the web of relations that unite so many nations cannot be taken apart and
reinvented in the future. They can, we hope, continue to
evolve.

We are left, therefore, with our imperfect selves, imperfect nations, and imperfect relations among them. And
it is upon this imperfect structure that the capability of
waging infinitely destructive nuclear war has descended.
Humanity has no alternative but to hold this threat at bay
and to learn to live with politics, to live in the world we
know: a world of nuclear weapons, international rivalries,
recurring conflicts, and at least some risk of nuclear crisis.
The challenge we face is not to escape to a fictional utopia
where such problems do not exist. It is to learn how to live
with nuclear weapons in ways that are successively safer
and in which the freedoms won by men and women are
kept secure and can grow.

Yet even this imperfect solution will not be achieved if
we ignore the incremental steps that are possible today or
if discouragement breeds despair. Indeed, that may be the
greatest danger of all.

## A PREVIEW

We hope this book can help clarify the issues involved in the nuclear weapons debate so that concerned citizens can better make their own judgments on current government policy. The two chapters that follow are about our pre-nuclear past and one possible nuclear future. Chapter 2 addresses the question "what is new about the nuclear world?" It provides the reader with some necessary political background information and discusses the historical traditions of the United States and the Soviet Union. Chapter 3 examines how a nuclear war might begin.

The next three chapters are about the nuclear arsenals of the two superpowers. Chapter 4 analyzes how we got to where we are today: what weaponry was built when, and why. Chapter 5 derives some lessons from this history. What nuclear weaponry currently exists throughout the world is the subject of Chapter 6. Chapter 7 is about the purposes behind atomic arsenals: What do we want from nuclear weapons?

The rest of the book explores what can be done about nuclear dangers. Chapter 8 discusses a number of nuclear weapons issues being debated in Washington and allied capitals and presents the current policy alternatives. Chapter 9 focuses on the role of arms control in reducing the nuclear peril: What can and can't be done? Nuclear proliferation, the spreading of nuclear weapons to other countries, is addressed in Chapter 10: Can proliferation be controlled?

The final chapter presents why we believe that there are reasons for hope in preventing nuclear war. The degree of hope will depend, in large part, on the actions taken by thoughtful men and women across the globe, today and in the coming years. Complacency will cancel hope; wise action will let it grow.

### Notes

1. CBS News/*New York Times*, May 19–23, 1982; *Public Opinion*, August/September 1982, p. 38.

2. Philip Green, *Deadly Logic* (Columbus: Ohio State University, 1966), p. 233.

3. Robert Jay Lifton, quoted in James Lardner, "Fear and the Bomb," *Washington Post,* April 16, 1982.

4. The speech is reprinted in Robert F. Kennedy's *Thirteen Days* (New York: Norton, 1969), pp. 163–75.

5. Jonathan Schell, *The Fate of the Earth* (New York: Knopf, 1982), p. 226.

# 2

# The Endless Balancing Act: What Is New About the Nuclear World?

In 13th-century Spain King Alfonso X is said to have declared, "Had I been present at the creation, I would have given some useful hints for the better ordering of the universe." Political leaders in the nuclear age certainly understand this sentiment. They too, if it were possible, could provide "useful hints" to the creator.

But no political leaders, of course—presidents and politburos, cabinets and kings alike—were present at the creation. Heads of governments enter their respective offices and inherit the political world as it is, a collection of sovereign states with no central authority above them. Preserving the security and promoting the interests of their countries is their primary duty. Maintaining or changing the often precarious order of the real world in order to serve these interests is their daily responsibility; "the better ordering of the universe" in the interest of the greatest number is only their long-range goal. Like all of us, statesmen may dream about another world, but they spend their wakeful hours living in the one world there is.

This world is an arena of politics. And all politics is about power. This is familiar in domestic politics: congressmen compete for votes, bureaucrats compete for their

22

supervisor's attention, government agencies compete for federal tax dollars. All are struggling for power of some kind, power to achieve their political objectives.

Although domestic political life is always competitive, the competition between nations often takes a more violent form—war. Why is this so? In order to prevent war in the future, the reasons for war in the past must be examined. How have statesmen in the past moderated the dangerous contest between armed nation-states? Can the methods used by earlier statesmen still be effective today? Have nuclear weapons, which make peace more necessary, made keeping the peace more difficult? That is the subject of this chapter: to examine what is new and what is old about international politics in the nuclear world.

## THE STATE OF NATURE

In domestic politics, competition is moderated by the existence of laws. Politicians still struggle for power, but the competition is governed by many rules. This has led many persons to believe that violent international politics would more closely resemble the relative peacefulness of domestic politics if there were more international laws for states to follow. Is this true?

The answer is yes and no. Law does moderate competition, but—in both domestic and international politics—the mere existence of laws is never enough. Laws need consensus and enforcement: the familiar figure of Justice holds a scale in one hand and a sword in the other. Without a government authority to ensure that laws are kept, individuals are free to follow or ignore the laws that exist. Without a consensus on common values and goals, or agreed-upon procedures for peaceful competition, government authority either breaks down or becomes tyrannical. In either case individuals will tend to disregard or rebel against the laws.

This is what happens in civil wars. And it is also largely the case in international politics. The relations between sovereign states are similar to what domestic life would be like if there was no consensus on maintaining a minimum of community and no central government and no police department to enforce the law. This point was understood by the 17th-century English philosopher Thomas Hobbes who imagined the "state of nature," a jungle of anarchy in which man without government had to "use his own power . . . for the preservation of his own nature." In such a world there would be "continual fear and danger of violent death; and the life of man [would be] solitary, poor, nasty, brutish and short."[1]

For citizens of a relatively peaceful society, life in "the state of nature" might be difficult to understand. But recall what daily life was like in the days of the Wild West on the American frontier: self-help was the only rule that existed and gunslingers often took the law into their own hands. Today, daily life can appear to be this desperate in urban slums all over the world. "The state of nature" also exists during civil war, as in Lebanon in 1975, when the domestic order completely collapsed. In such extreme circumstances fathers fight against sons, looting takes place throughout urban areas, political figures try to kill one another, and fear appears on every street corner.

## THE BALANCE OF POWER

International political life still looks more like the "state of nature" or civil war than it resembles peaceful domestic politics. There is little consensus on goals among states: nationalism remains the prevailing force and nations are separated both by conflicting interests and by varying prejudices and ideologies. Nor is there any agreement on settling all disputes peacefully through established procedures: in world affairs, war remains "one of the ways by which great human decisions are made."[2] There is no world government, no world police force to punish wrongdoers, no world court with binding authority. But peace can be kept, in international politics, if a nation can balance the power of others with its own strength. The life of a nation in this international jungle might be "nasty" and "brutish" at times, but it need not be "short." At least this is so if a balance of power against potential threats is maintained.

In periods when a balance of power exists, international law can develop. But what do people mean when they speak of the balance of power? The phrase has a multitude of meanings. It is sometimes used to describe any *distribution* of power among nations; sometimes it refers only to a roughly equal distribution of power. "Balance of power" is also often used to describe a particular kind of foreign *policy;* for example, Great Britain's traditional policy of not allowing any single government to gain control of the European continent (a policy which led the British into war a number of times). Finally, it refers to a certain kind of international *system,* to a pattern of relations among the principal states, in which any potential troublemaker finds himself deterred or defeated by a coalition of other states concerned with curbing his ambitions. Such a system has required flexible alignments among a number of major powers greater than two, a willingness on the part of states both to resist a rival's dangerous designs and to shift alliances as the origin of the threat changes. For some people, "balance of power" is an antiquated term, producing a history book vision of diplomats with top hats and walking sticks negotiating treaties around ornate conference tables. Still others believe that "the balance of power" is just a euphemism used by governments to justify a policy of preparing for the next war.

In its most general sense, however, all governments are concerned with the balance, that is, the distribution of power: it is an inevitable result of the independence of nation-states in international politics. In domestic politics, the checks-and-balances system is an attempt to ensure that no branch of the national government has absolute power over the others. The balance of power in international politics is, similarly, the result of the effort of nations to ensure that no power rules over all. It is a nation's only way of self-protection on a globe without a world government. We find balance-of-power politics practiced not only in the modern world, but in the long history of diplomacy, in ancient China and in India. Whenever there are competing independent actors, there will be concern with the balance of power.

## THE 19TH-CENTURY BALANCE

Since the fall of the Roman empire, no one power has gained such military preponderance that it could lay down the law to all other nations. Even the Romans held sway over only the Western world. A number of governments have tried to conquer the globe, however, and might have succeeded had not other nations joined together to stop them.

Louis XIV, the "Sun King" of France, sought a universal monarchy in the late 17th century. Napoleon Bonaparte, backed by the military powers unleashed by the French Revolution, was briefly the "master of Europe" until he was defeated by the harsh Russian winter and the allied armies of Britain, Prussia, Austria, and Russia. And in our century, Adolf Hitler came frighteningly close to building the Thousand-Year Reich, which would have held the world in a Nazi reign of terror partly because Britain and France, and an isolationist United States, failed to stop him before 1939 and preferred to "appease" Hitler by concessions that only fed his appetite.

Other periods of history have been less violent; other international orders have been more stable. Even the most tranquil periods of international relations, however, have not witnessed the kinds of shared values or laws found in peaceful societies. States have remained independent, with independent visions of justice, equality, and freedom. When an international order has been relatively peaceful, however, it has been largely because governments have followed principles of prudence and have sought only limited objectives either out of self-restraint, or because the operation of the balance of power obliged them to practice restraint.

When such a stability exists, states still compete but the balancing of power is made much easier. International law and cooperation among states and groups across borders can flourish. No nation is completely satisfied; but no nation seeks to dominate all others.

Many states might seek some readjustment of their borders or improvements of their status; they are called "revisionist powers" and can create considerable turbulence in world politics. But whenever a major state does not accept a balance-of-power order at all, it becomes a revolutionary power on the international stage.[3] A revolutionary state is more than a country; it is also a cause. It pursues its national interests as all states do, but in doing so, it seeks to alter the whole international order and influence the domestic politics of other states. A revolutionary state desires security for itself, but also believes that security cannot be ensured until international politics has been fundamentally changed.

In a world with a powerful revolutionary state, the balance of power is inherently precarious, for the state defines its security in ways which threaten the security of others. Napoleonic France may have sincerely desired peace, as Napoleon always said, but it sought peace in domination. Napoleon could not be satisfied with a mere balance of power. Metternich, the Austrian foreign minister and one of Napoleon's main rivals, best described the essence of a revolutionary power:

> Napoleon and I spent years together as if at a game of chess, carefully watching each other; I to checkmate him, he to crush me together with the chess figures.[4]

Napoleon was defeated in 1814 and, after the defeat of his final bid for power at Waterloo, the European diplomats who gathered at the Congress of Vienna could focus their energies on creating a more stable order in Europe. The scope of their success, creating a system that was maintained for one hundred years of relative peace, is naturally of great interest to us today.

How did the 19th-century balance-of-power system contribute to peace? First, the system had five major powers—England, France, Russia, Austria, Prussia—none of which could easily become dominant. Second, the resulting alliances were flexible: governments joined or left an alliance whenever another nation threatened to become too powerful. Many international conferences were held in which major powers could negotiate over their differences and act to prevent lesser countries from upsetting the established order; compensations were offered, often in the form of territory, to states that lost rights or provinces. Lastly, if wars were fought, they were kept limited in scope and violence through diplomatic efforts.

The hundred-year balance of power in Europe was not a century of absolute peace. Both Germany and Italy gained their unity, in the period of 1850 to 1871, through a series of wars; other wars broke out in the Balkans, where Russia supported the cause of nationalities trying to break out of the decaying Ottoman empire. But even wars between major powers—the Crimean War, which pitted Britain and France against Russia, or the Franco-Prussian War of 1870–71—were far less bloody than the American Civil War. It was a period of relative order without a major international war disrupting the progress of nations.

Such progress led many people to believe that a well-ordered international society was developing. The system, however, finally failed in 1914 and the First World War began. Territorial compensations were not continued in the last years of the 19th century and threats of war, not negotiating conferences, became the norm during the crises before 1914. But the cause of the First World War was not the balance-of-power system itself. Rather, war occurred because the balance broke down: The conditions that had made its operation successful had gradually disappeared. Alliances among modern states with intensely national feelings or popular involvement were no longer flexible. What was at stake in their contest was no longer limited ambitions, but the general credibility of each power's alliances, and in one case—Austria-Hungary—the very survival of a state composed of diverse and restive nationalities.

It was not the sheer size of the armies of 1914 that precipitated war. A major cause, rather, was the inflexibility of military mobilization plans coupled with what the historian Michael Howard has called "the bland ignorance among national leaders of the simple mechanics of the [military] system on which they relied."[5] Once political leaders ordered their military machines to take the first steps toward war, they could not control or reverse the process they started. When the armies began to march, the politicians wanted to put on the brakes, but did not know how. The industrialization of war ensured that a general conflict would be colossal and long, even though statesmen, after a century of relative peace, believed that the clash would be brief.

It is ironic, but the very success of the diplomats in the early 19th century may have contributed in two ways to the failure of statesmen to keep the peace at the start of the 20th. On the one hand, a century of order after

Waterloo allowed statesmen, soldiers, and citizens to assume that the balance-of-power system was stable, cast in iron, and would not be broken. On the other hand, this system had lasted only by curbing state ambitions and inducing restraint; many of the main actors, and several of the lesser ones, had been repeatedly frustrated, and were beginning to want to take off their gloves: the next time, it would be up to the adversary to show restraint. In 1914, in each camp—each of the alliance systems—the leaders thought that backing down now would put them in a far worse situation for the next crisis and that it would be easier for their opponents to back down. Each side thought time was on the other's side. And so time ran out for all. In the summer of 1914 war was no longer such a fearful thought. As Henry Kissinger has described it:

> [In] the long interval of peace, the sense of the tragic was lost; it was forgotten that states could die.[6]

## WHAT IS NEW ABOUT THE NUCLEAR WORLD?

Nuclear weapons are a stark reminder that states can die. They have made the horror of war more difficult to forget. In the summer of 1914, politicians on both sides envisioned their troops marching home by Christmas. Enthusiastic crowds gathered in the European capitals to greet the declarations of war with music and applause. Poets found gallantry in death, and even the famous recruiting poster—a young boy asking his father, "Daddy, what did *you* do in the Great War?"—assumed that the future world would be healthy and secure after the war was over.

Modern man has a different attitude toward world war. Our sense of the tragic is relentless. Our visions of a world after nuclear war are dreadful and horrifying. It is, therefore, understandable that many are tempted to look back into the hundred-year balance of power in Europe as a guide for the present. Indeed, the current international order, like the one which began in 1815, developed after an armed coalition of great powers defeated one man's bid to become ruler of the world.

The success of the 19th-century balance can only serve as a goal, however. It cannot serve as a guide. For no matter how strongly statesmen today would like to replicate their predecessors' success, two undeniable facts make the modern international order very different from that of the past. First, nuclear weapons exist and in very large numbers. Second, there are two superpowers today—not five or six relatively equal great powers as in the 19th century—and these two giants have different traditions and ideologies, different hopes and habits. In the past, contests between two major powers, in which both compete for influence or one tries to expand and the other attempts to contain its rival, have led not only to recurrent crises but to large-scale wars, such as the thirty-year Peloponnesian war between Athens and Sparta in the 5th century B.C.

Today, the mechanism that, in the 19th century, prevented general wars and kept other wars limited can no longer function. The two nuclear superpowers are too antagonistic to join forces against third parties, and the actual use of force between the superpowers risks destroying much of the world. Thus the containment of one side's ambitions is in the final analysis not a matter of coalitions, but a matter of nuclear deterrence by the other great power's nuclear weapons.

How different are these nuclear weapons? Anyone who has seen photographs of Hiroshima after the bombing may, even then, minimize the destructive potential of modern nuclear weapons. The death and destruction in that Japanese city on August 6, 1945, was horrible, but it stood beside equally appalling scenes of death from conventional attacks in Hamburg, Tokyo, and Dresden. The main difference is that Hiroshima was destroyed by a single fission bomb. Fusion bombs, developed since, are many times more devastating than the bomb that destroyed Hiroshima.

That these weapons are enormously powerful, everyone understands. Exactly how this destructive potential has affected military strategy is less well understood. What then is new about nuclear strategy?

Three major changes should be noted. First, with modern means of delivery, nuclear weapons make defense in the traditional sense of physically shielding oneself from attack extremely difficult, if not impossible. Throughout history, arms have been developed which seemed like "absolute weapons" at the time. The Romans thought there was no defense against their phalanx of advancing infantrymen; medieval English archers believed their long bow was an unstoppable weapon; military writers after the Franco-Prussian War thought the breech-loading rifle was impossible to resist. These prophets were wrong. The existence of the "absolute weapon" with offensive power produced a technological advance in defensive weaponry. So far, nuclear explosives have been "the absolute weapon." So far, at least, there is no defense against their power.

The immense difficulty of defending against nuclear attack is due to a combination of the weapon's destructive power and the "means of delivery," how the weapon is sent into enemy territory. During the Second World War, the British military did its best to shoot down the German V-1 rockets, or "buzz bombs," aimed at London. On their most successful day, August 28, 1944, 97 out of 101 rockets which approached England were destroyed.[7] This was a great success, but if the four bombs that were missed had been thermonuclear weapons, London would have been destroyed. For the defense of cities to be effective in the nuclear age, every incoming missile or bomber would have to be shot down, a rate of technical success which scientists in neither the Soviet Union nor the United States have been able to achieve; nor are they likely to achieve it in the future.

Second, nuclear weapons have greatly accelerated the historical trend toward making civilian populations the targets, intentional or not, in war. It is easy to forget how often wars in the past involved great civilian casualties. Carthage was turned into a barren wasteland by the Roman army; European cities were sacked and ruined during the Thirty Years' War in the early 17th century; and in the Second World War such cities as Leningrad, Dresden, Tokyo, Nanking, and Warsaw were bombed into rubble. Nuclear weapons, however, make population centers more vulnerable to attack in peace, and perhaps more likely to be attacked if war occurs. There was always the possibility that wars can be fought between the armed forces of the state without including the people. This is less likely today. Nuclear weapons, for the first time in history, offer the possibility of destroying a country before one has defeated or destroyed its armed forces.

Third, nuclear war would almost certainly be faster than war in the past, and this may make it even more dangerous. Conventional wars used to last for years and still do in many parts of the world. Nuclear war, or at least the most important acts of the tragedy, might be over in hours or days. It may be over before politicians have a chance to rethink their decisions and change their minds. It could be over before warnings of attack were discovered to be false alarms, or before two leaders could reach each other and negotiate an end to the conflict. The speed of modern missiles adds an extra obstacle to the political control over military conflict once it begins or even before it begins, a control which was often so tenuous even in the less dangerous past.

The existence of nuclear weapons also raises the value of "forces in being": the level of weaponry a nation has at the onset of war. Before 1945 there was often a time of safety between when war broke out and when the decisive battles were fought. Governments could, and usually did, use this time to mobilize resources and train and equip armies before fighting the final tests of strength. This was particularly true of the United States in both world wars, with its immense potential power protected by two oceans. The nuclear age does not give nations this period of grace.

## A CONDITION TO PUNISH

These factors have elevated an old idea, "deterrence," to a position of new prominence in strategy. Military deterrence simply means the process of convincing a potential enemy, by the threat of force, that he is better off if he does not use military force against you. The basic concept is ancient. It is what the Romans meant when they said, "If you want peace, then prepare for war." It was also understood by Thomas Jefferson, when he wrote,

[How] can we prevent those [wars] produced by the wrongs of other nations? By putting ourselves in a condition to punish them. Weakness provokes insult and injury, while a condition to punish often prevents it.[8]

A perfect ability to defend oneself might be the best solution if it were possible. But it is not. The difference between having an ability to defend oneself and being, as Jefferson put it, "in a condition to punish" is important and disturbing. Being able to defend oneself implies that one is safe *regardless* of what the enemy does with his military forces. Deterrence through punishment is about trying to influence the enemy's choices: one is secure not despite military attacks, but *only* if the enemy is dissuaded from attacking in the first place.

This is, therefore, a psychological strategy as much as a purely military one. It is the effort to use fear to ensure peace: the enemy's fear of our retaliation is meant to keep him from starting the war, because, given the enormous destructiveness of nuclear weapons, our retaliation would impose costs far in excess of any conceivable political gain he could hope to achieve. Thus deterrence, like beauty, is in the eye of the beholder. Because perfected defense does not seem possible or likely in the nuclear age, each side's security rests, in part, on the visions and decision of the other.

The old balance of power was best preserved when each nation had the power to defend itself successfully. Today, the balance of power takes the form of a balance of terror. Neither great power could avoid great destruction if it was attacked. Neither power believes it could escape painful consequences if it began a war, if it attacked first.

The concept of retaliation is, therefore, at the heart of the logic of the balance of terror. Deterrence is made necessary because the United States is *vulnerable* to any Soviet nuclear attack. Deterrence is made more secure when American retaliatory forces are *invulnerable* to any Soviet nuclear attack. Weapons by themselves may not add to security; weapons which cannot be destroyed by the Soviet Union can.

The idea is most readily understood through a metaphor. In stories about the old West, the balance of terror was never very stable between two gunslingers: whoever was the quickest draw shot first, killed the other, and walked into the sunset unscathed. In westerns, gunfighters shot first and talked later. But try to imagine some way of ensuring that the "quickest draw in the West" would still be killed by his dying opponent, that even he couldn't walk away safely. Under such circumstances, even the best fighter would hesitate. Imagine what a duel would be like between men armed only with darts tipped with slow-acting poison. With such weapons, "the winner" could be killed by "the loser." Talking first and shooting later, or never, might become the rule.

Both superpowers spend enormous sums of money to make their retaliatory forces invulnerable to enemy attack in order to ensure that whoever "shoots first" will not escape unscathed, and each one spends huge sums of money to try to make the other's forces vulnerable, in order to limit damage to itself if deterrence fails and war begins. But neither feels comfortable with these efforts, because it still leaves security up to the other side's rational decisions. And neither superpower wants to depend on these.

## CONTINUING DILEMMAS OF DETERRENCE

Relying on retaliation for security is extremely uncomfortable for two related reasons. We have termed the first the "usability paradox": *Nuclear weapons can prevent aggression only if there is a possibility that they will be used, but we do not want to make them so usable that anyone is tempted to use one.* It is an important objective to make sure that our nuclear weapons are never used by accident, through miscalculation or mechanical failure. But if weapons are made that could not be used at all, they would not contribute to deterrence at all.

The second dilemma can be called "the problem of credibility." The threat of retaliation which best deters aggression is a credible threat, one which the potential attacker believes the defender actually intends to execute if he is attacked. The credibility of nuclear threats is often in doubt, however, for this simple reason: a nation that retaliated might be attacked again and suffer even more.

Much of the history of American and allied defense efforts can be seen as an attempt to improve the credibility of our threats to retaliate. The problem is particularly profound in trying to deter limited nuclear attacks and attacks upon American allies. Would the president order a retaliation against the Soviet Union if it attacked the United States in a limited way, knowing that the Soviets could attack again if he retaliated? Would the president order a retaliatory strike against the Soviet Union if the Soviet Union attacked Western Europe? The answer to each question is that American policymakers don't know. But neither do the Soviets, which adds prudence to their calculations. This strategy still produces an uneasy state of affairs.

The American strategist Bernard Brodie has described the result in which sane statesmen are both cautious with nuclear weapons and uneasy with the results:

> It is a curious paradox of our time that one of the foremost factors making deterrence really work and work well is the lurking fear that in some massive confrontation crisis, it might fail. Under these circumstances one does not tempt fate.[9]

There is no escape from this paradox: it is the very character of nuclear weapons that has altered the stands powerful states must take to preserve peace. Because statesmen rarely are suicidal, nuclear weapons engender extreme prudence in action. Because statesmen do not like relying on a potential enemy's decisions, nuclear weapons have also engendered extreme discomfort even when the peace has been maintained. And the current international order is further complicated by the conflicting visions of the superpowers. Although the international "state of nature" remains as it was from 1815 to 1914—a contest of sovereign powers—the "nature of the states" is very different.

## THE SOVIET UNION

Winston Churchill's characterization of the Soviet Union as "a riddle wrapped in a mystery inside an enigma" is no less true for being repeated so often. The often sharp disagreements among American analysts about the nature of Soviet motivations are at least partly due to the penchant for secrecy in the Soviet regime, a habit born of both traditional Russian distrust of foreigners in general and an ideologically inspired distrust of the capitalist democracies in particular. In the Soviet Union, all publications are strictly censored by the central authorities, foreigners' access to government officials is highly restricted, and the information which is made available is always fragmentary, usually ambiguous, and sometimes false. Because the "facts" are ambiguous or impossible to discern, there is bound to be some debate over the meaning of Soviet actions. Some of the major disagreements, however, stem from the wrong questions being asked.

For example, many political debates revolve around the question of whether the Soviet Union's policy is motivated by defensive considerations or offensive intentions. The same Soviet action—say, the invasion of Afghanistan or the building of the SS-18 nuclear missile—is thus interpreted in two very different ways. Analysts believing the Soviet Union is "defensive" might find such actions disagreeable, but perhaps "understandable," at least not *too* frightening. Other analysts stressing "offensive" Soviet motivations might see such actions as the first steps toward something worse and as proof that basic Soviet policy is aggressive.

Such debates obscure the central issue, which is the effect, not the motive, of Soviet actions. We can never "know" exactly what motivates the Soviet leadership. What the West *can* know is that certain Soviet actions are not in its interests and the central issue is, then, how best to encourage Soviet restraint in such dangerous areas. An action undertaken for defensive reasons may provide an opportunity for a future offensive move; a "defensive" concern for one's security that entails the control of a neighbor, or concessions by that neighbor, cannot fail to have calamitous effects for that neighbor's own security. Thus, the Soviets may have invaded Afghanistan to preserve a friendly regime in power in that neighboring country, but their presence in Afghanistan has significant effects for Pakistan, Iran, and the Persian Gulf area, not to mention the Afghan people.

We can trust the Soviets in one sense. We can trust them to pursue their interests. The key to our security is, therefore, to ensure that it is never in the Soviets' interests to attack the United States or American allies. Even a "defensive power" can start a war if it miscalculates, if easy opportunities are presented, or if it is backed into a corner where it feels it has to fight. Even an "offensive power" can be deterred, if the opposite conditions prevail.

The actual policy choices which the United States faces are the subjects of later chapters. Here, the issue is the nature of the Soviet regime. Several important points deserve attention.

First, the Soviet regime is extremely sensitive to the possibility of foreign attack. This is partly a historical issue. Russia was invaded and almost conquered in 1812, 1918, and 1941. It is also the result of a fact of present-day life: the Communist leaders in Moscow feel that they are encircled by nations which, for whatever reasons, do not look kindly upon the Soviet Union. And they are right. The People's Republic of China to the East, NATO Europe to the West, and the United States across both oceans distrust and fear the Russians.

The Soviet regime came very close to being crushed by the Nazi armies in the Second World War. The Soviet people suffered to a degree that is still difficult to fathom in the United States. Twenty million Soviet citizens died in what they call "the Great Patriotic War," a figure which contrasts sharply with the American WW II losses of approximately 325,000 and the absence of warfare and occupation at home.

American specialists on Soviet policy disagree on how these terrible losses in past wars influence the Soviet regime today. Some believe that the experience of fighting the Nazi armies make the Soviets less sensitive to the prospect of large civilian casualties in the future. Others believe that the tragic experience of 1941–45 makes the Soviets more cautious, less willing to take risks which might bring about a similar disaster. What is certain is that the Soviet Union's wartime experience, especially the manner in which it was attacked after having signed a peace agreement with Hitler's Germany, makes it especially uncomfortable with having its security dependent on the decisions made in its rival's capital. A Soviet general, Nikolay A. Talensky, expressed this discomfort quite explicitly:

> History has taught the Soviet Union to depend mainly on itself in ensuring its security and that of its friends. . . . After all, when the security of a state is based only on mutual deterrence with the aid of powerful nuclear rockets it is directly dependent on the goodwill and designs of the other side, which is a highly subjective and indefinite factor.[10]

*Second.* Western specialists on the Soviet Union do agree that Moscow's security policy is not made in the same manner as is American security policy. In the United States the interplay between the civilian sector and the military bureaucracy is substantial and constant. The Soviets' military control over security policy, on the other hand, is greater than ours; civilian influence is restricted to the top leadership. The Communist political leadership, of course, still maintains control over the funds for and the use of the Soviet military machine, but the machine is a more autonomous entity than it is in the West, where the military have to cope not only with the civilian leaders but also with parliamentary surveillance, a free and often skeptical press, and critical pressure groups.

Third, analysts of the Soviet Union agree that—whether because of Russian traditions or Marxist-Leninist beliefs— the Soviet Union has a long-term perspective on international conflict. The Soviet Union continues to be a revolutionary state: its leaders still claim that communism will inevitably inherit the earth, but they are not acting on a short-term timetable. George Kennan, writing in 1947, noted the mixed results of this phenomenon:

> These considerations make Soviet diplomacy at once easier and more difficult to deal with than the diplomacy of individual aggressive leaders like Napoleon and Hitler. On the one hand, it is more sensitive to contrary force, more ready to yield on

individual sectors of the diplomatic front when that force is felt to be too strong, and thus more rational in the logic and rhetoric of power. On the other hand, it cannot be easily defeated or discouraged by a single victory on the part of its opponents.

Kennan also noted the implications for American policy suggested by the Soviet perspective on conflict:

> And the patient persistence by which it is animated means that it can be effectively countered not by sporadic acts which represent the momentary whims of democratic opinion but only by intelligent long-range policies on the part of Russia's adversaries—policies no less steady in their purpose, and no less variegated and resourceful in their application, than those of the Soviet Union itself.[11]

Fourth, while Western analysts disagree on the degree of continuity in Moscow's foreign policy—how different Soviet policy is from that of the tsars—they note a number of critical and dangerous points of continuity. There is the tradition of Russian pressure and expansion all around the periphery of that vast country: in the 18th and 19th centuries, this pressure led to the partition of Poland, wars against the Ottoman empire, expansion in central Asia, attempts at controlling Afghanistan, and forced Chinese concessions in Manchuria. Since 1917 Soviet expansion has led to the acquisition of all or part of Estonia, Latvia, Lithuania, Poland, Finland, Germany, Czechoslovakia, Romania, and Japan as well as the growth of a military presence in many other areas.

Continuity also exists, in Kennan's terms, in the Russian tendency to "cultivate and maintain armed forces on a scale far greater than any visible threat to their security would seem to warrant."[12] Last, autocratic rule has been continuous from tsarist Russia to the current Soviet regime. Throughout Russian history there has been a total absence of democratic experience, of checks and balances within the government, of an organized public opinion capable of affecting it from without.

## THE UNITED STATES

Continuity is not the most obvious feature of American foreign policy. The American system of government, with its relatively short presidency, its frequent elections, its intense competition of parties and interests, makes for frequent shifts and jolts. Neither this system nor American history train Americans in "patient persistence" in dealing with foreign nations. On the contrary, our impatience is encouraged through the lingering attractions of two traditions: idealism and isolationism.

The founding fathers were excellent players of balance-of-power politics during the American Revolution. Indeed, if they had not enlisted the military aid of England's continental rival, France, the outcome of the struggle might have been different. Ironically, we owe our independence to the balance-of-power system, but we also have a strong legacy of viewing it with suspicion. The luxury of being a new nation on a distant continent allowed us to forgo concern with the balance of power in Europe for well over a century. Alliances were not seen as "strengthening" aids to mutual security, but rather as "entangling" enterprises to be avoided at all times. Peaceful competition, which characterizes American domestic politics, was not seen as a distant goal to work for in international politics, but rather as the normal state of affairs.

George Washington's farewell address set the tone for American foreign policy:

> Europe has a set of primary interests. . . . Hence she must be engaged in frequent controversies. . . . Our detached and distant situation invites and enables us to pursue a different course . . . why forgo the advantages of so peculiar a situation?—Why quit our own to stand upon foreign ground?—Why, by interweaving our destiny with that of any part of Europe, entangle our peace and prosperity in the toils of European ambition, rival, interest, humor or caprice?[13]

As long as the United States could remain truly detached and distant from the European balance, the answer to Washington's question was isolationism. Remaining aloof from the competition of international politics was a realistic policy for that time. But the United States learned in the First and Second World wars that American security interests could not allow one power to conquer the rest of the globe. As President Roosevelt announced two days after Pearl Harbor, the attack proved "that we cannot measure our safety in terms of miles on any map any more." What was true in 1941 is even more manifest today in a world of nuclear weapons, economic interdependence, and alliance commitments. American idealism in foreign affairs was also the result of early America's secure position across the seas from the powers of Europe. American statesmen did not have to learn the painful process of adjusting ideals to what is possible in political affairs. If other nations did not agree with our vision of justice, we could simply not have dealings with them. Ideals, of course, can and should provide inspiration for foreign policy; they can make the difficult easier, and the improbable more likely. But idealism should not blind Americans to the necessity of compromise in a world of sovereign states, each with its own conception of its interests and its own ideals.

In the Soviet Union, discouragement over setbacks in foreign policy is dampened by Russian traditions—which include a patient, often heroic, acceptance of sufferings imposed from outside or above, enormous resilience, and not a little obstinacy—and by Marxist ideology, with its optimistic but dateless prophecy. America's ideals and traditions affect it in the opposite manner. Failure to achieve American objectives in any one round of international politics can lead to flirtation with the idea of withdrawing from the game altogether or of seeking "ideal" worlds that do not exist. Each superpower has, however, experienced some degree of both overconfidence and insecurity in the post-World War II era; fluctuation between the two breeds misperceptions.

## COMMUNICATION

Different national experiences, geographical positions, ideological assumptions, and political systems have not only given to the Soviet-American competition its distinctive features, they have also made the problem of communication and mutual understanding (by which we mean neither accord nor sympathy, but simply the ability to perceive correctly what goes on) particularly difficult between the two superpowers. Americans have often been exasperated by Soviet negotiating tactics, which require inexhaustible patience when confronting meticulous points of procedure or garrulous recriminations. The Soviets find it difficult to understand how a great power can take purely idealistic concerns (such as human rights, or the abolition of spheres of influence) seriously, and they see in such concerns nothing but hypocrisy, double standards, and a deliberate attempt to undermine Soviet positions.

Two factors—one external, one internal—contribute to the difficulty in an especially important way. The Soviet Union is a country that has played a major role in world affairs for several centuries. It is used to dealing with other great powers. But the experience has frequently been frustrating. Not only have there been invasions, but Russian dealings with the outside world have bred distrust and feelings of inferiority resulting from an often resentful, sometimes admiring contact with European culture and Western technology.

In contrast, the United States' experience in world affairs has been brief and, before the Second World War, episodic. The U.S. has rarely had to deal with equals. In the First World War, it intervened late, and President Wilson sometimes gave his European colleagues the impression of behaving like a supreme judge or arbiter. Since 1945, the only country capable of challenging American power has been the USSR; and the U.S. has, on the whole, remained confident in the superiority of its technological achievements, economic system, and appeal to other people.

Each nuclear superpower finds it difficult to predict the other's behavior, but for very different reasons. The

United States cannot predict Soviet behavior because it has too little information on what goes on inside the Soviet Union; the Soviets cannot predict American behavior because they have too much information. To Western observers the Soviet system is a "black box"; to Soviet observers the American system resembles "white noise."

The Soviet Union has a passion for secrecy. There is no free press, dissidents are persecuted, constitutional checks and balances are nonexistent. The information that does reach the United States is fragmentary at best and usually contradictory. Thus, the Soviet system appears like a black box: often observers in the West simply cannot know what the Soviet government is doing or why.

In contrast, the American system is so open as to be equally confusing to outsiders, and not just the Soviets. Political debates are loud and bewildering. It is often difficult for foreigners to separate the relevant information from the background noises. A fragmented executive branch, a legislative branch with little internal discipline, decentralized parties, multiple interest groups, assertive media, socially conscious religious groups, all have a say in government policy. And the noise and complexity all make it difficult for the Soviet Union to predict American future behavior.

## CONCLUSION: THE CRYSTAL BALL EFFECT

If one could gather together the skillful diplomats of the Congress of Vienna (1815) and ask their advice on how to build a stable order in international politics, they would certainly not suggest the characteristics of the present balance of terror. They would advise having many great powers, each willing to compete in limited ways for limited objectives. They would recommend against having two superpowers, and especially two powers with conflicting ideals and traditions. The statesmen of the past might suggest that technology be allowed to develop only weapons that could be used for defensive purposes, and even these should be limited in power. They would not recommend the nuclear revolution.

Yet since 1945 this anarchic order has been maintained without major war. It has been maintained despite the bipolar conflict, despite revolutionary governments, despite conflicts of interests and ideologies, despite technological advances that few predicted, and despite nuclear weapons.

Perhaps in one important sense, but only in this one sense, the balance of terror is more stable than was the balance of power in the 19th century. Nuclear weapons have created what we call the *crystal ball effect*. Imagine what would have happened if the statesmen who went to war in the summer of 1914 had possessed a crystal ball showing them the world of 1918. The political leaders in 1914 expected a short sharp war like their last one forty years earlier, to be followed by business as usual. One suspects that if the German kaiser, the Russian tsar, and the Austrian emperor had seen a picture of 1918 with their thrones vacant and their empires dismembered, they might have drawn back from the brink that fateful summer. Ironically, the enormous horror of nuclear weapons' effects means that modern leaders have the equivalent of a crystal ball showing them the devastation at the end of a major war. This crystal ball effect helps to give the nuclear world at least some measure of stability. Statesmen in the atomic age can envision the destruction of a full-scale nuclear war and it makes them determined to avoid it. Crises still occur, but when the statesmen of the nuclear age have gazed into the nuclear crystal ball they have, thus far, prudently retreated from the ultimate confrontation.

This crystal ball effect does not solve the problems of war and peace. It does not make war impossible. As long as political conflicts exist between sovereign and armed states, the temptation to use force as a way of deciding disputes will continue, as well as the hope to find uses of force that will not lead to the ultimate confrontation. For in the nuclear age, the crystal ball can still be shattered by accident, by negligence, by irrational blindness, or by miscalculation. Unfortunately, such failures of prudence are commonplace in history. Each must be avoided today. Nuclear weapons have not guaranteed peace; they have only made it more necessary.

## Notes

1. Thomas Hobbes, *Leviathan* (Baltimore: Penguin, 1968), p. 186.

2. Walter Lippmann, "The Political Equivalent of War," *Atlantic,* August 1928, p. 181.

3. Thus the word "revolutionary," in politics, is used in two meanings: it designates either a country *in* which a revolution has taken place, or a state that acts *outside* its borders in order to change the established international order. Often, as in the cases of France during the French Revolution or of Hitler, a country that is going through a revolution at home acts as a revolutionary power on the world stage.

4. Clemens Metternich, *Aus Metternichs Nachgelassenen Papieren* (Vienna, 1880), III:332, as quoted in Henry Kissinger, *A World Restored* (New York: Grosset and Dunlap, 1964), pp. 25–26.

5. Michael Howard, "Reflections on the First World War," *Studies in War and Peace* (New York: Viking, 1972), p. 106.

6. Kissinger, ibid., p. 6.

7. Bernard Brodie (ed.), *The Absolute Weapon* (New York: Harcourt, Brace, 1946), p. 29.

8. Thomas Jefferson, Correspondence, *Writings* 5, 95. As quoted in Arnold Wolfers and Laurence Martin (eds.), *The Anglo-American Tradition in Foreign Affairs* (New Haven, Conn.: Yale University, 1956), p. 158.

9. Bernard Brodie, *War and Politics* (New York: Macmillan, 1973), pp. 430–31.

10. N. Talensky, "Anti-Missile Systems and Disarmament," in John Erikson (ed.), *The Military-Technical Revolution* (New York: Praeger, 1966), pp. 227, 225, originally cited in Jack Snyder, *The Soviet Strategic Culture*, Rand R–2154–AF, p. 28.

11. George Kennan ("X"), "The Sources of Soviet Conduct," *Foreign Affairs,* July 1947, p. 575.

12. George Kennan, *The Nuclear Delusion* (New York: Pantheon, 1982), p. 44.

13. The farewell address is reprinted in Felix Gilbert, *To the Farewell Address* (Princeton, N.J.: Princeton University, 1961), pp. 144–47.

# 3

# The Shattered Crystal Ball: How Might a Nuclear War Begin?

The question is grisly, but nonetheless it must be asked. Nuclear war cannot be avoided simply by refusing to think about it. Indeed, the task of reducing the likelihood of nuclear war should begin with an effort to understand how it might start.

When strategists in Washington or Moscow study the possible origins of nuclear war, they discuss "scenarios," imagined sequences of future events that could trigger the use of nuclear weaponry. Scenarios are, of course, speculative exercises. They often leave out the political developments that might lead to the use of force in order to focus on military dangers. That nuclear war scenarios are even more speculative than most is something for which we can be thankful, for it reflects humanity's fortunate lack of experience with atomic warfare since 1945. But imaginary as they are, nuclear scenarios can help to identify problems not understood or dangers not yet prevented because they have not been foreseen.

Many commonly held beliefs about the likely origins of nuclear war are, however, misleading. Focusing on less likely ways that nuclear war might occur creates unnecessary worries and enhances the possibility that more probable dangers will be ignored. This chapter presents several scenarios—some more likely than others—each a conceiv-

47

able path to nuclear war. Although examining such horrible events can be frightening, creating fear is not the purpose of the exercise. Rather, constructing scenarios can underline actions already taken to reduce the likelihood of war and also point to actions that can minimize future hazards.

Nuclear war would most probably begin for reasons similar to those which began wars in the past. Governments might see opportunities for quick and easy gains and, misjudging enemy reactions, could take steps toward nuclear war without being fully aware of the risks involved. Governments might, under other circumstances, believe that beginning a war was the lesser of two evils, a plausible belief if the other evil is the enemy striking first. These and many other causes have led to war in the past.

Nuclear war is possible. It could occur through purposeful choice, through miscalculation, or through a variety of accidents. It could be started by a political leader, by a military commander, or by a group of terrorists. It could come as a sudden surprise in a time of peace or as the seemingly inevitable culmination of a prolonged conflict between nuclear armed nations. We chose the following kinds of scenarios (some of which are more plausible than others) to illustrate a gamut of possibilities as well as to explore popular and current concerns: (1) surprise attack by one superpower on all or part of the nuclear forces of the other; (2) pre-emptive attacks launched in desperation in time of crisis because one side believes (rightly or wrongly) that the other intends soon to strike first; (3) escalation of conventional wars to nuclear ones; (4) accidental uses of nuclear weapons resulting from malfunctions of machines or of minds; and (5) nuclear wars initiated by other nuclear armed nations or by terrorist organizations. These categories are not unique; additional scenarios involving elements from two or more categories could easily be constructed. Nor is the list of scenarios exhaustive; not all the possible paths to nuclear war can be foreseen. Murphy's law—which states that if something can go wrong, it will—applies here as in all other human activities: military plans go awry, controls fail, misjudgments occur, and one mistake often seems to lead to another, in peacetime and in war. This should not breed despair; it should serve as a constant reminder of the need to control events so that events do not control us.

## SCENARIOS

### THE BOLT FROM THE BLUE

Imagine the following conversation. The date is November 1, 1991; the location, inside the Kremlin.

General Secretary _____: "Comrade General, you have heard the debate. Some members of the Politburo favor your proposal for a surprise attack upon the United States. Others are highly opposed. We await your opinion. Can we go to war and win?"

General _____, Chief of Staff, Soviet Rocket Forces: "Yes! If war is to come, it must come soon, or all is lost. The counter-revolution in Eastern Europe has put our back against the wall. The American military buildup continues to threaten our socialist nation.

"But let me explain how we can triumph if we attack quickly, with all our power. The Americans suspect nothing. We have greatly improved our hunter-killer submarine force and now can closely follow all their submarines; our ballistic missile submarines can maintain adequate attack forces off the enemy's coast. In only seven minutes our submarine missiles could destroy American bombers on their runways, the American submarines in the ports, and, as importantly, American military and civilian command centers. Without orders from these command posts, the missiles in the United States will not be immediately launched and will be destroyed when our ICBMs arrive 23 minutes after the submarine missiles land on target.

"We have, of course, supreme confidence in our military strength. But if a small number of

America's nuclear missiles and bombers escape destruction from our overwhelming attack, our ballistic missile defense system and our air defense system will shoot them down. We can end the capitalist threat forever. Let us decide now to end this intolerable situation, destroy them before they gain in strength and threaten us even more."

General Secretary _____: "Thank you. Comrades, the day of destiny may be upon us. How do you vote?"

Is this scenario possible? Yes. Is it likely? No. This bolt from the blue, commonly the most feared prospect, is a most unlikely scenario for the start of a nuclear war *as long as* no Russian military leader could ever report to the Politburo that a Soviet victory in nuclear war was probable or that the damage from American nuclear retaliation could be reduced to acceptable levels.

What military, political, and economic conditions would have to exist before Soviet leaders would seriously listen to the imagined general's proposal? First, nearly *all* American retaliatory forces and the entire command system would have to be highly vulnerable to a Soviet first strike. Currently, most of the Minutemen ICBMs (intercontinental ballistic missiles), U.S. bombers on airfields and submarines in port, and the American command, control, and communications network are theoretically vulnerable. But the forces that would survive a Soviet attack would still be enormously destructive. Most importantly, the American submarine force routinely at sea, which carries more nuclear warheads than does the entire Minuteman force, cannot now or in the foreseeable future be located or quickly destroyed by the Soviet navy.

Second, both Soviet ballistic missile defenses and air defenses would have to be improved greatly, perhaps beyond what is possible, before they could be expected to reduce the damage of the American retaliatory missile and bomber attacks to an acceptable level. Third, technical difficulties would plague the prospects of success in such a surprise Soviet attack: not only would it be enormously difficult to coordinate the actions of Soviet missile-bearing submarines, ICBMs, and anti-submarine warfare forces, but success would hinge on complete surprise being maintained. If Soviet strategic forces were put on full alert status, the possibility that the American intelligence network would miss the warning is exceedingly remote. Strategic Air Command bombers would be alerted and dispersed, American political leaders and military commanders could be sent to safer locations, and some submarines in port could be sent to sea. These actions would reduce still further the probability that a massive Soviet nuclear attack would be answered with only token nuclear retaliation. Finally, the United States could choose to launch its ICBMs on warning of the attack (i.e., while the attacking missiles were in flight toward their targets) or after the first attacking warheads had arrived.

The bolt from the blue is thus not likely now or any time in the foreseeable future. This scenario is, indeed, so farfetched that it is useful to consider only in one sense: it points to a set of combined circumstances which, as a matter of long-range policy, the United States must seek to avoid. There is clearly no reason that such a dangerous combination of circumstances need ever develop. The bolt from the blue could become plausible only if there was a major deterioration of Soviet-American relations and if Soviet nuclear forces, defensive preparations, and anti-submarine capabilities were greatly enhanced, while American counter-measures were unilaterally restrained.

## A LIMITED ATTACK ON THE MINUTEMAN MISSILES

Some defense specialists believe that while American nuclear retaliatory capabilities might successfully deter surprise attacks on American cities, as well as bolt-from-the-blue attacks on all of the nuclear forces, limited attacks on portions of America's nuclear arsenal are substantially more likely. This is one of the concerns that has fueled the debate over the basing mode for the MX missile, a replacement for the vulnerable Minuteman system. The feared scenario often runs something like this:

*The decision in Moscow:* In a deep crisis over the status of Berlin, the Politburo decides not to launch an all-out pre-emptive attack against American forces and command centers, but only to attack the Minuteman silos. A hot-line message is sent as soon as the warheads land: first, the Soviet Union will spare American cities if the United States refrains from retaliation and, second, the United States is urged to give in to Soviet demands in Europe.

*The decision in Washington:* The president asks the Joint Chiefs of Staff what military options exist, now that 90% of the Minuteman force is destroyed. They say that fifteen million Americans have just died in the Soviet attack and that an American response will likely trigger a Soviet attack on population centers. Should the president launch a retaliatory strike? Or should he give in to Soviet demands?

This Minuteman-only scenario rests upon a very questionable premise: that the Soviets would believe that the president of the United States would choose not to launch the ICBMs on warning or retaliate after 2,000 Soviet nuclear warheads have exploded here. The American submarines, moreover, could attack many Soviet military targets. A Soviet leader probably would assume that retaliation of some sort would be launched after 15 million Americans were killed. In such circumstances, it would be likely that the Soviets would try to reduce the American retaliation to whatever extent they could.

Thus, if the Soviets were to attack the United States on a large-scale basis, they would have great incentives to attack not only the land-based missiles, but also other American strategic forces and the American command, control, and communications network. There is little Soviet advantage to be gained by attacking the U.S. ICBMs alone, for they contain less than one-fourth of America's strategic nuclear warheads. It is not surprising that Soviet military doctrine, as far as American intelligence sources can determine, stresses that if nuclear war occurs, their nuclear forces would be used on a massive scale.

This Minuteman-only scenario, like the full-blown bolt from the blue, is far less likely than many other possible paths to nuclear war. These surprise attack scenarios preoccupy all too many defense analysts whose talents would be far better applied to preventing more likely dangers. And the attention of the public would be better directed to more realistic scenarios and more probable perils.

## A PRE-EMPTIVE WAR

Not all wars begin with coolly calculated decisions. Indeed, under certain circumstances, a nuclear war could originate from a series of hasty decisions made in the midst of uncertainty. In fact, a nuclear exchange could be precipitated by a mistaken action, originally intended to deter war, which could produce a counter-decision to launch a pre-emptive strike.

Consider the following scenario. It is the opening page of an imaginary historian's future best-seller, *The Missiles of August: The Origins of World War Three:*

> What was the cause of the war? The Greek historian Thucydides, in his history of the conflict between Athens and Sparta, differentiated between the immediate causes and the underlying causes of war. The latter can be compared to the mass of combustible material; the former is the match that sets the material ablaze.
>
> On August 2, 19__, none of the American leaders in Washington knew that they were lighting such a match. A number of years earlier, Soviet Premier Brezhnev had warned the United States that, if NATO deployed Pershing II and cruise missiles in Western Europe, the Soviet Union would "take retaliatory steps that would put the other side, including the United States itself, its own territory, in an analogous position." On the last day of July, American intelligence satellites spotted cruise missiles being unloaded onto Cuban soil from Soviet ships and on August 1 Pre-

mier Andropov announced that he would remove the missiles only if the United States withdrew the NATO deployments.

The sole surviving member of the National Security Council later reported that the president's decision to attack the Cuban dockyard and the Soviet ships was taken overnight. "We had no choice. In a few days, those missiles—we didn't know how many—would have been scattered all over Cuba. This was the only way to get rid of the missiles. We told the Soviets that there would be no attack on Russia itself. Our nuclear alert was only meant to signal our strength."

This was not the view from Moscow. Two Soviet staff officers who survived reported that the Politburo was informed that the Americans must be about to launch a nuclear attack. The head of the KGB told the Politburo that if the Americans launched first, the vast majority of Soviet ICBMs would be destroyed and eventually up to 100 million Soviet citizens might die. But if the Soviet arsenal was used immediately to destroy American nuclear forces and command centers, the casualties after retaliation would probably be "only" between 10 and 20 million. He even told the group that there was a small chance that a pre-emptive attack would "decapitate" the American giant and that no response would come.

He was wrong. The Russians thought war was unavoidable and launched first in desperation and fear. Thirty-five million Americans were killed instantly. The retaliation was perhaps smaller than the first strike the Soviets feared, but it still left 25 million Russians dead.

Perhaps, however, it is misleading to start this history with the immediate cause of the war. The deeper causes go back to 1945. At the close of the Second World War, Soviet and American relations deteriorated rapidly . . .

How plausible is such a pre-emptive war scenario? Although no precise probabilities can be given, of course, it is at least a possibility that in a deep and apparently irresolvable crisis the Soviets (or the United States) might launch their nuclear weapons first with full knowledge that many of its citizens might die, but fearing far worse casualties if they allowed the other side to attack first. A desperate decision indeed, but a possible one.

What conditions would increase the likelihood of such a tragic decision being made by the leaders of a superpower? First, the leaders would have to believe that the other side intended to strike first, and soon. This would require that the adversary's forces be at or moving toward (or be perceived to be at) a high state of alert—a condition likely to be met only in times of crisis. Second, the leaders would have to believe that the other side could carry out a relatively successful disarming first strike—a judgment which would depend upon the capabilities of the adversary's forces and the vulnerabilities of their own. Lastly, the leaders must be convinced that by launching a pre-emptive attack against the other side's nuclear forces, they could substantially reduce the casualties and damage that would ultimately be suffered by their own nation.

The possibility that such a scenario might happen does not, by itself, mean that the United States should never put its forces on alert in a crisis or that we should always back down in dangerous circumstances. Nor does it mean that American nuclear forces should not be aimed at Soviet weaponry. But the possibility of such an occurrence should, at a minimum, promote great caution in times of crisis, highlight the importance of clear and unambiguous military orders, and stress the need for retaliatory forces that are invulnerable and are perceived as such by both sides. Moreover, it should serve as a constant reminder that the security of both sides is diminished by either side's fear of being struck first or by either side's temptation to strike first.

## ESCALATION: CONVENTIONAL STEPS TO NUCLEAR WAR

It is difficult, though clearly not impossible, to outline a credible scenario in which, during peacetime, a Soviet or an American leader would decide to launch an all-out nuclear attack. It is less difficult to imagine a war occurring between the conventional forces of the two superpowers. And once American and Soviet troops met in combat, the likelihood of the use of nuclear weapons would be increased.

The process by which a war becomes incrementally more violent, either through the plans of the combatants or unintentionally, is called escalation. Escalation from conventional fighting to nuclear war has been a continuing concern of defense planners since the Soviets developed their nuclear arsenal. This fear has, thus far, produced prudence: each superpower has been reluctant to use even conventional forces against the other. Can this prudence continue indefinitely? What would happen if Soviet and American conventional forces did clash somewhere?

We do not know. And this inability to know whether conventional war would escalate to a nuclear exchange both enhances prudence and perpetuates fear. Consider two possible scenarios for nuclear conflict developing through escalation:

*War in Europe*
Step 1: East German workers, organized by an underground labor union, go on strike, demanding political changes in the government of their country. Martial law is imposed and riots ensue throughout the country. Russian troops help in the "police action." East Germans flee across the border into West Germany.

Step 2: Fighting breaks out between West German military units, who are aiding the refugees, and East German security forces. Soon Soviet forces join in the fighting. Two days later Soviet divisions cross into West Germany and the Soviet premier publicly warns the United States to "refrain from self-defeating threats."

Step 3: Other NATO forces—American, British, and Dutch—become involved in the fighting as the Soviets advance further into West Germany. As the Allies are being pushed back by the superior numbers of Soviet divisions, NATO leaders gather to decide on further military action.

They publicly warn the Soviets to withdraw immediately or "suffer the gravest consequences." Four airfields along the Polish-Soviet border are attacked with nuclear-tipped cruise missiles, a communiqué announces, "as a demonstration of NATO resolve."

Step 4: The Soviet Union immediately fires nuclear missiles to destroy nuclear weapons sites in West Germany.

Step 5: ?? Does the war escalate to a full nuclear exchange or is a settlement possible? What would the United States do? What would the Soviet Union do next?

*War in the Persian Gulf*

Step 1: The Iranian Communist party overthrows the increasingly unpopular government of Ayatollah Khomeini. Civil war breaks out throughout Iran and the new government requests that Soviet troops enter the country "to help restore order." Despite American warnings against such action Soviet forces cross into Iran and move toward Teheran.

Step 2: American troops are immediately sent to southwestern Iran to protect the West's oil supply sources. Advance parties of the two armies meet and engage in combat.

Step 3: As Soviet reinforcements begin to move into Iran, the president orders aircraft from an American aircraft carrier in the Indian Ocean to "close the mountain passes" along the Soviet supply route. Told that nuclear bombs might be needed, he refuses to give weapons release authority to the local commander. "The United States will not be the first to go nuclear," the president's message concludes.

Step 4: The American military commander orders six conventional air strikes against mountain passes in Iran. The next morning, Soviet bombers fly south and attack the American carrier task force with nuclear-tipped missiles. The

aircraft carrier and many of its supporting ships
are destroyed instantly.
    Step 5: ?? Does the president escalate further?
Does the Soviet Union stop fighting? What happens next? How does the war end?

These paths to nuclear conflict (or others like them)
are more likely than the previous scenarios of initial
homeland-to-homeland exchanges for an obvious reason:
once war begins, the balance between political and military
considerations shifts decidedly toward the military side.
The leader of a government is far more likely to authorize
use of a small number of nuclear weapons during a conventional war than to initiate a full-scale nuclear conflict.
But unless the war is somehow terminated, there will be
continued incentives for further escalation.
    Once a conventional war began, there would be two
other factors, in addition to possible decisions to take incremental escalatory steps, that could lead to nuclear war.
First, there would be increased possibilities of miscalculation leading to nuclear war. It is possible that at some
stage in a conventional conflict a field commander might
be given "pre-delegation of authority," the president's option of allowing commanders to decide themselves when
to use tactical nuclear weapons. Once this is done, the
likelihood of use through miscalculation or mistake in the
"fog of battle" would greatly increase. Second, the pressures for pre-emptive nuclear strikes would likely be enhanced after the line between superpower peace and
superpower war was crossed. Once the fighting began,
one or both governments might decide that full-scale use
of nuclear weapons was inevitable or very nearly so; thus,
despite the terrible risks involved, a pre-emptive attack
might be chosen, on the basis that striking first is better
than being stricken first, though both are worse than the
unavailable option of no nuclear war at all.
    The maintenance of a conventional-nuclear "fire-
break"—an often used metaphor borrowed from forest
fire-fighting techniques—is most strategists' goal here. If a
conventional conflict between the superpowers does someday occur, every effort should be made to terminate the
war without the use of nuclear weapons; escalation to full

thermonuclear war should be avoided. Withdrawing tactical nuclear weapons from sites near borders, where they might be used quickly in a war, and keeping strict political control over weapons release authority widen the firebreak between conventional and nuclear war. It is not clear, however, exactly how wide such a firebreak should be because of what was earlier described as the "usability paradox": if nuclear weapons are too usable, they might be used when and in a manner not controllable by government leaders; yet if it is certain that weapons will not be used, might this not encourage conventional aggression?

## TRAGIC ACCIDENTS

Could nuclear war begin purely by accident? Mechanical failures do occur, after all, even with (and perhaps especially with) the most sophisticated machinery. Human frailties always exist as well. And such frailties can produce highly irrational behavior at times, even when (and perhaps especially when) the psychological pressures to behave cautiously are enormous.

It is a common assumption that nuclear weapons are likely to be used, not through decisions of rational government leaders, but through mechanical or human accidents. Jonathan Schell, for example, has written that "the machinery of destruction is complete, poised on a hair trigger, waiting for a 'button' to be 'pushed' by some misguided or deranged human being or for some faulty computer chip to send out the instruction to fire."[1] Is this true? Are the following scenes possible?

*The Faulty Computer Chip War*
Deep inside a multimillion-dollar computer, used to process the military intelligence coming from American satellites, a 35-cent computer chip malfunctions. Suddenly the radar screens begin to flash. A thousand Soviet missiles appear to be coming over the horizon. "Oh, my God," the radar screen operator says. "This is it."

In the White House, the president is informed of the warning, now ten minutes old. "In twenty minutes the missiles will destroy our retaliatory forces, sir," his military aide informs him. As the president leaves the White House for his specially equipped command post airplane, he orders that all land-based missiles be launched immediately.

"I am not going to let our missiles be destroyed on the ground," he says as he climbs aboard the helicopter. "We'll fight. But the Russians started this war. Let the history books record that fact."

### The Strangelove Scenario

Individuals under pressure cannot always withstand the strain. Sometimes men snap. Late one night, a Soviet submarine commander walks into the control room of his new *Typhoon*-class submarine and, before the astonished ensign can react, he pushes a button sending a single SLBM, with twelve nuclear warheads in the nose cone, on its way to the United States.

"What have you done?" the ensign cries as he tackles the commander, wrestling him to the floor.

The commander appears startled. Then he smiles, looks up, and says, "That missile is going to down a Nazi bomber. I'm teaching those fascists a lesson. Remember Stalingrad!"

Although such imaginative scenarios are often discussed, they are, fortunately, extremely unlikely if not impossible. This is not because the problem of accidental war is not a serious concern. Rather the opposite is the case: precisely because the possibility exists that nuclear weapons could be used accidentally, the United States government has devised numerous precautions to prevent such accidents. Indeed, contrary to a popular belief, the chances of an American weapon being used accidentally are probably much less today than they were in the 1950s. For along with more sophisticated and more numerous weapons, more sophisticated and more numerous precautionary policies have been developed.

Four kinds of measures intended to minimize the chances of unauthorized or accidental use are worth noting. First is the "two-man rule," which requires parallel actions by two or more individuals at several stages in the process of communicating and carrying out any order to use nuclear weapons. Second is the system of Permissive Action Links (PALs), including a highly secure coded signal which must be inserted in the weapons before they can be used. Third, devices internal to the weapon are designed to ensure that an attempt to bypass the PALs system will disarm the weapon. Finally, the nuclear warheads themselves are designed to preclude accidental detonation as a result of exposure to heat, blast, or radiation. The Soviets share our concern with unauthorized and accidental nuclear war, and there is reason to believe that they too have taken measures to prevent it.

In this light, how credible are the two scenarios outlined above? There have been, it is true, many false alarms in the American nuclear attack warning system. Some of them have been traced to such minuscule components as an inexpensive computer chip. But none of these false alerts has even come close to leading the nation into war because the government has built redundancies into the system, precisely so that no president will ever have to rely on a single computer or single radar screen to make such important decisions. For this kind of accident to lead to war, several warning systems of different kinds (e.g., infrared sensors on satellites, and radars on land) would have to fail simultaneously. Even that by itself would be unlikely to cause the president to order an immediate launching of ICBMs. His incentives to do so might indeed be small if the missiles were relatively invulnerable and if he had other nuclear systems at sea, not under attack. It is even possible to maintain a policy of not launching missiles in a retaliatory strike until after the damage of the enemy's first strike is assessed.

Of course, it is possible that a military commander could go insane (although the stability of American officers with such responsibilities is carefully tested). An insane American officer could not, in peacetime by himself, arm and deliver the nuclear weapons under his command. In the submarine case, to give but one example, it would take the simultaneous insanity of a number of American submarine officers for an unauthorized American launch to be possible. Given the Soviets' strong propensity for tight political control of their nuclear weapons, there is no reason to believe that the chances of unauthorized Soviet use are any greater.

Thus it is a mistake to believe that a simple accident or an unstable commander could easily lead to a nuclear exchange. In reality, the probabilities of such an event are very low. This should not, however, breed complacency about the prospect of accidental war, for two reasons. First, it is only through continual concern that the likelihood of accidental use of weapons is kept so low. Second, mechanical accidents and human frailties could become increasingly dangerous in times of deep crisis or conventional war, during which time command centers could be threatened or destroyed.

There will continue to be an uneasy balance between the degree of control required to ensure that weapons are not used accidentally and the degree of "usability" required to ensure that the weapons can be used if needed. Preventing accidental use is an important goal, but it cannot be the only objective of a nuclear weapons policy. Nuclear weapons must be usable enough to provide credible deterrence, but not so usable as to invite unintended use.

## REGIONAL NUCLEAR WAR

One important reason why the world has seen nuclear peace since 1945 is that there has been no conventional war between the United States and the Soviet Union. In the future, if nuclear proliferation continues, there will be an increased danger of nuclear war breaking out between two nuclear armed Third World countries. Such an event might be more likely than nuclear war between the superpowers because many of the conditions that have led to the maintenance of nuclear peace—such as invulnerable second-strike forces, strong leadership control of nuclear weapons, and stable governments in nuclear weapons states—may be absent. The following is an imaginary future newspaper report of a nuclear war which neither Washington nor Moscow would be in a position to stop.

INDIA USES THE BOMB, PAKISTAN SUES FOR PEACE

New Delhi, India.—The Indian government this morning announced that four nuclear bombs were dropped on Pakistan late last night. At noon, a Defense Ministry spokesman in Islamabad read a declaration over the radio accepting "unconditional surrender" on behalf of the Revolutionary Islamic Council of Pakistan. Thus it appears that the week-long war between India and Pakistan has come to a sudden end.

Sources inside the Indian Ministry of Defense have revealed that India's entire nuclear arsenal was used in this morning's pre-emptive attack against Pakistan's three major military airfields and its nuclear weapons assembly facility. When the Pakistani forces crossed the Indian border last week, Radio Islamabad announced that any Indian use of nuclear weapons would be met in kind. After last year's Pakistani nuclear test, the government in New Delhi took the threat seriously, the Ministry of Defense officials reported, and only decided to attack pre-emptively when Indian intelligence warned that Pakistan's weapons were being readied for use. "We had no choice," an official said. "The enemy was preparing for an attack. Fortunately, we knew where the bombs were kept, and destroyed them and their bomber aircraft simultaneously."

Meanwhile, in New York, the UN Security Council met throughout the night and . . .

Somehow this scenario appears less farfetched than most of the previously outlined scenarios for superpower nuclear war. It also appears less apocalyptic (at least from a non-Pakistani perspective). Indeed, its less-than-apocalyptic nature may be precisely the characteristic that makes it less farfetched. The dangers of this kind of nuclear war may be comparatively small today, but they will increase in the future as more countries acquire nuclear weapons. (Nuclear proliferation and policies designed to reduce its dangers are more fully discussed in Chapter 10.)

It is tempting, but incorrect, to think that a nuclear conflict between any two countries would not affect other nations. There is the possibility that one government at war would be allied to the Soviet Union and the other government to the United States, thereby raising the specter of the superpowers becoming involved in the war. Moreover, there is a danger that a nuclear armed country could use a weapon, intentionally or not, against a superpower.

## CATALYTIC WAR

There is yet another way in which the superpowers could be dragged into nuclear war by the actions of a third party. Imagine the two scenarios described below:

> *The French Connection*
> A conventional conflict between NATO and the Warsaw Pact erupts and, despite the imminent collapse of the NATO front, the United States does not use nuclear weapons. The French government, however, launches a small number of its nuclear-tipped submarine-launched ballistic missiles against military targets, hoping to bring a halt to the Soviet advance. The Soviets do not know who launched the missiles, and respond by launching a nuclear attack against NATO military targets throughout Europe. The American president orders that NATO's Pershing IIs be used against military targets in the USSR. . . .

> *Mistaken Identity*
> A war in the Persian Gulf has broken out between the United States and the Soviet Union. After a week of conventional fighting, nuclear-tipped cruise missiles are launched against the American carrier task force. The planes are Soviet models and bear Soviet markings; they are not manned by Soviet pilots nor are they otherwise under Soviet control. Some other country has intentionally and successfully disguised its aircraft, and the Americans mistakenly conclude that it is the Soviets who have initiated use of nuclear

weapons. Does the American president escalate further? What might the Soviets do in the midst of this confusion? What happens next?

Clearly, such scenarios are possible. Under a number of circumstances another nuclear power might trigger a strategic nuclear exchange between the superpowers, a war that they had thus far avoided. The possibilities of such an event are greatly increased if conventional war occurs. Few strategists place the danger of catalytic war as high as nuclear war through escalation or pre-emption, but it still is a serious concern. Indeed, during the SALT I negotiations, the Soviet Union mentioned its concern that the growing Chinese nuclear arsenal might someday be used with such results.

## NUCLEAR TERRORISM

What if a terrorist organization gained possession of a nuclear bomb? Could nuclear war occur as a result? Consider the following scenario, which was invented in the best-selling novel *The Fifth Horseman*:[2]

On a snowy December evening, the President of the United States is told by his National Security Adviser that a tape recording in Arabic has just been delivered to the White House. It appears to be a message from Muammar al-Qaddafi, President of Libya, and claims that a nuclear weapon has been placed somewhere on Manhattan. Unless the United States forces Israel to withdraw to its 1967 borders, the bomb will be detonated.

"I must further inform you that, should you make this communication public or begin in any way to evacuate New York City, I shall feel obliged to instantly explode my weapon," the message concludes.

"A man like Qaddafi has got to know we have the capability to utterly destroy him and his entire nation in retaliation. He'd be mad to do something like that," the President tells his adviser.

But what should the president do? Is nuclear terrorism possible? How could it come about?

Terrorists might gain possession of an atomic bomb in one of several ways, including theft, purchase, or manufacture. If they were to steal it, and if it were of American origin, then the Permissive Action Links should frustrate any attempt to detonate it. But it is not at all clear just how confident a president might be in the ability of the PALs to resist a concerted attempt to bypass them, especially in light of the high stakes involved. And suppose the stolen bomb was not an American one. Other current and future nuclear weapons states may not have equipped their warheads with safety systems comparable to those developed by the United States.

A terrorist organization might purchase an atomic bomb from (or be given one by) a government that shares the terrorist group's goals. Indeed, this possibility is reason enough to work to inhibit the spread of nuclear weapons to additional countries.

Finally, terrorists might fashion their own nuclear explosive device. The highly enriched uranium or plutonium essential to the project might be stolen or bought, and a crude but workable bomb assembled. (See Chapter 10.) The task would be difficult, but not impossible. In any event, how confident could a president be that the terrorists' bomb would not work? And against whom could he threaten retaliation?

## CONCLUSION: CONTINUING ISSUES

How should one think about the various paths to war outlined in this chapter? Five points need to be stressed. First, the set of scenarios presented here is not exhaustive. Surely each reader can think of other ways in which a nuclear war might begin. How probable are such scenarios? What can be done to minimize the likelihood of their occurrence? Also, the dangers of these scenarios could be compounded. Suppose, to give but two examples, mechanical failures in warning systems developed during a deep superpower crisis, or human frailty produced unstable commanders during a conventional war. Thus, when thinking of the potential dangers to be avoided in the future, one must not assume that decisions will always be deliberate, or that accidents will always develop when they can do the least harm.

Second, this chapter suggests that it is usually misleading to concentrate one's attention on the number of nuclear weapons when analyzing the likelihood of war. It is widely assumed that changes in the numbers of weapons in the superpower arsenals—either upward or downward—are the major determinant of the risks of war. Sheer numbers, however, matter far less than factors such as the vulnerability of weapons, the credibility of commitments to allies, and imbalances in conventional forces. In the short run, to give but one example, making command and control systems less vulnerable can be as important, and probably more so, in reducing certain risks of war than would changes in the numbers of weapons: improved command and control could reduce an enemy's incentives for a "decapitating" attack, and could improve our ability to follow a policy of "no retaliation until specifically ordered." And the long-run risk of nuclear war is likely to depend more on our ability to stem proliferation than on any other single factor. The common fixation on numbers of weapons in the superpower arsenals misses such important issues.

Third, there is no reason to assume that an all-out nuclear exchange, certainly the most frightening scenario, is either the only kind of nuclear war possible or even the most likely type of nuclear war. Nuclear war occurring through the escalation of conventional conflict appears more probable. Avoiding conventional war is, therefore, one of the most important ways of avoiding nuclear war. And maintaining strong and credible conventional forces may thus be an important component of preventing nuclear war. One should never forget that, despite the incentives to keep a conventional war limited, once fighting begins it would be difficult to control escalation to the nuclear abyss. But escalation should not be considered inevitable, for that could prove to be a self-fulfilling prophecy.

Fourth, it is noted that in none of these scenarios do leaders of the United States or the Soviet Union act insanely. But departures from rationality are not inconceivable; they must be taken into account in the design of measures to prevent nuclear war.

Finally, this glimpse at the shattered crystal ball should breed neither complacency nor despair. A horrible nuclear future is not inevitable, but only because great efforts have been made in the past to decrease its likelihood. The good news for the present is, then, that nuclear war is not probable. The bad news is that nuclear war is, and will continue to be, possible. To make sure that the possible does not become more probable is the continuing task of nuclear policy.

## Notes

1. Jonathan Schell, *The Fate of the Earth* (New York: Knopf, 1982), p. 182.

2. Larry Collins and Dominique LaPierre, *The Fifth Horseman* (New York: Simon and Schuster, 1980), pp. 13–19.

# PART II

## The Current Condition

# 4

# Weapons and Rivalry: How Did We Get Here?

For the more than three decades since the Second World War the United States and the Soviet Union have been at peace. Peace between nations, however, does not necessarily mean the absence of rivalry. Throughout these years the two superpowers have competed with each other, politically, ideologically, diplomatically, economically, and militarily. The military dimension has not included armed conflict between Americans and Russians. It has primarily been competition in development and deployment of military force, particularly nuclear weapons. Each power has created an enormous nuclear arsenal aimed at the other: thousands of nuclear warheads atop intercontinental missiles, in long-range bombers and in submarines, on board ships in the ocean and with troops on land. It has been a competition in arms—without conflict by arms, which both sides have wanted to avoid.

## THE FIRST NUCLEAR ARMS RACE AND NUCLEAR WAR

Why was the atomic bomb first built? Three factors need to be understood: scientific advances in nuclear physics which made a bomb possible; political and military pressures to build whatever weaponry was possible during

71

the second World War; and ever present anxiety that the enemy would develop atomic weaponry first. The U.S. nuclear experience began in August 1939 with a letter from Einstein to President Roosevelt. "The element uranium may be turned into a new and important source of energy in the immediate future," Einstein wrote, "and it is conceivable—though much less certain—that extremely powerful bombs of a new type may thus be constructed."[1]

Einstein's letter initiated the world's first nuclear arms race. It was not a race between the Soviet Union and the United States, although Soviet scientists were working on atomic weapons development as early as 1942. The race was between Nazi Germany and the United States and Britain. The Allies won, to no small degree because of the minds and labor of scientists exiled from Hitler's Europe.

It was more than three years before these scientists, led by Dr. J. Robert Oppenheimer, tested a nuclear device in July 1945. By that time the original motivation of the project—fear of Nazi Germany's atomic weapon program— had vanished; on April 30 Hitler had taken his own life and seven days later the war in Europe ended.

The war in the Pacific continued. In the summer of 1945 President Harry S. Truman had to decide if the United States should use the atomic bomb on Japan. His views were shaped by several considerations. American policymakers wanted the unconditional surrender of the Japanese regime responsible for the Pearl Harbor attack. The alternative to dropping the bomb, a planned invasion of the main Japanese islands, was expected to result in as many as a million American and many more Japanese casualties. Compared to such expectations, the bomb seemed like a "miracle of deliverance" (see the box).

The American decision makers considered using the bomb merely as a demonstration, in an uninhabited area, but rejected the proposal for four reasons. They wanted the Tokyo government to know that the bomb could destroy cities and were concerned that even a successful demonstration explosion would not convince them of the bomb's potential. They feared that if the Japanese government was warned when and where an atomic demonstration bomb would be dropped, American prisoners of war might be brought to the site. They also feared that an

---

### Winston Churchill on the Decision to Drop the Atomic Bombs in 1945

I had in my mind the spectacle of Okinawa Island, where many thousands of Japanese, rather than surrender, had drawn up in line and destroyed themselves by hand-grenades after their leaders had solemnly performed the rite of *hari-kiri*. To quell the Japanese resistance might well require the loss of a million American lives and half that number of British. . . . Now all this nightmare picture had vanished. In its place was a vision—fair and bright, indeed it seemed—of the end of the whole war in one or two violent shocks. . . . To avert a vast indefinite butchery, to bring the war to an end, to give peace to the world, to lay healing hands upon its tortured peoples by a manifestation of overwhelming power at the cost of a few explosions, seemed, after all our toils and perils, a miracle of deliverance.

SOURCE: Churchill, *Triumph and Tragedy*, pp. 638–39.

---

advertised but unsuccessful demonstration explosion would lend encouragement to the Japanese to continue fighting. Lastly, the men in Washington knew what the Japanese did not: the American arsenal contained no more than three atomic bombs. If the demonstration failed to achieve the desired results, the odds were high that the American military would have no choice but to invade Japan.

President Truman decided to use the new weapon as soon as possible on Japanese cities containing defense industries. On August 6, 1945, an atomic bomb was dropped on Hiroshima. Three days later, the second bomb destroyed Nagasaki. The same day, the Soviet Union declared war on Japan and invaded Manchuria. A few days later Japan surrendered. World War II was over.

Did use of the bomb cause Japan's surrender? Probably. Whether the Tokyo government would have surrendered quickly if only one bomb had been used will never be known with certainty, but three points are clear. First, use of the bomb undoubtedly contributed to the decision to

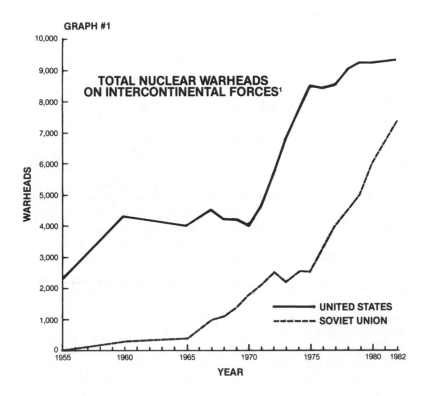

GRAPH #1

TOTAL NUCLEAR WARHEADS
ON INTERCONTINENTAL FORCES[1]

UNITED STATES
SOVIET UNION

YEAR

[1] Warhead estimates are unavoidably uncertain because (1) the number of bombers in service and the number of bombs loaded on each bomber vary considerably and (2) some warheads are stockpiled, but not deployed on delivery vehicles. Some studies have estimated that U.S. warheads exceeded 7,000 in the early 1960s and 11,000 by the mid-1970s.

SOURCES: International Institute for Strategic Studies, *Military Balance 1982–83;* Stockholm International Peace Research Institute, *SIPRI Yearbooks 1976–1980;* and Robert P. Berman and John C. Baker, *Soviet Strategic Forces,* (Washington: Brookings Institution, 1982) pp. 42–43.

**GRAPH #2**

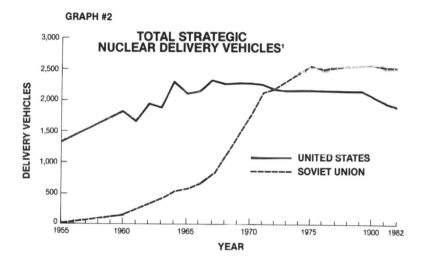

[1] Comprising ICBMs, SLBMs, and intercontinental range bombers (including the U.S. B-47). U.S. bombers able to reach the Soviet Union only from foreign bases are excluded.

SOURCES: International Institute for Strategic Studies, *Military Balance 1960–1982–83*; and Robert P. Berman and John C. Baker, *Soviet Strategic Forces* (Washington: Brookings Institution, 1982), pp. 42–43.

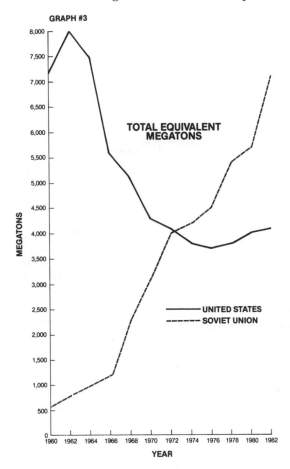

[1] "Equivalent megatons" (EMT) measure aggregate destructive power.

SOURCE: *Ground Zero, Nuclear War* (New York: Pocket Books, 1982), Table C.1.

surrender. Second, however the American decision is judged today, dropping the atomic bombs in 1945 was a far easier choice to make than starting a nuclear war would be today, simply because the United States did not have to fear a counter-attack from the Japanese. Third, the decision makers in Washington had another, although clearly secondary, reason for wanting to use the atomic bomb in war. Besides wanting to defeat Japan, they hoped that a demonstration of atomic force now would aid in keeping the peace later. As Karl Compton, one of Truman's advisers, wrote at the time: "If the bomb were not used in the present war the world would have no adequate warning as to what was to be expected if war should break out again."[2] This warning was aimed especially at the Soviet Union.

## THE SOVIET-AMERICAN NUCLEAR ARMS COMPETITION

The competition in nuclear arms that began at the end of World War II was only one element in a broader, pervasive rivalry between two superpowers that embody entirely different philosophies of how to organize politics, the economy, and society. At the end of World War II the interests of these two powers necessarily came into conflict in central Europe, the eastern Mediterranean, and the Middle East.

At stake were the futures of Iran, Turkey, Greece, Yugoslavia, Italy, Austria, Poland, Czechoslovakia, and, most important to the winners, Germany. Given these stakes, it was natural for each side to look to its nuclear arms. The U.S.-Soviet nuclear arms competition began in this atmosphere. Later it took a variety of forms, but its basic causes lie in this political rivalry that eventually spread to virtually every other region of the globe.

This competition in the development of nuclear arms and forces is illustrated in three graphs. Graph 1 represents the total numbers of intercontinental nuclear warheads; Graph 2, the total number of strategic nuclear delivery vehicles; and Graph 3, total explosive power measured in equivalent megatons.

This competition is often referred to as an "arms race," a somewhat appropriate metaphor that is also misleading. It implies a grueling contest between two runners straining to do their utmost, which will end when one staggers across the finish line first or when they both drop from exhaustion. The nuclear arms competition is more like a track meet than a simple race. In a track meet there are many events; a team may do well in some, poorly in some, and may not even bother to compete in others; the teams may decide to exclude certain competitions. Most important, in a track meet there may not be a clear winner: overall standings depend upon a purely arbitrary allocation of points to different competitions and different performances.

The Soviet-American nuclear arms competition is a complex contest in which each country has competed intensely in some areas and conceded the other's advantage in others. The events in the meet have changed over time, and the parties have agreed to limit or prohibit some forms of competition. In the history of the competition, these topics need to be explored:

1. the evolution of the nuclear forces of both sides;
2. the announced policies of the U.S. government on the use of nuclear weapons ("declaratory policy") and the actual military plans for their use ("targeting policy");[3] and
3. the efforts by the U.S. and the Soviet Union to set limits on the nuclear arms competition (arms control policies and agreements).

This U.S.-Soviet nuclear track meet has moved through five historical phases, which will now be discussed.

## U.S. SUPERIORITY AND INVULNERABILITY: 1945–57

From 1945 until 1949 the United States had a monopoly of nuclear weapons. By 1949, though, the U.S. arsenal included only 100–200 bombs. Each bomb was under the control of the Atomic Energy Commission, and required a team of 24 technicians to assemble. American bombers could not reach the Soviet Union from the United States; the B-29 bomber, with its 4,000-mile range, would have had to embark from European airfields in order to strike the Soviet homeland.

In 1949 the Soviets detonated their first atomic explosive. American nuclear superiority and effective invulnerability, however, continued for many years. The Soviet explosion led President Truman to order the development of a much more powerful weapon called the fusion, thermonuclear, or hydrogen bomb. The U.S. exploded a thermonuclear device in November 1952; the Soviets achieved a comparable result in August 1953. These tests made it clear that bombs 10 to 1,000 times as powerful as the Hiroshima bomb could be made. During the 1950s both sides stockpiled these weapons. By 1957 the United States probably had slightly more than 2,000 nuclear bombs, and the Soviet Union a few hundred.

During the early 1950s American superiority was most marked in nuclear delivery systems. The Soviet Union had to rely on a relatively small number of TU-4 and Badger bombers, which could reach the U.S. from Soviet bases but could not then return home. The United States had an increasingly overpowering fleet of bombers that could reach the Soviet Union from the United States or from overseas bases: the B-29, then the intercontinental B-36, then the medium-range B-47 jet bomber (2,000 of which were eventually produced), and then in 1955 the first intercontinental jet bomber, the B-52, later versions of which are still in the Strategic Air Command.

The declared purpose and the actual, planned purpose of U.S. nuclear forces during these years was to deter and, if necessary, help defeat a Soviet attack on Western Europe, which before 1951 was thought to be virtually defenseless against Soviet attack. (A wry joke of the times was: "Question. What does the Red Army need to reach Paris? Answer. Shoes.") If Stalin had any desire to march to Paris, however, he was deterred from doing so by the threat of U.S. nuclear retaliation. American nuclear war plans gave primary emphasis to attacks on Soviet cities. If war had occurred in 1948, at the time of the crises over Czechoslovakia and the Berlin blockade, U.S. B-29s probably could have transformed most major Soviet cities into Hiroshimas. For a country just beginning to recover from the physical destruction and the death of 20 million people in World War II, it was a persuasive deterrent.

As the Soviets began to develop their nuclear forces,

the U.S. and its allies in NATO (North Atlantic Treaty Organization, formed in 1949) wanted to create conventional forces in Europe that could defeat a Soviet conventional attack without recourse to nuclear weapons. This proved, however, not to be feasible. Instead, the U.S. began deploying less powerful, tactical nuclear weapons to Europe in order to strengthen the deterrent effect of its forces there and also to re-emphasize the deterrent role of its overwhelming nuclear superiority.

The principal deterrent against a Soviet attack in Europe remained the threat of nuclear retaliation and U.S. war plans were drawn up accordingly. In 1955, for example, the Strategic Air Command war plan, as one military officer summarized it at the time, was designed to reduce the Soviet Union to "a smoking, radiating ruin at the end of two hours."[4] After its major military buildup in 1951 and 1952 prompted by the Korean War, the U.S. began to cut back significantly on defense spending. This led unavoidably to an emphasis on nuclear weapons, which was publicly enunciated by Secretary of State John Foster Dulles in January 1954 as the doctrine of "massive retaliation." The U.S., he suggested, might use nuclear weapons not only in response to a major Soviet attack on Europe but in response to smaller types of aggression elsewhere. It remains unclear, however, whether this threat helped to deter Communist aggression in the Third World and whether, if such aggression had occurred, the threat would have been carried out.

From 1945 to 1957, the United States thus used its nuclear superiority to compensate for what it assumed to be conventional inferiority in areas adjacent to the Soviet Union. Throughout this period, despite American concerns over Soviet nuclear weapons, the United States remained relatively safe from Soviet attack. The Soviet Union, on the other hand, remained extremely vulnerable to American attack. This state of imbalance did not provide many opportunities for agreements limiting the nuclear competition.

The first effort to control nuclear arms was the Baruch Plan of 1946. The U.S. proposed the creation of an International Atomic Development Authority to be given sole control over all aspects of nuclear energy development, ownership of fissionable materials, and power to punish transgressors (presumably with nuclear weapons, if need be, since it would be the sole possessor of such technology). Once the Authority was set up, all stockpiles of nuclear weapons were to be destroyed. The Authority's actions would be immune from UN Security Council veto, the only means then available to the Soviet Union to influence what was a decidedly pro-Western organization. The USSR rejected the U.S. plan, and proposed instead that all stocks (that is, U.S. stocks) of atomic weapons be destroyed, that an international entity (subject to the veto) be established after that to share atomic energy technology, and that each state should punish transgressors within its borders.

Neither the American nor the Soviet proposal had much chance of success, given the growing political mistrust between the two countries. The U.S. offered to give up its monopoly before any other country had a chance to develop the bomb. However, it would have retained knowledge of bomb construction while other countries would not have been given the "secret." The Soviets saw the Baruch Plan as a way for America to keep a nuclear monopoly, in a latent rather than an active form. The Soviet counterproposal, on the other hand, allowed Soviet nuclear weapons development to continue undetected after U.S. nuclear capabilities had been dismantled.

In 1953, with the end of the Korean War, the death of Stalin, and a change of U.S. administration, the door was opened to renewed discussion of nuclear disarmament measures. In 1954–55, under UN auspices, the world's major powers traded proposals for general and complete disarmament. But the underlying political hostilities of the Cold War—given active form in the Soviet invasion of "counter-revolutionary" Hungary and the U.S. overthrow of radical regimes in Iran and Guatemala—ruled out the kinds of political accommodation necessary for successful disarmament agreements. Neither side trusted the other and neither had much reason for trust. American proposals for "open skies" aerial reconnaissance were judged by the Soviets as an invitation for espionage. Soviet proposals for total disarmament were viewed by the Americans as propaganda aimed at weakening support for defense in the Western democracies.

By 1955, ten years into the Nuclear Age, extensive testing of hydrogen bombs had conveyed to all the enormous increase in explosive power. Both sides were busy developing long-range ballistic missiles to deliver these weapons. For nine years the U.S. had made the elimination of nuclear weapons its main objective in disarmament negotiations. This goal no longer seemed technically achievable. President Eisenhower acknowledged this in a mid-1955 statement to the effect that it had become impossible to construct an international control system capable of detecting all nuclear weapons and materials. All previous U.S. disarmament proposals that assumed this to be possible were withdrawn. The emphasis on finding an acceptable comprehensive disarmament program came to an end. In the next two years both sides developed alternative proposals that would not have to wait for an agreement on a comprehensive program. Among them was a U.S. proposal for an agreement dealing with surprise attack. These detailed partial measures marked an important transition from disarmament, that is, doing away with nuclear weapons, to arms control, or limiting the number, types, and possible uses of nuclear weapons. However, the differences between U.S. and Soviet positions still made agreement impossible.

## U.S. INVULNERABILITY ENDED, SUPERIORITY CHALLENGED: 1957–62

The second phase in the nuclear arms competition opened with a series of shocks for the United States which involved the end of U.S. invulnerability to nuclear attack as well as what seemed a major challenge to U.S. nuclear superiority. These shocks prompted momentous and rapid changes in U.S. nuclear forces and strategy. Twenty years later, U.S. forces and strategy remain largely in the mold set in the early 1960s.

In 1957 new Soviet bombers, the Bison and the Bear, which had begun to worry Americans in 1955, were deployed in operational squadrons. The era of American safety from significant attack was over. More dramatically, in August 1957 the Soviets flight-tested an intercontinental ballistic missile at full range. A few months later they launched Sputnik I, quickly followed by Sputnik II. The

U.S. did not match these achievements until late the following year. Not only were American cities now vulnerable, but the ability of the U.S. to retaliate was in question because overseas bases of the U.S. B-47 fleet were vulnerable to a Soviet first strike. To worried Americans, it appeared that the Soviet Union had gained a substantial lead in ballistic missiles. The Soviet leaders used deception and propaganda to make their nuclear striking power appear much stronger than it was. These factors combined to make the "bomber gap" and the "missile gap" major focuses of American strategic concern.

All three U.S. military services had ballistic missiles under development. Their programs were given top priority and the missiles rushed into production. By 1962 the U.S. had a massive force of intercontinental bombers and ballistic missiles (see table, p. 87). Total U.S. nuclear warheads, including bombs, rose from 2,000 in 1955 to over 4,000 in 1962. Although the Soviets had begun to deploy long-range bombers and had introduced ICBMs, they were very slow to expand their strategic forces between 1957 and 1962. They decided to forgo the creation of a large long-range bomber force and to move directly to ballistic missiles. They gave priority to shorter-range missiles aimed at Europe rather than intercontinental missiles aimed at the United States. At the same time, Prime Minister Khrushchev was reducing the overall size of the Soviet defense forces and attempting to hold down military spending. As a result, by 1962 the United States was far ahead of the Soviet Union in nuclear warpower, and, due to the new "spy" satellites, both Soviet and American leaders knew this was so.

Vulnerability hastened a reconsideration of American strategy. If the Soviets could launch a nuclear attack on the United States, the United States clearly would not want to make a nuclear response to a Soviet conventional attack unless truly vital American interests were at stake. This was not likely to be the case in the Third World—but what about Europe? If Soviet troops invaded Western Europe, would the U.S. launch its missiles and bombers against Soviet cities knowing that the Soviets could retaliate with a weaker but still devastating attack against New York, Washington, Chicago, and other cities? French President Charles de Gaulle did not think so, and pushed rapidly ahead with the creation of a French nuclear deterrent. Everyone had to assume that the credibility of the U.S. nuclear guarantee had decreased. As a result there were three major changes in U.S. strategic policy.

First, to ensure the survivability of U.S. strategic forces against a Soviet first strike, the U.S. had to have an "assured second-strike capability." The U.S. could do little or nothing to protect its cities against a Soviet attack, so it was essential to be able to protect the strategic forces against such an attack, since the safety of U.S. cities depended upon the ability of the strategic forces to retaliate. To ensure survivability the U.S. diversified its strategic forces, initiating the "triad" of land-based ICBMs, submarine-based SLBMs, and long-range bombers. The theory was that while the Soviets might develop a defense against one force or develop the ability to destroy it in a first strike, it was most unlikely that they would be able to do one of these things to all three forces. A large part of the U.S. submarine force was kept continuously at sea; a portion, varying over the years, of SAC (Strategic Air Command) bombers was kept on alert, and ICBMs were placed in hardened silos. During the 1960s these measures ensured that a substantial part of the U.S. strategic force would survive a Soviet first strike.

Second, in 1960, for the first time, the Defense Department drew up a Single Integrated Operations Plan (SIOP) for the conduct of a nuclear war by ICBMs, SLBMs, and bombers in a single overpowering attack. In 1961 and 1962 this plan was modified to make more limited attacks—in particular, separate attacks on military and industrial targets—possible. In 1962 at Ann Arbor, Michigan, Secretary of Defense Robert McNamara enunciated the "no-cities" doctrine, a major shift from the "city-busting" emphasis of the 1940s and 1950s. In case of a major Soviet attack on Western Europe, he said, the principal objective of the American nuclear response "should be the destruction of the enemy's military forces, not his civilian population." Thereafter, military planning for nuclear war put primary, although not exclusive, emphasis on military targets, including nuclear and conventional forces. Now the United States could conceivably respond to a Soviet attack in Europe with a nuclear attack on Soviet military forces, without necessarily starting a mutual exchange of attacks against cities.

The third major change in U.S. strategy concerned the circumstances in which a U.S. nuclear response might be triggered. In the 1950s it was assumed that this would be very early in any conflict. With the development of Soviet nuclear capabilities and the vulnerability of the U.S., however, there was a clear U.S. interest in delaying resort to nuclear weapons in a war. The United States consequently began developing a strategy of "flexible response" to replace massive retaliation. Under this strategy, NATO conventional forces in Germany would be strengthened in order to resist a Soviet conventional attack as long as possible. If the Soviet attack was succeeding, low-yield tactical nuclear weapons might be brought into action. If the Soviets pressed ahead, there could, under the amended operations plan, be limited strategic nuclear attacks against Soviet military targets. If the Soviets still continued their advance, the full weight of the U.S. strategic forces might have to be applied. Under "massive retaliation" strategic weapons would be used quickly; with "flexible response" such action would only be the last recourse. This new policy was adopted by the U.S. government in the early 1960s and was ratified as official NATO doctrine in 1967.

The late 1950s and early 1960s also saw the emergence of nuclear arms control as a central issue of national policy. U.S. vulnerability increased the interest of both political leaders and citizens in finding ways to reduce the probability and/or destructiveness of nuclear war. In 1961 the U.S. created an autonomous Arms Control and Disarmament Agency. The leaders of the Soviet Union could also see the advantages of attempting to limit nuclear risks.

The major accomplishment of this period was the 1963 Limited Test-Ban Treaty banning nuclear weapons tests everywhere except underground. Atmospheric nuclear tests had increased to a peak of one every four days in 1958. The debris from these tests entered the atmosphere, settled out as fine radioactive dust, eventually affected food sources, and significantly raised the level of worldwide radiation. The consequence was a certain increase in cancer and genetic diseases.

The natural desire to prevent this coincided with growing public opposition to nuclear testing. Negotiations on a nuclear test ban were intermittent from 1957 to 1962. Then the combination of growing public pressure, plus the impetus of the Cuban missile crisis, led to the resumption of negotiations and the treaty in 1963. The treaty prohibited above-ground nuclear tests. This immediately lowered the level of radioactive contamination. It also slowed the development of nuclear weapons by about three years. Both sides learned how to carry out nuclear tests underground. But they never again conducted as many weapons tests as in 1958 and 1962. Therefore, many experiments which would have been used for military planning could not be explored.

The agreement also underlined the importance of verification, of determining whether the other country was complying with an agreement. There was no problem verifying a ban on tests in the atmosphere, hence it was possible to reach an agreement to ban such tests. Since it was not possible, with the same degree of certainty, to verify constraints on below-ground testing, it was impossible to agree to ban such tests, despite elaborate negotiations.

## FROM SUPERIORITY TO PARITY: 1962–70

The consequences of the rapid U.S. buildup of its strategic nuclear forces and the laggard Soviet increase became clear in October 1962. During the summer of that year, Soviet Premier Khrushchev began to deploy intermediate-range nuclear ballistic missiles to Cuba. Khrushchev knew of U.S. military strength, but he was undoubtedly motivated to take this action both by the impression he had formed of the weakness of U.S. political will, particularly that of President Kennedy, and by Soviet military weakness which would be compensated for by posing this new and close-in threat to American security. He expected that once these missiles were in place, the U.S. would not dare go to war to remove them. He misjudged the determination of the American President and the temper of the American people. The Soviet deployment was discovered while it was still under way. The U.S., obviously, possessed overwhelming conventional superiority in the Caribbean. At the strategic level, while the U.S. was now vulnerable to Soviet nuclear attack, it also, thanks to the rapid U.S. and slow Soviet buildups between 1957 and 1962, had overwhelming nuclear superiority:

### The Perceived Nuclear Balance in 1963[2]

|                    | U.S.  | USSR            |
|--------------------|-------|-----------------|
| ICBM launchers     | 229   | 44              |
| SLBM launchers     | 144   | 97              |
| MR/IRBM launchers  | 105   | (20–40 in Cuba) |
| Strategic bombers  | 1,300 | 155 +           |

SOURCE: Raymond L. Garthoff, "The Meaning of the Missiles," *Washington Quarterly*, Autumn 1982, p. 79.

Historians still debate whether U.S. conventional superiority in the Caribbean or overall U.S. nuclear superiority was responsible for the outcome of the Cuban missile crisis. In fact, both played roles. The outcome was also the product of both sides' intense desire to avoid nuclear war, of skillful diplomacy, and of some compromise: the Soviets removed their missiles from Cuba, but the U.S. promised not to invade Cuba and implemented a previous decision to remove medium-range missiles from Turkey.

Overall, the missile crisis was an American victory and most observers, including the Soviets, perceived it as such. And this outcome was secured even though, if nuclear war had occurred in 1962, some American cities would probably have been obliterated. In 1962 American nuclear superiority was clear and played some role in the outcome of the crisis, but the kind of superiority that contributed to the outcome of the Cuban missile crisis disappeared forever as both sides pursued their nuclear buildups during the 1960s.

During most of the 1960s the United States maintained a significant lead in overall nuclear capability over the Soviet Union, building up its ballistic missile forces until 1967 when they leveled off at 1,054 ICBMs and 656 SLBMs deployed in 41 submarines. These numbers did not change throughout the 1970s. Also during the late 1960s the U.S. retired all of its B-47 medium-range bombers and about half of its B-52 long-range bombers. By 1970 the United States had fewer launchers, fewer warheads, and less megatonnage than it had earlier in the decade, but it also had much more modern and sophisticated nuclear forces which were capable of imposing overwhelming damage on the Soviet Union.

While the U.S. was shifting in these directions, the Soviet Union was beginning to move rapidly to develop a nuclear capability at least equal to that of the United States. Soviet leaders became determined never to let a humiliation like the Cuban missile crisis happen to them again. They began a substantial (3%–4% a year) and sustained increase in defense spending, strengthening their military capabilities across the board. In the late 1960s the Soviets carried out a dramatic increase in their nuclear forces comparable to what the U.S. had undertaken in the first half of the decade. In 1966 the Soviet Union had only 292 ICBMs. Four years later, in 1970, it had 1,300 ICBMs, with 300 more under construction, and had surpassed the United States. It also began a rapid buildup of SLBMs, although it did not surpass the U.S. in numbers of those launchers until 1974. Throughout this period Soviet long-range bombing capability remained quite limited, but the Soviets also greatly expanded their defensive capabilities, including construction of an immense air defense system to bring down U.S. B-52s. They initiated a major push on anti-ballistic missile systems designed to counter U.S. ICBMs and SLBMS, and upgraded their civil defense system to provide some protection for Soviet leaders, workers, and industry in case of a nuclear war.

From 1962 to 1970 the declaratory policy of the United States on the use of nuclear weapons changed significantly. In the mid-1960s Secretary of Defense McNamara increasingly began to talk in terms of an "assured destruction" strategy. Under this strategy the U.S. should be able to destroy in a massive nuclear retaliatory strike one-quarter to one-third of the Soviet population and 50%–75% of Soviet industry. If the U.S. had that capability, it was argued, nuclear deterrence would work. This strategy seemed on the surface to be the opposite of the "no-cities" strategy McNamara had articulated in 1962. In fact, the shift in declaratory policy was not matched by a shift in targeting policy. McNamara set forth his new assured destruction strategy not to destroy Soviet cities in wartime but to hold down the U.S. military budget in peacetime. To counter Soviet military forces weapon for weapon could require an ever-expanding U.S. nuclear arsenal. An assured destruction strategy, on the other hand, set a ceiling on military requirements which could be met at the levels U.S. strategic forces had achieved in 1966.

Despite this declaratory policy, throughout the 1960s the American nuclear forces remained targeted primarily on Soviet military forces. In the early 1960s, indeed, U.S. superiority was so overwhelming that the Soviet nuclear forces could have been substantially destroyed in a first strike. By the end of the decade, however, the growth of Soviet strategic forces had markedly reduced their vulnerability: both sides had strategic forces which could not be substantially damaged by a first strike. The U.S. could no longer minimize damage to American cities by first attacking and destroying a substantial portion of Soviet strategic forces. Now, clearly, the principal use of one side's nuclear forces was to deter the other side from using its nuclear forces. The era of mutual assured destruction (or MAD) had arrived.

Efforts to negotiate arms control agreements have always faced the problem of how each side can verify to its satisfaction the capabilities of the other side. In the 1950s the absence of acceptable verification measures prevented the negotiation of limits on strategic weapon systems. In the late 1950s the United States used its U-2, an airplane that cruised at 70,000 feet, to spy on Soviet forces. This program ended when U-2 pilot Francis Powers was shot down in May 1960.

By that time, however, the United States was developing spy satellites. The U.S. first successfully used photo satellites in 1960 and the Soviets in 1962. With this revolution in verification technology, together with the expectation that the Soviets could catch up with the U.S. in weaponry, more ambitious efforts at negotiated arms control were desirable. After much preliminary sparring, Strategic Arms Limitation Talks were launched in late 1969 and led to the SALT I agreement in 1972. The SALT process had to reflect the limitations of verification technology: it therefore chose as its basis delivery vehicles which were large enough to spot from space (for example, ICBM silos) and which, if mobile, could only operate from relatively few, known bases (heavy bombers and strategic submarines).

## PARITY, ARMS CONTROL, AND DIVERGING PROGRAMS: 1970–77

In 1970 it began to make sense to speak of strategic parity between the superpowers. The strategic balance between the superpowers was far different from what it had been in the 1962 Cuban missile crisis. This did not mean that the nuclear forces were mirror images, but that the advantages of one side could be counter-balanced by comparable advantages of the other side:

|  | U.S. | USSR |
|---|---|---|
| ICBM launchers | 1,054 | 1,300 |
| SLBM launchers | 656 | 240 |
| Long-range bombers | 520 | 140 |
| Warheads/bombs | 4,000 | 1,800 |
| Total megatonnage | 4,300 | 3,100 |

Later in the 1970s the number of U.S. strategic launchers remained fixed at 1,054 ICBMs, 656 SLBMs, and roughly 350 long-range bombers. Beginning in 1970, however, the U.S. began to replace single-warhead missiles with missiles with several warheads that could be aimed at separate targets. Such a missile is said to be equipped with MIRV (Multiple Independently Targetable Re-entry Vehicles). During the early and mid 1970s 550 Minuteman III missiles, each with three nuclear warheads, were substituted for a like number of single-warhead ICBMs. Similarly, Poseidon missiles, each with about ten warheads, replaced un-MIRVed Polaris missiles on submarines. As a result, the total number of U.S. strategic warheads rose sharply from 4,000 in 1970 to 8,500 in 1977.

Why did the United States put these additional warheads on its missiles? First, the Soviets were clearly about to equal the U.S. in total launchers. By MIRVing its missiles, the U.S. could re-establish a substantial lead in warheads, capitalizing on a technology in which the U.S. was significantly ahead. Second, adding warheads to missiles was a relatively cheap way of multiplying nuclear strength. Third, the additional warheads, many believed, would be essential to overcome the ABM system the Soviets had started to deploy. More warheads, particularly in submarines, would ensure that the U.S. would always have an assured destruction capability to retaliate against the Soviet Union.

In the mid-1970s the Soviets began the deployment of a fourth generation of ICBMs, the SS-17s, SS-18s, and SS-19s. Later versions deployed in larger numbers carried multiple warheads. All these missiles were larger than U.S. Minuteman missiles: the SS-18 was a giant "heavy" missile, with a payload seven to eight times that of the U.S. Minuteman III. ("Payload" refers to the useful weight the missile can lift into space, including nuclear explosives and guidance system.) By 1977 Soviet MIRVing had outpaced that of the U.S. for land-based missiles, and the Soviets had more warheads on their ICBMs than did the United States. Because of their size, the Soviet missiles could carry much more powerful warheads than could U.S. missiles.

During the 1970s the Soviets also significantly increased the number of SLBMs on submarines, surpassing the United States in this category in 1974. The Soviets did not in that period, however, MIRV their sea-based missiles, and with the deployment of its Poseidon missile the U.S. had many more sea-based warheads than the Soviet Union. In the mid-1970s the Soviets also began to deploy a new bomber, the Backfire, undoubtedly designed primarily for use against targets in Western Europe and China and against U.S. carrier task forces operating off the Eurasian continent. If refueled in flight, however, it could deliver atomic bombs against the United States from Soviet bases. This mixture of characteristics made it a major issue in the strategic arms limitation talks (SALT) of the 1970s.

Mutual assured destruction—that is, the ability of each side to absorb an attack on its nuclear forces and still retaliate massively against the other side—deterred all-out nuclear exchanges. Given the Soviet strength in conventional forces, particularly in Europe, the U.S. also felt the need to rely on the threat of the use of nuclear weapons to help deter other lesser forms of aggression. As Soviet strategic capabilities increased, the problems of providing such "extended deterrence" increased accordingly. The Kennedy and Johnson administrations developed the concepts of counter-force targeting and flexible response to help deal with this problem. In the early 1970s Secretary of Defense Schlesinger elaborated this policy further and stressed the importance of the U.S. having the capability to respond to Soviet aggression with a variety of "limited nuclear options," from a small single-weapon strike against advancing Soviet tank forces to more complex strikes against broader ranges of military targets. This policy was designed to make the NATO deterrent in Europe more credible, although its critics argued that by doing so it also made nuclear war more likely. It reflected the fact that the U.S. no longer had the ability it had had earlier in the 1960s to launch a disarming first strike against the Soviet nuclear forces.

The most important forward steps on arms control occurred precisely during the years when the strategic balance between the superpowers was approaching parity. The central achievements were the SALT I agreements, which were signed in 1972 after three years of intense negotiations. An "interim agreement" due to expire in 1977 set a ceiling on ICBMs and SLBMs at their 1972 levels. To the casual observer, this agreement might have looked decidedly lopsided (see box, p. 94), but it was widely regarded as justified because it stopped Soviet weapons programs that would have gone much further and because bombers, where the U.S. had an advantage, were not part of the agreement. However, in ratifying the SALT I Treaty and Interim Agreement, the Senate added the Jackson amendment, which stipulated that any future agreements on strategic arms should not permit American inferiority in "levels of intercontinental strategic forces."

The offensive missiles agreement was a stopgap measure, as its title implies. The more significant achievement of SALT I was restriction of the development, testing, and deployment of anti-ballistic missile systems. What led the two sides to agree on this? First, technical problems on the effectiveness of ABM systems were giving both sides second thoughts. Second, the Soviet Union may have decided not to compete in such an expensive undertaking where the U.S. had the technological lead. Third, an arms race stability argument may have had some appeal: If ABM were deployed by country B, country A might have to assume as a worst case that it would work, causing it to build more ICBMs and SLBMs to compensate for those that might be destroyed. And the reciprocal situation applies as well. Whatever stability had been achieved would be sacrificed. Finally, political conditions nudged both sides toward agreement. The Soviets were worried about growing Chinese strength and interested in better relations with the U.S. The Americans felt they lacked domestic support for a massive ABM buildup, and that an agreement codifying parity at a very low level was in their interests.

The ABM Treaty limited the two countries to two ABM sites of 100 launchers and a specified number of radars. The two sites were cut, by agreement, in 1974 to one site protecting either an ICBM deployment area or the national capital. The U.S. elected to build its site near the Minuteman ICBM field at Grand Forks, North Dakota, but then dismantled it. The USSR elected to maintain its ABM site at Moscow.

The SALT Agreement also established a unique institution, called the Standing Consultative Commission (SCC), to deal with questions of implementation and compliance. Normally, the SCC meets twice yearly and provides a regular forum for discussion of SALT-related matters with neither the publicity nor the political posturing that often accompanies the meeting of high-level delegations. As a vehicle for examining detailed technical matters related to the control of strategic arms, it is widely considered an unqualified success.

The period that began with the Limited Test-Ban Treaty and ended with SALT I also began with U.S. escalation in Vietnam and ended with the withdrawal of the last American combat troops and the return of prisoners of war (in January 1973). As the United States moved into the post-Vietnam period, SALT seemed to signal the beginning of a new period of cooperation with the USSR,

## The Salt I Agreements in Brief

### ABM TREATY

- Entered into force on October 3, 1972. (Modified by a protocol on May 24, 1976.)
- Duration: unlimited.
- Numerical limits:

  One ABM deployment area, either at the national capital or at an ICBM field

  100 ABM launchers and 100 ABM interceptor missiles at launch sites

  Six ABM radar complexes at national capital or 20 ABM radars at ICBM field

- Prohibitions:

  No development, testing, or deployment of ABM components which are sea-based, air-based, space-based, or mobile land-based

  No deployment of ABM components based on exotic physical principles and capable of substituting for ABM launchers, ABM interceptor missiles, or ABM radars

  No development, testing, or deployment of ABM interceptor missiles with more than one independently guided warhead

### INTERIM AGREEMENT ON OFFENSIVE FORCES

- Entered into force on October 3, 1972
- Duration: five years. (Expired October 3, 1977.)
- ICBM limits:

  No construction of additional fixed launchers for ICBMs and no relocation of such launchers. (U.S. had 1054 ICBM launchers; USSR had 1608.)

  No conversion of launchers for light ICBMs to launchers for heavy ICBMs. (U.S. had no launchers for heavy ICBMs; USSR had 308.)

- SLBM limits:

  SLBM launchers limited to number operational and under construction. (U.S. had 656 SLBM launchers; USSR had 740.)

  Additional SLBM launchers permitted as replacements for older ICBM launchers. (U.S. permitted maximum of 710 SLBM launchers on 44 submarines; USSR permitted maximum of 950 SLBM launchers on 62 submarines.)

not only in limiting strategic arms, but in other fields. That spirit was not to last long.

## PARITY DISPUTED: 1977–

By the end of the 1970s many Americans were becoming concerned about the trends in the nuclear arms competition that seemed to threaten strategic parity as well as by the apparent willingness of the Soviet Union to take advantage of opportunities to expand its influence in the Third World. In the late 1970s the U.S. improved the capabilities of 300 of its 550 Minuteman II missiles, doubling the explosive power of their warheads and improving their guidance systems. In 1980 the U.S. began deploying in its Poseidon submarines new Trident I missiles which carried larger warheads and had much greater range than the older Poseidon missiles. The total number of U.S. warheads did not increase, however, and the total number of U.S. launchers decreased somewhat as older bombers and older submarines were retired from service. In 1980 the Carter administration set forth what it termed its "countervailing strategy" in Presidential Directive (PD) 59. This represented a refinement and elaboration of Schlesinger's limited nuclear options idea, giving greater stress to flexibility in targeting, the ability to change targets during the course of a prolonged nuclear war, and the central importance of secure facilities for command, control, communications, and intelligence.

To many of those concerned with the strategic balance, these developments on the U.S. side appeared to be an inadequate response to the growth in Soviet nuclear capabilities. The deployment of Soviet heavy missiles continued, and with improvements in accuracy the Soviets developed the theoretical capability substantially to destroy U.S. land-based missiles in a first strike. The growth of the Soviet air defense system raised questions about whether a significant number of the U.S. B-52s, deployed between 1956 and 1962, would be able to carry out their retaliatory mission. The MIRVing of Soviet ICBMs also greatly narrowed the gap in numbers of warheads between the U.S. and the Soviet Union. In the past, the U.S. had led in accuracy and warhead numbers; both of these advantages seemed to be on the wane. In addition, in 1977 the Soviet Union began deploying a new mobile, intermediate-range missile, the SS-20, which carried three warheads and was aimed at Western Europe. NATO had nothing comparable, and this imbalance aroused concerns on both sides of the Atlantic.

The principal issues of nuclear weapons policy which the United States confronted at the beginning of the 1980s rose out of these trends in the strategic balance. The Ford, Carter, and Reagan administrations made arms control proposals to the Soviet Union designed to limit the prospective vulnerability of the U.S. land-based missiles. Through 1982, the Soviets consistently rejected these proposals. All three administrations attempted to deal with this problem by development of a new ICBM (the first since 1970), which could carry ten warheads and thus pose a threat to the survivability of the Soviet Union missile force. To be an effective deterrent, however, this missile, the MX, would have to be survivable itself, and as of early 1983 no administration has been able to devise a basing mode that both ensured its survivability and was politically acceptable.

Throughout this period two remedies were advanced to compensate for the decreased ability of the B-52s to penetrate Soviet defenses. One was cruise missiles: slow, low-flying, terrain-hugging missiles that could be launched from B-52s or other planes outside the Soviet defensive perimeter. The other was a new bomber, the B-1, with greater capabilities to penetrate Soviet defenses. President Carter canceled the B-1 and approved the cruise missiles.

In the fall of 1981 President Reagan announced his strategic weapons program which involved continuing the cruise missile programs, building 100 B-1 bombers, deploying 100 MX missiles (compared to 200 proposed by Carter), improving command, control, and communications systems, pushing ahead with the Trident submarine program and development of a larger, more accurate, and longer-range Trident II (D-5) missile, placing cruise missiles on submarines and surface ships, and expanding the U.S. defenses against nuclear weapons.

In response to the SS-20 threat against Europe, the United States followed up on an initiative taken by Ger-

## Salt II Agreement in Brief

TREATY

- Would remain in force until December 31, 1985
- Numerical ceilings
    - 2,250 ICBM launchers, SLBM launchers, heavy bombers, and long-range ASBMs (i.e., air-to-surface ballistic missiles with ranges greater than 600 kilometers)
    - 1,320 launchers for MIRVed ICBMs, launchers for MIRVed SLBMs, MIRVed ASBMs, and heavy bombers equipped with long-range cruise missiles
    - 1,200 launchers for MIRVed ICBMs, launchers for MIRVed SLBMs, and MIRVed ASBMs
    - 820 launchers for MIRVed ICBMs
- Prohibitions
    - No construction of additional fixed launchers for ICBMs and no relocation of such launchers
    - No conversion of launchers for light ICBMs to launchers for heavy ICBMs
    - No mobile launchers for heavy ICBMs
    - No heavy SLBMs and no heavy ASBMs
    - No increases in the numbers of reentry vehicles on existing types of ICBMS
    - No flight-testing or deployment of new types of ICBMs, with an exception of one new type of light ICBM with no more than ten reentry vehicles
    - No flight-testing or deployment of SLBMs with more than fourteen reentry vehicles

PROTOCOL

- Would have expired on December 31, 1981
- Prohibitions
    - No flight-testing of ICBMs from mobile launchers
    - No deployment of mobile launchers for ICBMs
    - No flight-testing or deployment of ASBMs
    - No deployment of long-range cruise missiles on land-based or sea-based launchers

man chancellor Helmut Schmidt in 1977 and proposed the deployment in Europe of 108 Pershing II ballistic missiles that could strike the Soviet Union from Germany and 464 ground-launched cruise missiles (GLCMs) to be deployed in five West European countries. NATO agreed to these deployments in December 1979 conditional upon the U.S. also attempting to negotiate an arms control agreement with the Soviet Union limiting theater nuclear weapons. The Reagan administration continued this approach, on the one hand engaging the Soviets in intermediate-range nuclear weapons talks and on the other endeavoring to bolster European resolve to go ahead with deployment of the weapons on schedule in 1983–84.

The end of detente between the superpowers was marked by Soviet support of Cuba's overseas military activities. In late 1975 the Soviets equipped and helped to transport a Cuban expeditionary force sent to support one faction in the Angolan civil war. This action influenced the presidential campaign of 1976 and, in conjunction with attacks on the Ford administration from the Republican right, put the SALT II talks on ice for a year. In 1978 a second Cuban-Soviet intervention in Ethiopia put severe strains on all of the arms control initiatives of the Carter administration. Finally, public dispute over the significance of a Soviet brigade in Cuba in September 1979 served to delay ratification of the SALT II Treaty just long enough for it to be killed by the Soviet invasion of Afghanistan in December 1979.

In this atmosphere, arms control succumbed to political linkage. Three treaties negotiated with the USSR in 1974, 1976, and 1979—the Threshold Test-Ban Treaty, the Peaceful Nuclear Explosions Treaty, and SALT II— were not ratified by the Senate: they were, indeed, never brought up for a vote.

The Threshold Test-Ban Treaty and its companion agreement governing "peaceful" nuclear explosions would have limited underground nuclear tests to 150 kilotons. In 1977, however, the Carter administration set these aside in favor of resuming negotiations, dormant for 15 years, on a comprehensive test ban. Those talks went on for three years and came near to an agreement that would have permitted placement of automatic seismic monitors in each country and certain kinds of on-site inspection. The Reagan administration inherited these talks, waited 18 months to decide on a policy, and in July 1982 decided not to pursue the negotiations any further.

The best known of the treaties in limbo is, of course, SALT II (see box, p. 97). Six and a half years of negotiations produced an agreement that outraged many hawks and sorely disappointed many arms controllers. The treaty did "ratify" many weapons deployments of the 1970s, including MIRVs, "heavy" missiles, and super-accurate counter-force warheads. It also, however, put a cap on the number of warheads that could be installed on missiles, and prevented the biggest Soviet missile, the SS-18, from being tested or deployed with more than 10 warheads (theoretically, it could carry 20 or 30). Although each side at different times urged a ban on any new ICBMs, in the end one was allowed to each side. Moreover, SALT II forbade the construction of new silo launchers for ICBMs as well as the enlarging of smaller silos to accommodate "heavy" ICBMs. Since the USSR already had 308 "heavy" ICBM silos and the U.S. had none and wanted none, these provisions seemed to legitimize a Soviet advantage. Finally, SALT II froze strategic nuclear delivery vehicles at a high level, 2,250, above the U.S. number but 10% lower than the Soviet number.

The complex provisions of the treaty were a product partly of American politics, partly of Soviet behavior, and partly of weapons technology and the pace of its development. These same factors were, in the end, also responsible for the failure to ratify SALT II. Arms control negotiations are particularly vulnerable to a hostile political climate, such as began to emerge after 1973. The contrast between the decade beginning with 1963 and the following one is stark. Ten treaties relating to controlling nuclear arms were ratified in the first (see p. 192); none of any consequence in the second.

## CONCLUSION

Thirty-five years of nuclear arms competition have changed the nature of the nuclear arms balance in four significant ways.

First, the absolute number of weapons increased tremendously, as did the sophistication of delivery systems. Well into the 1950s, U.S. strategic warheads numbered less than 2,000; the Soviets still had less than 500 warheads as late as 1965. In the early 1980s, the United States had 9,000–10,000 strategic warheads, and the Soviets were close behind.

Second, the relative balance between the countries changed dramatically. As we have seen, the U.S. was substantially invulnerable to attack through the mid-1950s and had a meaningful superiority through the early 1960s. By the mid-1970s strategic parity existed and, given the absolute numbers, it was difficult to see how either side could expect to achieve a meaningful margin of superiority in the future. U.S. society and the land-based U.S. strategic forces were vulnerable to attack.

Third, the introduction of ballistic missiles in the 1960s reinforced the primacy of the offensive over the defensive. In a nuclear conflict, a few weapons can cause unprecedented devastation. Conceivably, air defenses could bring down a large proportion of an attacking bomber force. In the early 1980s, however, neither country had an effective defense against ballistic missiles and both were bound by the ABM Treaty not to deploy any large-scale defense. Both technology and the treaty appeared to guarantee the dominance of offensive forces.

Fourth, arms control negotiations and some measure of arms control restraint have become permanent features of the U.S.-Soviet rivalry. Thirty-five years of competition have produced a more stable and regularized pattern of both weapons innovation and weapons control than existed in the early phases of that rivalry. The lessons to be learned from this history of competition are the subjects of the next chapter.

## Notes

1. The Einstein letter is reprinted in Morton Grodzins and Eugene Rabinowitch (eds.), *The Atomic Age* (New York: Simon and Schuster, 1963), 11–12.

2. As quoted in Martin J. Sherwin, *A World Destroyed* (New York: Knopf, 1975), p. 213.

3. The "black box" surrounding Soviet decision making and strategy makes it difficult to analyze the development of Soviet policy in the same way one can American policy. No public information is available on Soviet targeting policy, and it is impossible to say to what extent Soviet declarations on strategy actually reflect Soviet policy or are simply designed to influence Western policy. For a discussion of some aspects of Soviet military doctrine and strategy, see Chapter 7.

4. David Alan Rosenberg, " 'A Smoking Radiating Ruin at the End of Two Hours': Documents on American Plans for Nuclear War, 1954–55," *International Security*, Vol. 6, No. 3, Winter 1981–82, p. 25.

# 5

# Nuclear Lessons: What Have We Learned?

This brief review of the history of the Soviet-American arms competition and attempts to control it demonstrates that some widely held beliefs about the arms race and arms control are not entirely accurate. These beliefs have some validity, but they are half-truths which all too often are offered and accepted as full truths.

## HALF-TRUTHS ABOUT THE ARMS RACE

Among the popular beliefs about the arms race are that it has continued at an ever-increasing rate, that the United States has always been in the lead and the Soviets merely struggling to catch up, that the United States government invariably has overestimated and overstated the nature and extent of the Soviet military threat, and that the fundamental driving force for the race is runaway technology. Each of these beliefs deserves discussion.

It is widely believed that the arms race has been continuously "accelerating," the numbers and destructiveness of weapons on both sides have been constantly increasing, and the money and resources devoted to these weapons steadily growing. This notion is at least half-true. Since the early 1960s, so far as we can tell, the resources the Soviets have devoted to their nuclear forces have increased regularly. Certainly the capabilities of those forces increased in almost all dimensions through the 1960s and 1970s. Presumably this upward movement will level off at some point, but there seems to be little reason to think that it will be reversed.

For the United States the picture is much more complex. On many of the accepted measures of nuclear capabilities, the U.S. peaked during the 1960s. In other cases, the lines on each of the graphs in Chapter 4 may be fairly horizontal with occasional rises and dips. Consider, for instance, the following figures for various aspects of U.S. nuclear capabilities in 1982, as compared to selected earlier years:

|  | Earlier Year | 1982 |
|---|---|---|
| Strategic launchers | 2,271 (1964) | 1,888 |
| SLBMs | 656 (1967–1977) | 520 |
| Strategic warheads | 4,500 (1967) | 9,200 |
| Total nuclear warheads | 32,000 (1967) | 26,000 |
| Equivalent megatonnage | 8,000 (1962) | 4,100 |

The point of these figures is not to argue that the numbers and destructiveness of U.S. nuclear forces are steadily declining. Clearly they are not. Moreover, in some respects the U.S. had more effective nuclear arms capabilities in 1982 than at any earlier time. For very good reasons, however—such as the retirement of one weapon system and the introduction of another—the numbers and destructiveness of weapons have changed over time. As the table indicates, many indexes of U.S. nuclear strength reached their high points in the 1960s. The total destructive power of the U.S. arsenal, as measured in equivalent megatonnage, peaked in 1962 and then declined sharply as a result of the replacement of large bombs by smaller missile warheads; in 1982 it was only about half of what it had been twenty years earlier. On the other hand, the

U.S. had about 4,500 strategic warheads in 1967 and about 9,200 in 1982. In between, in 1970, it had about 4,000 strategic warheads because some bombers had been retired and the MIRVing of U.S. missiles was just beginning. The point is simply that it is incorrect to think that all the lines necessarily go upward on the chart and that the arms competition is always accelerating. The one general trend is for nuclear weapons and their delivery systems to become increasingly sophisticated technically, increasingly accurate, and increasingly diversified in their purposes.

Nor has money spent on U.S. strategic forces shown any consistent pattern of increase. Although it is often alleged that spending for nuclear arms drives the defense budget upward, in fact the strategic forces hardly ever account for more than 15% of the defense budget and often for considerably less. The amount of money spent on nuclear forces goes up when major investments, as in the early 1960s and now in the 1980s, are made in new weapons systems. At other times, it requires relatively little money and manpower to keep the strategic forces operating. In the late 1970s, for instance, the U.S. was spending, in real terms, on its strategic nuclear forces, only one-third what it had in the early 1960s. The relative "cheapness" of nuclear forces is one reason why serious efforts to reduce defense spending have often led to increased emphasis on nuclear rather than conventional forces. If the U.S. is to maintain an effective defense establishment, there is often a trade-off between reducing defense spending and reducing reliance on nuclear weapons.

The second half-truth of the arms race is that the United States has always been the first to build new weapons with the Soviet Union then being compelled to follow the American lead. For example, George Kennan has stated that "we Americans . . . at almost every step of the road, have taken the lead in the development of this sort of [new] weaponry."[1]

This statement, however, is only part correct. It is true that the United States has often been first to introduce new weapons. Two powerful factors are, in large part, responsible for this. First, in most areas of the relevant technology the United States is more advanced than the Soviet Union. Qualitative technological superiority is the U.S. strong suit, just as the Soviets normally lead in building bigger weapons and more weapons. Second, the U.S. technological drive is fueled by the "black box" of Soviet secrecy. With little information available on what the Soviets are doing, a natural tendency for American decision makers is to assume the worst and try to make sure that it does not happen.

Despite these factors, the United States has not always been the first with new weapons. The Soviets tested the first intercontinental ballistic missile in 1957 and deployed the first anti-ballistic missile system in 1968. They deployed the first anti-satellite (ASAT) missile and warhead. They also were the first and, so far, the only country to build "heavy" ICBMs and reloadable ICBM silos. The Soviets also were the first in testing two developments in nuclear weapons that were later abandoned: the "super H-bombs" (over 59 megatons) in 1961 and fractional orbital bombardment systems in 1967. Here, the Soviets were obviously not merely reacting to American initiatives.

Even where the Soviet Union acquired a new form of weaponry or delivery system after the United States, it may not have been merely in reaction to American actions. For example, the H-bomb was tested first by the United States, but the corresponding Soviet test took place only a few months later. The timing of the Soviet H-bomb test does not reflect a belated decision in Moscow to build the hydrogen weapon, but merely American ability to build it more rapidly. All the available evidence indicates that U.S. "firsts" were due to superior technology, not to the Soviets hanging back and then reacting to the U.S. In general when they can be first, the Soviets are first.

A third common half-truth about the arms race is that the United States government has continually overestimated Soviet military power and then, reacting to such misperceptions, has built more weaponry than was necessary. It is true that the "bomber gap," which frightened many in the mid-1950s, and the "missile gap," which was a major issue in the 1960 election, were both later discovered to be illusory. As we have indicated, however, Soviet officials encouraged Americans to believe these illusions.

On the other hand, U.S. officials consistently underestimated the growth of the Soviet missile force in the 1960s, when the Soviets built more accurate missiles more rapidly and in larger numbers than was predicted. For example, in 1965 Defense Secretary McNamara reported:

> The Soviets have decided that they have lost the quantitative race, and they are not seeking to engage us in that contest. . . . There is no indication that the Soviets are seeking to develop a strategic nuclear force as large as ours.[2]

McNamara was wrong. The Soviets built an arsenal much larger than the U.S. expected. The historical record is thus mixed on the question of American estimations of Soviet nuclear power. Future warnings of a potential "gap" in American nuclear strength vis-à-vis the Soviet Union, therefore, should neither be dismissed out of hand as another misperception nor accepted unquestioningly.

A fourth half-truth of the arms race is that political rivalries do not really matter and that the problem is merely one of runaway technology. Lord Solly Zuckerman, once chief science adviser to the British government, for example, has argued:

> The nuclear world of today has come about because basic scientific enquiries into the nature of matter led to an understanding of atomic structure, and so to the demonstration that the atom could be split with the release of vast amounts of energy. From that moment technology assumed command.[3]

The notion that technology controls politicians, rather than the reverse, is insidious; it shifts responsibility from men of free will to the impressive but utterly dependent fruits of their labors. Technology has no mind of its own; it is developed only through choice. Technological advances in weaponry have sometimes begun without a prior request from political authorities. But that merely shifts the responsibility among officials; technology itself is blameless. Moreover, political authorities have at times limited "runaway" technology (as when the United States and the Soviet Union negotiated a limit on ABM systems in 1972) and at other times have proceeded with developing new technology only after active consideration of the probable political and military results of such technological advances. Technology is difficult to control; it creates temptations and momentum. But blaming current problems on technology is only slightly different from our predecessors' tendency to blame the stars for their misfortunes.

It is also wrong to believe that all technological innovations are necessarily destabilizing and undesirable. The development of satellite technology was a prerequisite for meaningful and enforceable arms control agreements. The development of nuclear propulsion for submarines and SLBM technology made it possible for both sides to have highly invulnerable retaliatory forces, the existence of which would clearly contributes to stability in diplomatic crises. The world would be far less safe if the U.S. and the USSR had only vulnerable forces, a situation where each side would be under pressure "to use 'em or lose 'em" in a crisis. Technological developments have also made possible the Permissive Action Links and other devices designed to minimize the possibility of accidental nuclear firings or the unauthorized use of nuclear weapons. Thus, technology is a means that can be used for good or ill.

## THE "OVERKILL" ARGUMENT

There is an often made argument that massive "overkill" capacity exists in the American and Soviet nuclear arsenals, that the current stocks of explosive power are enough to destroy every man, woman, and child on earth ten times over. This overkill argument captures the essence of mankind's nuclear danger, but does so in a possibly misleading way. It captures the essence of the problem because it points to the horrible consequences of a nuclear war fought with the enormous nuclear arsenals in the U.S. and the USSR. The "overkill" argument can be misleading, however, in two ways.

First, the "overkill" argument can lead one to think that nuclear weapons are, in fact, aimed at every man, woman, and child on earth. This is not the case. As will be discussed in the following two chapters, most of the nuclear arsenal of each side is aimed at the nuclear arsenal and military power of the other side. If either superpower planned to kill as many people as possible, enormous overkill capacity would exist. But contemporary nuclear forces are not targeted deliberately to kill enemy civilians, although enemy military targets could not be destroyed without killing large numbers of civilians. The reason such large forces exist goes back to the usability paradox discussed in Chapter 2. Threats to destroy each other's populations are so suicidal in a world of mutual vulnerability that they are simply not credible for all types of deterrence. Threats against military targets have a greater credibility that has the virtue of enhancing deterrence. At the same time, with the absence of arms control, this has led to increased numbers of weapons: as each side adds weapons to its arsenal, the other adds forces to aim at those weapons. And if these additional weapons *were* to be used deliberately against populations, it would certainly be enormous overkill.

Also, the "overkill" argument leaves the impression that any new building of weaponry is redundant and therefore unnecessary. Some nuclear weapons programs are unnecessary; others have been created in response to the bureaucratic needs of competing military services. But the argument misses the point that having some redundancy in nuclear forces is a virtue that every American president and every Soviet leader appears to have understood. Political leaders have a responsibility to try to deter war, not just today, but in the future as well. They want to ensure as much as possible that future technological advances by the adversary will not threaten their entire retaliatory force, thereby creating crisis instability and increasing the likelihood of war. Thus both the United States and the Soviet Union have deliberately built some redundancy into their nuclear arsenals. Each superpower has placed nuclear weapons on land-based missiles, in bombers, and in submarines, creating a "triad" of forces. Once again, the result is larger numbers of weapons than would be needed to kill populations if that were the objective; but in fact the objective is to avoid *any* nuclear war. Keeping more than one form of invulnerable retaliatory forces is, from one perspective, an exercise in "overkill"; from another perspective, it is an effort to safekeep tomorrow's deterrent.

## HALF-TRUTHS ABOUT ARMS CONTROL

The more prevalent half-truths about Soviet-American arms control are that it is technologically unrealistic, that it requires trusting the Russians, that it weakens and distorts U.S. defense efforts, and that it inevitably benefits the Soviet Union. Consider these in turn.

First among the arms control half-truths is that efforts to constrain technology by means of political instruments such as arms control agreements are doomed to failure. (This belief comes naturally to those who view the arms race itself as driven primarily by technological innovation rather than political rivalry.) A few examples serve to demonstrate the fallibility of this half-truth: the technologies needed to station nuclear weapons in space are available, but the Outer Space Treaty (1967) prohibits such action; the technologies needed to emplace nuclear weapons on the bottom of the world's oceans are available, but the Seabed Arms Control Treaty (1971) prohibits such action; and the technologies needed to build extensive (if not effective) defenses against ballistic missiles are available, but the ABM Treaty (1972) prohibits such action.

The argument that arms control cannot constrain technology is imperfect but it is not entirely wrong. That *some* technologies have been constrained through negotiated arms control agreements does not mean that all technologies could be constrained in this way, or that they should be. Such judgments on the feasibility and desirability of constraining specific technologies must be case by case.

The second half-truth about arms control is that it requires trusting the Russians. Given the nature of the Communist system and known tradition of secrecy and concealment as instruments of defense in Russian history, few if any Americans would be willing to rest their nation's security on such trust. But arms control agreements need not, and should not, rely upon trust to assure compliance: an American ability to verify that the Soviets are keeping their promises is essential. In fact, arms control agreements can reduce the "black box" effect of the secretive Soviet system. Modern arms control agreements to which both superpowers are parties often include specific provisions designed to enhance verification of compliance. For example, the Antarctic Treaty (1959) guarantees that designated observers will have access to all areas of the Antarctic; the Non-Proliferation Treaty (1968) provides for international safeguards, including on-site inspections, to deter diversion of nuclear materials from civilian to military use; and the SALT I (1972) agreements prohibit deliberate concealment measures and other forms of interference with national technical means of verification including photographic satellites. Trusting the Russians is not a prerequisite for Soviet-American arms control; indeed, Soviet secrecy would be an even greater problem for U.S. defense planners without the bonus of information that comes with verifiable arms control agreements.

A third complaint is that arms control weakens and distorts American defense efforts. Proponents of this belief maintain that arms control develops a momentum of its own, is poorly integrated with defense planning, and lulls the Western democracies by relaxing the public support for defense spending. They allege specifically that the SALT process stopped the United States from responding to the Soviet military buildup in the 1970s. History indicates that this is a half-truth at best: the Soviets have tried to use arms control offers to produce such a lulling effect or to split the Western alliance. Still, though arms control did not cure the imbalance between Soviet and American defense spending that developed in the 1970s, arms control was also not the cause of that imbalance. The impetus to cut defense budgets grew from reaction against the Vietnam War and from domestic social changes—a ferment which began well before the SALT I agreements were completed. If anything, the debate on SALT I increased attention to strategic issues and defense budgets in the years that followed.

Rather than undermining defense efforts, arms control can enhance them by reducing uncertainties associated with projected military threats. Defense planners can make more efficient use of the resources available to them if they do not have to employ worst-imaginable-case assumptions for every conceivable contingency. Arms control can also help to create public confidence that the nuclear balance is being prudently managed. In short, arms control is not in competition with national security planning; it is, or should be, an integral part of that effort.

A fourth argument against arms control is that arms agreements inevitably benefit the Soviet Union. This notion unlike the others, is entirely true: it is, however, misleading. There is no doubt that the Soviet leaders enter into only those agreements which they judge to be in their interest; they would be foolish to do otherwise. The same can be said about the United States (or any other sovereign nation). Fortunately, arms control agreements can be in the interest of more than one party. (If this were not the case, there would be no agreements.) The observation that Soviet-American arms control agreements benefit the Soviet Union is as self-evident as the observation that they favor the United States. Without such *mutual benefit*, there would be no meaningful accords. Future agreements, if there are to be any, will be like previous ones, benefiting both superpowers.

## IS THE NUCLEAR ARMS COMPETITION INEVITABLE?

The history of the nuclear arms competition and attempts to curb it necessarily leads one to ask: Why can't the competition be stopped? What are the forces that have compelled the Soviet and American governments to act as they have for over thirty years?

Analysts have set forth a number of theories which attempt to identify the underlying cause and motivation for the continuation of the competition. All of them have some claim to plausibility; no one of them, however, is totally sufficient, although one is undoubtedly more fundamental than the others. Five such theories deserve mention.

One approach emphasizes how the *genuine security requirements* of the superpowers produce incentives for arms buildups. Through much of the postwar era, for example, American policymakers have seen nuclear arms as a way of compensating for relative weakness in conventional military power. This issue was expressed perhaps most simply in the late 1940s by Secretary of Defense James Forrestal, who noted that "the only balance that we have against the overwhelming manpower of the Russians, and therefore the chief deterrent to war, is the threat of the immediate retaliation with the atomic bomb."[4] A related argument also stresses security requirements as the prime cause of arms buildups and emphasizes the desire that nuclear superiority be exploited to limit the damage that would occur to one's own country if a war occurred despite all efforts to the contrary. These views of the competition find the root cause to be one side seeking a military advantage through arms spending, and the other spending in order to deny the first that possibility.

A second theory stresses *uncertainty and misperceptions* between the superpowers as the main source of arms increases. The holders of this view believe that each side chronically overestimates the adversary's strength, and then overcompensates by starting a massive arms program. An action-reaction cycle results. While the first theory stresses competition stemming from genuine security interests, this theory finds the competition to be based on illusions, mistakes, or inadequate military intelligence. Military officials on both sides undoubtedly do tend to focus on the "worst case" and to highlight the actual and potential capabilities of the presumed enemy. Soviet secrecy encourages this tendency. Yet, as we have seen, intelligence estimates have sometimes underestimated the opponent's military forces.

A third explanation focuses on the role of *domestic political pressures* which are quite unrelated to the Soviet-American military balance. Such pressures include politicians urging defense increases in times of popular support for arms expenditures, the various military services lobbying not to have their budgets reduced, and industrialists promoting the economic benefits of defense spending. Here the main cause of the arms race is not found in competing national interests, but rather in powerful private interests: the interests of the so-called "military-industrial complex" in the United States and the "metal-eaters" in the Soviet Union. These interests undoubtedly do play a major role in both countries. In the U.S. such pressures often have significant influence in determining which weapons will be built, but much less influence on broader questions of overall policy and strategy. In addition, one recurring phenomenon in U.S. politics has been pressure to hold military spending down and cut defense spending, if possible. The strength of such pressures is reflected by the fact that in 1981 the United States was spending less on defense in real terms than at any time from 1951 to 1971.

A fourth school of thought emphasizes what can be called *technological determinism.* Here the focus is on neither international political rivalry nor domestic political pressure, but rather on the scientific habit of improving technology and the political habit of making use of what is developed. "If it can be built, it will be built" is the underlying idea of technological determinism. As we have indicated, however, this theory gets at only a portion of the truth.

Finally, there is the theory that emphasizes the *international political rivalry* between the United States and the Soviet Union inherent in the global balance of power. The United States and the Soviet Union embody fundamentally different philosophies and purposes. Each is in a position to do unprecedented harm to the other. In such a situation it would be anomalous, if not miraculous, for rivalry, including arms competition, not to occur. The existence of large numbers of nuclear weapons on both sides, however, has given both countries a common interest in avoiding nuclear war. In such a situation, it would be surprising if both countries did not make some effort to control or manage their arms competition.

Unless the philosophies and purposes of the two countries become more compatible, each will have to assume that the other will do what it can to promote its own interests and to weaken its opponent. This fundamental impetus to arms competition is well reflected in an exchange which occurred early in 1951 when President Truman was meeting with his advisers to decide whether or not to build the hydrogen bomb. The president asked: " 'Can the Russians do it?' All heads nodded yes they can. 'In that case,' Truman said, 'we have no choice. We'll go ahead.' "[5] So long as the political competition between the United States and the Soviet Union continues in its present mode, statesmen on both sides will continue to be driven to say, "We have no choice. We'll go ahead."

## Notes

1. George Kennan, "A Modest Proposal," *New York Review of Books*, July 16, 1981.

2. *U.S. News & World Report*, April 12, 1965.

3. Solly Zuckerman, *Nuclear Illusion and Reality* (New York: Viking, 1982), p. 108.

4. *The Forrestal Diaries* (New York: Viking, 1951), p. 538.

5. As quoted in McGeorge Bundy, "A Chance to Stop the H-Bomb," *New York Review of Books*, May 13, 1982, pp. 14–15.

# 6

# Nuclear Arsenals: What Is the Balance?

What is the balance between the American and the Soviet nuclear arsenals? Who is ahead?

When the question is asked in this manner, it might appear easy to give a definitive and objective answer. Unfortunately, this is not the case. No definitive answer is possible.

This can best be understood by way of an analogy. Comparing the nuclear arsenals of the superpowers is like comparing the strengths of two football teams. Each team may be stronger in some departments: one in running, the other in passing; one in special teams, the other in placekicking. Specialists try to predict the winner by comparing, for example, one side's aerial attack with the other side's pass defense. This is a better comparison than contrasting the quarterbacks or the receivers. But the accuracy of such complicated predictions cannot be known until the game is over.

Similarly, as long as nuclear peace is maintained, it is impossible to measure the complex balance between two nuclear arsenals with any certainty. Given this fortunate uncertainty, different individuals can hold very different beliefs about the nuclear balance. Such differences are usually not about what numbers of weapons exist in the arsenals of the two superpowers, but about how to interpret the differences between the arsenals and the importance of certain kinds of nuclear advantages and disadvantages.

The purpose of this chapter is both to present the "facts" about the current arsenals and to examine various opinions on how to interpret them.

Some attention to detail is required for at least two reasons. Only by taking a trip through the inventories of the arsenals of the U.S. and USSR can the complexities and differences between the two arsenals be grasped. And only then can the dimensions of the physical threat be appreciated. This inventory check can also help explain the difficulty in deciding who is ahead. It also underlines the magnitude and complexity of the task of bringing these arsenals under control.

A second reason for a close look at the arsenals is that these weapons with their differing numbers and characteristics are the basis of defense budget arguments and votes, and of arms control negotiations. Decisions about nuclear weapons policy can be improved by a better understanding of the complex arsenals. Knowing the numbers of weapons involved is not enough, however; their characteristics, accuracy, and basing modes are equally important.

## HOW TO BEGIN

Although defense specialists may disagree on the current nuclear balance, they agree on one major point about how to judge the arsenals: looking at total numbers of weapons in peacetime may tell one little about what would be the outcome of a war. If one side could destroy the other's weapons in a first strike, for example, then a balance in numbers would not produce stable deterrence. Thus it is necessary to examine the vulnerability of weapons as well as their numbers.

Measuring the balance of the nuclear arsenals must therefore include not only the numbers of weapons, but an assessment of what the weapons are aimed at. Both sides' weapons—their numbers and their ability to destroy other weapons—must be assessed.

How many nuclear weapons exist in the superpowers' arsenals? What are they aimed at?

The number of nuclear weapons in the U.S. inventory is near 26,000, down from 30,000 in the mid-1960s. There are no reliable public figures on weapons total in the Soviet nuclear arsenal: it may be as high as ours, but is probably somewhat lower. Only a little more than a third of the U.S. total are strategic weapons capable of hitting the USSR from the U.S. or from submarines; the others have shorter ranges. Clearly the strategic weapons, if even a small percentage could escape destruction in a Soviet first strike, would be more than enough for retaliation against Soviet cities. The great majority of American weapons, however, are aimed at Soviet military and industrial targets.

What targets? The answer is known in some detail, after congressional testimony by the Department of Defense in 1980:[1]

1. *Nuclear forces*
   ICBM and IRBM launcher facilities
   Strategic command and control centers
   Nuclear weapon storage sites
   Strategic air bases
   Submarine bases

2. *Command and control facilities*
   Command posts
   Key communication facilities

3. *Conventional military forces*
   Supply depots
   Airfields
   Tank and vehicle storage yards
   Rail and road systems used by military

4. *War-supporting industry*
   Ammunition factories
   Military vehicle factories
   Refineries
   Railyards and repair facilties

5. *Industries that contribute to economic recovery*
   Coal
   Steel and aluminum
   Cement
   Electric power

This list, which is far from complete, shows a wide range of targets. Are all these military and industrial targets of nearly equal value? Of course not, as all strategists stress.

Some targets would be more important in trying to stop a Soviet attack against Western Europe, others to counter the Soviet nuclear war-fighting ability, and still others to slow Soviet recovery from a nuclear war. If targeting enemy missile silos has high priority, then many weapons will be assigned for this purpose. Other high-priority targets may include bomber bases, submarine bases, and military command centers. But with so many weapons in the arsenal, eventually the military value of adding a new target to the war plan declines. Indeed, at some point there will be little need to be able to destroy new targets. It is a matter of some dispute whether this point has been reached, but the diminished value of new targets is not in doubt.

How similar are nuclear weapons in terms of destructive power? Weapons now in inventory have yields that cover an enormous range, from less than a kiloton to more than 10,000 kilotons, and it may be believed that they cannot be compared. However, most of them are in the relatively narrow range of 40 to 1,000 kilotons. Both the U.S. and the USSR maintain a few very large weapons as well. Most strategic weapons are approximately equivalent for destroying unprotected targets; very large or very accurate weapons are required to destroy specially hardened targets.

The next generation of strategic weapons will be capable of extraordinary accuracy, on the order of a few hundred yards or less, well within the circle of total destruction. Before, high-yield weapons were planned to compensate for larger miss distances. As accuracy improved, the explosive power of modern weapons aimed at soft targets diminished. For example, 25 years ago the U.S. and Soviet bombers carried bombs of 5 to 20 megatons. These have largely been replaced by bombs of 1 megaton and missiles with smaller yields. In 1962 the average yield of ICBM warheads was 1 megaton for the U.S. and 2 megatons for the USSR. Today the average yields are one-fourth as large. As concern about hardened targets increased, the U.S. is again increasing the size of some of its warheads.

## AN OVERVIEW OF THE STRATEGIC ARSENALS

Both sides deploy their strategic arsenals in three ways: on land-based missiles (ICBMs), submarine-based missiles (SLBMs), and long-range bombers. Each side emphasizes different weapons. This can be understood by comparing (1) number of launchers, (2) number of warheads, including bombs on bombers, (3) destructive power of warheads, and (4) launcher payload.

The current strategic nuclear capabilities of the two sides are displayed in the figure:

1. *Launchers.* For both sides, ICBM launchers are most numerous, followed by SLBM launchers and then bombers. Soviet launchers exceed U.S. launchers by about 25%. (Had the SALT II Treaty been ratified the Soviet force would have had to reduce the difference by half; the U.S. could have closed the gap to a common ceiling of 2,250 launchers. Since launchers are large and easily detected, arms control agreements have focused on controlling nuclear capability by restricting numbers of launchers.) In 1982 the number of U.S. SLBM launchers is lower than usual by 136, due to early decommissioning of old Polaris submarines. Otherwise the total numbers of U.S. and Soviet launchers have remained essentially the same since 1974.

2. *Warhead numbers.* The Soviets have three to four weapons per launcher for all three types of launchers. The U.S. has fewer weapons per ICBM and considerably more per SLBM or bomber. Indeed, the loading of our heavy bombers accounts for the 25% more warheads the U.S. has. If bomber weapons are excluded, the number of warheads is about the same for the two sides.

3. *Destructive power.* A more direct index of nuclear capability which is related to the estimated area the weaponry would destroy, which is called equivalent megatonnage (EMT).[2] The third panel shows that the Soviet force has about 6,000 EMT and the U.S. force nearly 4,000 EMT. This index displays great differences among the three components of the strategic forces. For the Soviets, 75% of the destructive power is carried by ICBMs, 20% by

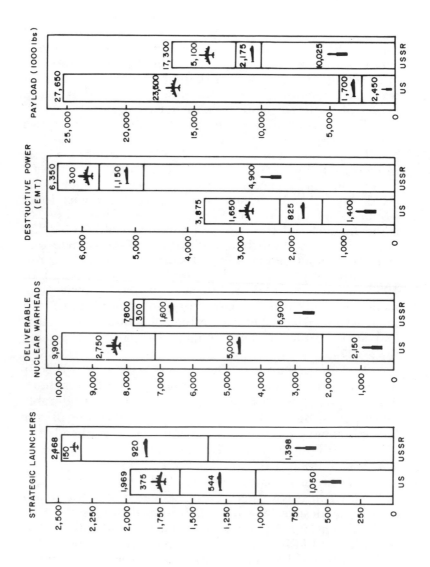

SLBMs, and only 5% by long-range bombers. U.S. destructive power is much more evenly divided.

4. *Payload.* Another measure of nuclear capability is the weight that each side's strategic force can direct toward the other's targets. This is known as payload: it includes not only the weight of the warheads but also the guidance systems. To the extent that U.S. and Soviet warheads of equal yield have different weights, the interpretation of this index is uncertain. The U.S. has a substantial advantage in overall payload because of its bomber force. But the Soviets are far ahead of the U.S. in ICBM payload.

In sum, the Soviet forces emphasize missile delivery and neglect the bomber component; the U.S. forces are more evenly balanced. The U.S. leads in warheads and payload, the Soviets in launchers and destructive power.

## LOOKING AT THE STRATEGIC FORCES IN MORE DETAIL

Other aspects of the nuclear forces must also be examined. Some of the indexes may be more important than others. If destructive power and number of launchers are the crucial indexes, or if the contributions made by heavy bombers should be discounted because of their vulnerability to air defenses, then the Soviet forces are ahead. This position has been argued by conservative military analysts for some time and it is a central tenet of Reagan administration policy. It stresses that the momentum of force improvement lies with the Soviets and that the apparent balance shown in our overview will be lost if an active U.S. buildup is not undertaken.

U.S. forces are being improved. The larger destructive power of Soviet weaponry is a diminishing asset as high accuracy takes over. Indeed a much larger fraction of their destructive capabilities would become vulnerable if the Americans continue to deploy highly accurate missiles, because the Soviet missiles are too big to be made mobile. The superior U.S. bomber force is becoming more effective as it is equipped with air-launched cruise missiles (ALCMs) which permit bombardment from well outside the Soviet homeland, far from Soviet air defenses.

As for the Soviet lead in launchers, it could have been corrected by ratifying SALT II.

The claim of greater Soviet momentum in maintaining and improving strategic forces deserves a closer look. The strategic forces of the U.S. were modernized during the 1960s and faced the 1970s without much need for replacement. The improvements of the 1970s were on existing missiles and launchers: MIRVing and adding short-range attack missiles to the bombers. More recently, the U.S. is replacing 300 Minuteman III warheads with more accurate, more powerful ones.

The Soviet forces at the beginning of the 1970s were in substantial need of modernization: this the Soviets carried out with gusto, replacing their missile systems with at least 16 new types or modifications and deploying their new bomber, the Backfire, as well. By 1980 it was obvious that the U.S. forces had begun to age and required another cycle of replacement and modernization over the next decade or so if parity was to be maintained (as the Carter administration claimed) or restored (as the Reagan administration claimed). For the Carter administration this meant an 18% real increase in the strategic forces budget for fiscal 1982; for the Reagan administration it meant a 34% real increase for fiscal 1983. Thus, without arms control, it was evident that the U.S. would be quickening its pace of military spending in the 1980s if the challenge of the continuing Soviet buildup was to be met. In 1983 this is well under way. The same would have happened in a second Carter administration, but more slowly. The difference between the administrations is largely one of prudence in choosing the optimal rate of increase and the choice of weapons being added or replaced.

## OTHER FACTORS AFFECTING THE STRATEGIC BALANCE

Other factors, besides these four indexes, must be considered in any judgment of the strategic balance. For the most part, however, these factors are not expressible in numbers.

1. The Soviet Union is at the center of the world's largest landmass and has very poor access to the oceans.

The ports it does have require passage through narrow waterways, and in consequence its submarines cannot easily go and come without detection. The USSR has been unable to obtain bases for its submarines at advantageous ports abroad, as the U.S. has. Consequently, even if its strategic submarines were technically the equal of those of the U.S. they would have to be judged more vulnerable, less reliable. In an effort to compensate for this geographical disadvantage, the Soviets are deploying long-range submarine-based missiles. With a dozen neighbors, some with considerable grievances, the USSR, unlike the U.S., has potential border problems. These geographical disadvantages are only partly compensated by the Soviet Union's advantage of short supply lines in wars fought on its periphery.

2. Contrary to widespread opinion, the industrial activities of the Soviet Union are more concentrated than those of the U.S. and therefore far fewer weapons would be needed for equivalent destruction. Moreover, the Soviet transportation system has far less capacity than ours and consequently is more vulnerable and less readily restored.

3. If nuclear war between the two superpowers escalated beyond the exchange of a few weapons, the efficient, controlled use of the vast remainder would depend on the survivability of the network of command, control, communications, and intelligence facilities that serve as the eyes, ears, and nervous systems of each strategic force. No one can know if these facilities, which number only in the low hundreds, would be destroyed early in such an encounter. If they were, each side would be blinded and the effectiveness of the weapons counted in the overview above would be greatly and unpredictably diminished.

4. Throughout the nuclear age the U.S. has been more inventive and technologically advanced than the USSR and has used this to make up for some numerical disadvantages. However, as the Soviet Union concentrates more of its technical ability in the military sphere and learns how to incorporate new technology from abroad into its military design, the gap is narrowing. It is a matter of active dispute whether the technological gap is nearly closed or not. In any event, technological ferment in new weaponry is evident on both sides. As a result, static judgments

on nuclear balance may be more subject to change than in the recent past. Meanwhile, the U.S. will continue to benefit from some of its past technological triumphs, such as having much quieter, less detectable submarines, an anti-submarine capability widely recognized as superior, and a head start on modern cruise missiles.

5. The United States has two allies with modest nuclear capabilities; the Soviet Union has none. As France and the United Kingdom shift to MIRVed weapons in the late 1980s their forces will become more destructive. While still only a few percent of the U.S. force, these forces provide a significant deterrent in their own right.

Judgment of the balance of nuclear forces is often carried out in an obsolete framework, reminiscent of judging the likely outcome of a 19th-century artillery duel where each shell was of equal value. The most important task for deterrence is to deter the initial use of strategic weapons, and this is unlikely to be influenced by the total inventory. And in an all-out nuclear exchange the last half of the weapons fired would most likely be used against targets of relatively little military value. Numbers taken alone fall short of measuring the balance; but this does not reject or negate all the ground covered above. Weapons remain the coin of the nuclear realm, even if the exchange rate is not clear.

## DIFFERING INTERPRETATIONS OF THE STRATEGIC BALANCE

Assessment of the strategic balance is complicated and uncertain; it is not surprising that different views are expressed by knowledgeable persons well acquainted with the facts just presented. Even a full examination of the state of the strategic balance leads different specialists to quite different interpretations and prescriptions for nuclear policy.

Some defense analysts find the emerging state of balance dangerously off center in favor of the Soviet Union. They stress that the apparent state of near-balance is deceptive. It overestimates the contribution of the American lead in strategic bombers and numbers of warheads because Soviet air defenses would prevent most U.S. bomb-

## Thoughts on the U.S.-Soviet
## Strategic Balance

In the field of strategic nuclear weaponry, the U.S. and the Soviet Union continue to be in a position of rough equivalence. New U.S. systems such as the cruise missile are beginning to reverse an adverse trend. . . . More is needed for defense, but when leaders claim that the U.S. is weaker than it is, they make a mistake. This can encourage the Soviets to commit aggression, and it can dispirit allies and our own people, frightening them into thinking Russia is the dominant power. It is not.

—Harold Brown,
Secretary of Defense,
1977–80

The Soviets do have a significant lead in counterforce capabilities. That is one—but only one—of the dimensions of strategic forces. . . . [We] are less concerned about the capability of our strategic forces to deter attack against North America than to provide extended deterrence for our allies. Particularly for this reason, I think it is ill-advised for the President of the United States baldly to state that we are inferior in strategic forces.

—James Schlesinger,
Secretary of Defense,
1973–75

How you determine who's ahead, who's behind is not an easy question, because the missions of the forces are not symmetrical. On balance, however, I have to give the edge to the Soviet Union—and it's growing.

—Sen. John Tower,
Chairman, Senate Armed Services Committee

SOURCE: *U.S. News & World Report,* January 10, 1983, pp. 18–19.

ers from reaching their targets and many of our warheads are too small for their intended targets. The superior Soviet payload also allows for future growth in their warhead numbers. More important, these defense analysts view American land-based missiles as totally vulnerable. These analysts argue that counting missiles on each side in peacetime is the wrong way to measure the balance; instead, one must imagine what the balance would look like if the

Soviets struck first. After this first stage of war the Soviet Union would have more weapons left that would be capable of striking hardened targets than we would have.

Other specialists interpret the balance quite differently. They believe that the problem of land-based missile vulnerability is exaggerated and that the strategic forces of both sides are vastly larger than any rational military needs. Arms control negotiations, these specialists argue, deserve high priority and speedy execution in order to draw down the two arsenals at a substantial rate. If this should fail, many urge that U.S. strategic forces should be restructured and reduced so as to provide a robust but smaller deterrent. This would allow for a wide range of options that have in common a leaner strategic force, or at least one that is under no compulsion to mimic all Soviet deployments.

## THEATER NUCLEAR WEAPONS

In the U.S. the term "strategic" refers to weapons that can hit the USSR from the United States or from American submarines at sea and vice versa. Other weapons, which are deliverable only at shorter ranges, are often referred to as "theater" weapons. The theater category contains most U.S. nuclear weapons, covering a wide spectrum from intermediate- and medium-range ballistic missiles and medium bombers, with ranges of 1,000–4,000 miles, to shorter-range systems, both missile and bomber, with ranges of 100–1,000 miles, to battlefield weapons of less than 100-mile range, to demolition mines. A large number of theater weapons are deployed in naval forces for sea combat and land attack.

U.S. non-strategic weapons number about 16,000 and are deployed at home, in Western Europe, in South Korea, at one or more Pacific bases, and on shipboard. Nearly half of them are in Western Europe. In the interests of brevity we will examine only these, analyzing the theater nuclear arsenals of Britain, France, and the USSR.

## NUCLEAR WEAPONS IN EUROPE

In reviewing the strategic balance we find a rough parity between the forces of the two superpowers and a manageable number of weapons systems.[3] In the European theater we find a striking Soviet superiority in numbers, a larger array of weapon systems, and additional complications such as dual purpose bombers which can deliver nuclear or conventional bombs and thus resist simple counting procedures.

Long-range theater systems have ranges of 1,000–4,000 miles. In Table 1 the relevant inventories for the Warsaw Pact Organization and NATO are listed as of mid-1982. All of the Warsaw Pact weapons are Soviet weapons under Soviet control. The nuclear weapons of Britain and France are included under NATO even though this is not precisely correct. Britain has assigned its submarine-based weapons to NATO command permanently but its bomber-delivered weapons remain under its own command until released to NATO at time of war. France, having separated from the NATO military organization in 1966, keeps its forces entirely under its command and is not obligated to release them to NATO command in time of war. Nevertheless, there is close practical cooperation between the French force and NATO and it seems more appropriate to include French weapons than to exclude them.

The first entries in Table 1 are of Soviet missiles, beginning with the SS-20 carrying three MIRVed warheads and deployed over the last five years in large numbers, about two-thirds in the western Soviet Union and one-third in the Far East. The second column shows the number of launchers, and the third the maximum number of weapons that can be carried by the launchers. The Soviet SS-5 and SS-4 missiles are quite old, large-yield missiles of low accuracy. They are being slowly phased out and are unlikely to be usable after a few more years. Next the medium bombers are listed. The Backfire is currently being deployed; the Badger and Blinder are quite old.

The NATO missiles are British and French, mostly submarine-based. There are only two entries for medium bombers: the British Vulcan which is nearing obsolescence and the U.S. F-111 which is aging. In long-range nuclear systems, the Warsaw Pact deployments greatly exceed those of NATO both in launchers and in warhead totals.

As for medium-range weapons systems (100–1,000 miles) in Europe, there are more types, larger numbers,

Table 1

*Warsaw Pact–NATO Nuclear Weapons in Europe
(ranges greater than 1,000 miles)*

| Type | Launchers | Warheads/ Bombs |
|---|---|---|
| *Warsaw Pact:* | | |
| SS-20 | 345 | 1,035 |
| SS-5 | 16 | 16 |
| SS-4 | 275 | 275 |
| Missiles | 636 | 1,326 |
| Backfire | 100 | 400 |
| Badger | 310 | 620 |
| Blinder | 125 | 250 |
| Bombers | 535 | 1,270 |
| Total | 1,171 | 2,596 |
| *NATO:* | | |
| Polaris A–3 (UK) | 64 | 64 |
| M-20 (France) | 80 | 80 |
| SSBS S-2 (France) | 18 | 18 |
| Missiles | 162 | 162 |
| Vulcan B-2 | 48 | 96 |
| F-111 E/F | 156 | 312 |
| Bombers | 204 | 408 |
| Total | 366 | 570 |
| *Warsaw Pact/NATO ratio:* | 3.2 to 1 | 4.6 to 1 |

SOURCE: *The Military Balance, 1982–83* (International Institute for Strategic Studies, 1982). The figure for SS-20s has been updated to November 1, 1982. The 60 U.S. FB-111A bombers based in the U.S. but designated for deployment to Europe in a crisis have not been included. The 400 warheads in the U.S. strategic forces assigned to NATO have not been included here, since they are counted in SALT/START and the corresponding Soviet assignment is unknown. However, French forces have been included.

and more uncertainty due to dual capable aircraft and varying estimates of aircraft ranges. The Warsaw Pact missiles are present in impressive numbers (Table 2), and there are numerous medium-range bombers and fighter-bombers. For NATO the only missile is the Pershing I with a range of about 400 miles. A variety of aircraft make up the major NATO force. The A–6E and A–7E are planes on two aircraft carriers normally assigned to the Mediterranean. Whether these would be withdrawn in an emergency or others brought in is unpredictable. But this item would surely be larger in a Soviet version of the table.

Again, Soviet superiority in numbers of medium-range systems is clearly evident: 2.6 times as many launchers, and 2.7 times as many weapons in maximum loading.

There can be no comparable tabulation of battlefield nuclear weapons because the relevant Warsaw Pact and NATO data are not publicly known. Some observers believe that most battlefield weapons for the Warsaw Pact would be flown from the Soviet Union at time of crisis. All that can be said is that presumably several thousand battlefield weapons would be available to each side in the form of artillery shells, bombs, air defense missiles, short-range missiles, and mines.

The remarkable disparity between the two sides has its origins in the force deployments of the 1960s, when the U.S. had a substantial lead over the Soviet Union in strategic weapons and the local unbalance in Europe was therefore of little concern. But since rough strategic parity was reached in the 1970s the compensation no longer exists. Whether this should become a cause for alarm and action should be taken to redress the situation has divided NATO and defense specialists in the West for nearly a decade. The issue was crystallized by West German chancellor Helmut Schmidt in 1977, who advocated action to redress the balance. By the end of 1979 NATO governments had agreed to modernize their long-range theater systems by replacing other nuclear weapons with 108 Pershing II missiles with a range of 1,100 miles and 464 ground-launched cruise missiles with a range of 1,500 miles. It was agreed to make serious, parallel efforts to obtain arms control agreements with the Soviet Union on limiting long-

## Table 2

*Warsaw Pact–NATO Nuclear Weapons in Europe*
*(ranges 100–1,000 miles)*

| Type | Launchers | Warheads/Bombs |
|---|---|---|
| *Warsaw Pact:* | | |
| SS-12 | 70 | 70 |
| Scud | 593 | 593 |
| SS-22 | 100 | 100 |
| SS-23 | 10 | 10 |
| SS-N-5 | 57 | 57 |
| Missiles | 820 | 820 |
| Fencer | 550 | 1,100 |
| Flogger | 550 | 550 |
| Fitter C/D | 688 | 688 |
| Fitter A | 265 | 265 |
| Fishbed | 100 | 100 |
| Bombers | 2,153 | 2,703 |
| Total | 2,973 | 3,523 |
| *NATO:* | | |
| Pershing IA | 180 | 180 |
| Missiles | 180 | 180 |
| Mirage IVA | 34 | 34 |
| Buccaneer | 50 | 100 |
| F-104 | 290 | 290 |
| F-4 | 424 | 424 |
| F-16 | 68 | 68 |
| Mirage IIIE | 30 | 30 |
| A-6E | 20 | 40 |
| A-7E | 48 | 96 |
| Super Étendard | 16 | 32 |
| Bombers | 980 | 1,114 |
| Total | 1,160 | 1,294 |
| *Warsaw Pact/NATO ratio:* | 2.6 to 1 | 2.7 to 1 |

range weapons so that only a reduced deployment, or perhaps no deployment of new NATO weapons, would be necessary.

## CONCLUSION

Even this brief discussion of the superpower arsenals illustrates the complexity of the subject and the reasons why specialists disagree about the nuclear balance. It is worth repeating that the actual numbers involved are rarely in dispute. The meaning of the numbers is the prime source of disagreement.

Despite deep disagreements between specialists, two important points of consensus exist. First, the current arsenals are so large that the nuclear balance between the U.S. and the USSR is insensitive to minor changes in numbers of weapons. A *minor* advantage in one of the many weapons systems is unlikely to influence the probability of war or its outcome.

Second, specialists agree that the nuclear balance is not cast in iron, even at these high numbers. *Major* imbalances in particular nuclear systems can be destabilizing. To understand why this is so, we must move beyond focusing on the sheer numbers of weapons in the superpower arsenals to analyze the purposes which the weapons are meant to serve. We must ask not only "What is the balance?" but "What do we want from nuclear weapons?" That is the subject of the next chapter.

### Notes

1. Testimony of William J. Perry, Under Secretary of Defense for Research and Engineering, before the U.S. Senate Committee on Armed Services, *Department of Defense Authorization for Appropriations, Fiscal Year 1981, Part 5: Research and Development.* 96th Congress, 2d session, March 1980, p. 2721.

2. The equivalent megatonnage (EMT) is related to the megatonnage (MT) of a weapon by $EMT = (MT)^a$, where $a = \frac{2}{3}$ for $MT \leq 1$, and $a = \frac{1}{2}$ for $MT > 1$.

Thus five weapons of 100 KT would have an EMT of about 1.08, a destructive power roughly equal to that of a single 1000-KT (1-MT) weapon.

3. For the U.S.: 3 ICBMs, 2 SLBMs, and 2 bombers. For the USSR: 5 ICBMs, 4 SLBMs, and 2 bombers. *The Military Balance, 1982–83*, p. 140.

# 7

# Military Power and Political Purpose: What Do We Want from Nuclear Weapons?

Weapons are tools. And like other tools, they should serve a purpose or they should not be built. They should be means to an end and not ends in themselves.

The plan for using a tool is usually called an "instruction"; the plan for effective use—or skillful non-use—of military weaponry is called a "strategy." The difference is important and exists because weaponry is meant to influence not an inanimate object, but rather other individuals or governments, objects that react. The possibility of reaction means that weaponry can be useful without being used. Indeed, if the threat of using a weapon makes another government react in the way one wants it to, this is generally to be preferred to actual use.

The possibility of reaction also means that the usefulness of a weapon often depends on the perceptions, weapons, and counter-moves of a potential adversary. Strategy in peace and war is therefore always a more uncertain and more difficult process than merely following instructions. But strategy is still about how to utilize military tools to achieve national objectives.

How can nuclear weapons help the United States to achieve its foreign policy and national security goals? What does the United States want its nuclear weapons to do?

The simple answer, that we want our nuclear weapons not to be used, is both accurate and misleading. It is accurate because no American government wants to use the nuclear arsenal; it is misleading because if the only U.S. goal was for *our* nuclear weapons not to be used we could simply do away with them. But then the Soviet Union would also not fear our nuclear forces and the U.S. and its allies would certainly fear Soviet military might.

The United States wants its nuclear forces to serve the purposes of American foreign policy. It wants from them many of the same things it wants from its conventional military forces. The basic goal is to protect the security of the United States and its allies from attack or coercion by a hostile power. Nuclear weapons should serve that primary purpose.

Although deterrence is the nation's most important objective, nuclear strategy does not end when fighting begins. War, conventional or nuclear, could be forced upon the United States despite all efforts to avoid it. Besides trying to design the best possible deterrent policy, strategists, therefore, must always consider the possibility that deterrence might fail. "Thinking the unthinkable" is part of their job; if war occurs, what then do we want from nuclear weapons?

The box on the opposite page lists the principal goals for U.S. nuclear weapons that have been identified by administrations and strategists. Not everyone, however, would necessarily agree that each of these goals should be on this list. In addition, major differences often exist over two questions: first, the relative importance of the seven goals and to what extent achievement of one purpose should be sacrificed to achieve another; and second, the most desirable and effective means of achieving each goal, particularly the extent to which conventional forces can reduce dependence on nuclear weapons.

We will deal with each goal in turn. But first it will be useful to consider what happens on "the other side of the hill." How do the Soviets think about nuclear war? What do they want from their nuclear forces?

## Goals of Nuclear Policy

Deter nuclear attack by the Soviet Union on the United States ("basic deterrence").

Help deter a nuclear or conventional attack on U.S. allies ("extended deterrence").

Minimize the incentives for either side to strike first in an international crisis ("crisis stability").

If deterrence fails, help defeat nuclear or conventional attacks on the United States or its allies and minimize damage to them ("war-fighting," "damage limitation," "escalation control").

If deterrence fails, help terminate conventional or nuclear war in the manner least damaging to American and allied security ("war-termination").

Support U.S. foreign policy in peacetime and prevent nuclear coercion of the United States and its allies ("diplomatic support," "counter-deterrence").

Provide support for U.S. policies in arms control negotiations and be amenable to limitation by arms control agreements ("bargaining chip," "arms control impact").

## SOVIET NUCLEAR DOCTRINE AND STRATEGY

For many years American observers often assumed that the central dilemmas of the nuclear age—the extraordinary destructiveness of nuclear weapons and the absence of meaningful defenses against them—would lead Soviet and American strategists to similar views on the proper role of nuclear weapons in their countries' policies. They tended to believe that Soviet nuclear strategy would be the mirror image of American nuclear strategy. If this was clearly not the case, it was often assumed that Soviet strategic thinking was "lagging" behind American thinking and that American strategists should attempt to educate their Soviet counterparts on the facts of life in the nuclear age.

The Soviet approach to nuclear strategy is, however, shaped primarily by distinctive Soviet influences: Marxist-Leninist political theory, Russian and Soviet historical experience, traditional Russian military strategy and doctrine, the geopolitical position of the Soviet Union in the Eurasian landmass surrounded by potentially hostile states. These factors make Soviet strategy look different from American strategy. Concepts that are central to American strategy—such as mutual assured destruction, assured second-strike capability, flexible response, crisis stability, escalation control, arms control—are less frequently used in Soviet strategic writings, and other concepts such as strategic parity and nuclear deterrence play a different role in Soviet thought. Still, one must be careful not to exaggerate the differences between American and Soviet nuclear strategy.

From the beginning, the central concept of American nuclear strategy has been deterrence. The overriding purpose has been to prevent aggression and war. War-fighting has played a role in the American approach—particularly in targeting policy—but Americans have generally seen a conflict between what is needed for deterrence and what is needed to fight and win a nuclear war. Soviet strategy, in contrast, stresses war-fighting ability as the means to achieve deterrence. It does not see a conflict between the requirements for deterrence and the requirements for war-fighting. The Soviets appear to believe that preparing to fight a nuclear war is the best way to deter nuclear war.

Because the Soviet approach to deterrence is different, and its domestic system dissimilar, the Soviet Union, unlike the United States, has put great emphasis on the development of strategic defenses to limit damage to the Soviet economy, people, war-making capability, and leadership from nuclear attacks. The Soviets see no advantage in the mutual vulnerability of American and Soviet societies. The Soviets have also placed great emphasis on the need to destroy quickly the war-making capabilities of the West. As a result, Soviet strategy emphasizes the importance of initiating hostilities with a massive attack against enemy military forces. (It should also be noted, however, that Soviet strategic forces are kept at lower levels of alert than American strategic forces, so that such an attack is less likely to come as a "bolt from the blue" than after a period of increasing tension and crisis.) Such an attack, stimulated by a crisis in Europe, would aim primarily at NATO nuclear weapons depots and facilities in Western Europe and the United States, command and control centers, communications facilities, radar stations, and intelligence satellites. If necessary to achieve success, nuclear weapons would be used and their use would not necessarily be limited to Europe. These attacks would be followed by a massive offensive by Soviet forces into Western Europe.

For many years Soviet doctrine did not recognize the possibility of a major war between the superpowers in which nuclear weapons were not used. In the late 1960s, however, Soviet strategic writers began to refer to the possibility of a conventional phase in such a conflict. More generally, however, the Soviets remain dubious about the possibility of either a limited conventional war or a limited nuclear war.

The Soviet focus on nuclear war-fighting does not imply blindness to the catastrophic destruction that would result from any nuclear war. Since Khrushchev in the 1950s, Soviet leaders have emphasized the destructiveness of nuclear war. But they do view nuclear weapons as the "decisive" weapons in modern war, and however destructive nuclear war might be, they shape their strategy toward minimizing as much as possible the destruction they will suffer as well as forcing their opponent to accept their demands as quickly as possible. While American goals in war are often phrased in terms of "damage limitation," "escalation control," and "war termination," the Soviets speak of the quick defeat of the enemy.

## AMERICAN PURPOSES

### BASIC DETERRENCE

In discussing nuclear weapons policy it is perhaps natural that many people focus exclusively on the most frightening prospect: a full-scale Soviet nuclear surprise attack against the American homeland. The horrifying vision of "a bolt from the blue" attack has been part of the American consciousness ever since December 7, 1941, when the Japanese navy launched its surprise raid on Pearl Harbor. But this, the most feared possibility, may also be the least likely possibility. Why?

Dissuading Soviet leaders from launching such an attack is called the "basic deterrence" objective. Most strategists believe that basic deterrence is the easiest goal to achieve because the Soviets would have every reason to believe that our threat to retaliate with any remaining nuclear forces would be fulfilled after such an attack. The concern cited earlier, that American threats of nuclear retaliation might appear to be bluffs, would be least manifest if the American homeland were the target of a surprise Soviet missile attack.

The credibility of the American threat to retaliate if American society is attacked is, therefore, rarely questioned. Questions are raised, however, about the credibility of basic deterrence against a Soviet attack limited to U.S. missile silos or U.S. strategic forces generally (missile silos, SAC air bases, command and control centers, submarine bases). These facilities have become increasingly vulnerable as a result of Soviet deployment of large, MIRVed missiles. The argument is that such a Soviet attack, particularly if limited to U.S. ICBM silos, could destroy perhaps 90% of U.S. land-based missiles. Most U.S. missile bases are in relatively unpopulated areas, and it is difficult to say how many civilian casualties such an attack would cause. Estimates vary from 2 million to 20 million. In a diplomatic crisis the Soviets, it is argued, might launch such an attack and thus pose to the American president the undesirable choice of either—

1. ordering full retaliation by the remaining U.S. SLBM missiles and bombers on the Soviet Union, in full knowledge that this would trigger a second Soviet attack directed at American cities, which would cause the deaths of many tens of millions of Americans; or
2. accepting the loss of one-quarter to one-third of the U.S. retaliatory force and negotiating terms with the

Soviets after this humiliation and from this disadvantageous position.

The counter-argument challenges the plausibility of this scenario on the grounds that the Soviets could never be sure—

1. that their attack on U.S. missile silos would achieve the results they hoped for (and there is, happily, no way in which they can experiment to improve their confidence that it would work);
2. that the president would not order U.S. missiles to be fired before all the Soviet missiles hit their targets (30 minutes would be available for this "launch on warning" or "launch under attack"); and
3. that the president would not order a limited retaliation by U.S. bombers and submarine-based missiles against selected Soviet military targets, thereby imposing comparable punishment on the Soviet Union but avoiding attacks on cities, or
4. that the president would not order full-scale retaliation with the bulk of the U.S. nuclear force—bombers and submarine-based missiles—which would totally destroy the Soviet Union, even though the Soviet Union could still retaliate in similar fashion against the United States.

In matters of such consequence, however, there is much to be said for taking as few chances as possible. Hence the issue of whether the U.S. land-based missile force can be invulnerable is one of the policy issues now under debate. (See Chapter 8.)

Preventing nuclear attack on the United States is not the only Soviet threat we try to deter. The other security objectives the U.S. hopes to achieve may seem less dramatic than basic deterrence, but they are also of fundamental importance and, in many ways, more difficult to realize.

## EXTENDED DETERRENCE

The United States has a number of commitments, by formal treaty and by common interest, to the protection of allied nations and other countries whose security is vital to us. Deterring Soviet aggression against such nations is called extended deterrence. This goal existed before basic deterrence was a problem for the United States. Indeed, in the 1940s and early 1950s, the primary purpose of American nuclear forces was to dissuade Soviet leaders from taking advantage of the military opportunities provided by their conventional superiority in Europe. As long as the American homeland was largely invulnerable to the Soviet nuclear threat, our commitment to retaliate with nuclear forces if our allies were attacked was rarely questioned. But as Soviet nuclear forces gained sufficient range, and later sufficient invulnerability, so that any American nuclear attack on the Soviet Union could result in a counter-retaliation by Soviet rocket forces, the credibility of the American nuclear guarantee to allies became less certain. A debate has continued on how far the American nuclear deterrent threat can and should be extended.

Extended deterrence takes two forms. First, there is the commitment to protect NATO Europe and the American allies in the Far East—Japan and South Korea—from possible Soviet nuclear attacks. Second, there is the need to deter Soviet conventional attacks against American allies and interests. What should the role of nuclear forces be here?

Most strategists still consider American nuclear forces absolutely essential to deter Soviet nuclear attacks against, and nuclear blackmail of, American allies. Questions about the credibility of the American strategic guarantee contributed to the decisions of two allies, Britain and France, to build nuclear arsenals. No other U.S. allies, however, have nuclear weapons. Of particular importance, West Germany, on the front line of the NATO–Warsaw Pact frontier, does not possess them, nor does Japan.

If our only concern was to deter nuclear attack against the United States, it might be advisable to withdraw our nuclear guarantee to our allies. But the risks produced by such an action would in the long run probably be far worse than the risks the U.S. faces today. Not only would American influence overseas be reduced, but the whole postwar settlement of 1945 could be overturned. American nuclear isolationism would dangerously increase the likelihood of eventual Soviet aggression against or coercion of U.S. allies.

The second form of extended deterrence is the contribution of American nuclear forces to deterring Soviet conventional aggression against American allies and vital interests. The policy of the American government has been to decrease, but not entirely remove, NATO's reliance on nuclear weapons to deter Warsaw Pact conventional attacks. The evolution of NATO military strategy from "massive retaliation" in the 1950s to "flexible response" dating from the 1960s to current discussions of more conventionally oriented strategies for extended deterrence illustrates a decreasing reliance on nuclear weapons.

Strategists differ on the proper role of nuclear weapons in deterring Soviet conventional aggression, partly because of different views on the conventional military balance in Europe. Most Western observers agree that the Warsaw Pact's conventional strength is greater than NATO's: the disparity in numbers of divisions (2:1 Pact advantage) and in numbers of tanks (2.5:1 Pact advantage) is disturbingly large. Some strategists believe, however, that NATO's real conventional disadvantages are less pronounced than these numerical differences suggest. They point to qualitative advantages in NATO's weaponry, to the traditional advantage of defensive positions, and to the modest advantage (1.2:1) the Pact is estimated to have in overall ground combat power. They stress the dubious reliability of East European forces—particularly in a prolonged conflict. They claim that a credible conventional "deterrence by denial" posture is militarily plausible.

Other strategists believe such a defense posture is desirable but not politically or economically possible. They cite the continued disadvantages in NATO strength vis-à-vis the Warsaw Pact. They point out that, for example, for political reasons NATO troops are strung out all along the inter-German border (and hence vulnerable to Soviet concentrations of force), but that—also for political reasons—strong fortifications have not been built along that border. They argue that only the threat of a nuclear response can serve as a credible deterrent.

Different strategies are proposed by those who stress deterrence through nuclear punishment and those who stress denial. A pure "punishment" approach would need to maintain only enough nuclear forces to retaliate against the Soviet Union; a pure denial approach would stress forces capable of stopping Soviet tank divisions on the West German border. Positions combining both approaches might stress the need for theater nuclear forces to serve as a link to the threat of continued nuclear escalation. The fear of ultimate nuclear consequences serves as the foundation of deterrence.

Do nuclear forces play a role in deterring Soviet military intervention in the Third World? The answer is ambiguous. The United States made an implicit nuclear threat in October 1973 when it placed its nuclear forces on increased alert as part of an effort to deter Moscow from sending ground forces into Egypt at the close of the Yom Kippur War. In 1980, after the Soviet invasion of Afghanistan, President Jimmy Carter announced that American military force would be used, if necessary, to defend the Persian Gulf. Soon thereafter, administration officials leaked reports that the use of nuclear weapons might be required if Soviet forces moved toward the oilfields of the region.

It is difficult to measure the effect of such nuclear threats. There are at least some grounds not to believe that the United States would take risky steps toward nuclear war in order to stop Soviet aggression against these areas. The danger also exists that the Soviets might find U.S. statements incredible and launch an attack to which the U.S. would feel it had to respond, using nuclear weapons if necessary. On the other hand, in deterrence residual uncertainty can help the defending side. When the risks of miscalculation are so enormous, and the stakes are high for the defending power, a potential aggressor may be deterred by threats with less than perfect credibility.

## CRISIS STABILITY

Besides deterring premeditated Soviet aggression, the U.S. wants to minimize the probability of a pre-emptive attack by the Soviet Union, an attack made not from a belief in Moscow that the costs of war would be low or that victory would be probable, but from great desperation. In a deep crisis—such as a repeat of the Cuban missile crisis of 1962—Soviet leaders, fearing an attack that would destroy much or all of their capability to retaliate, might launch their missiles first.

Reducing incentives for pre-emptive nuclear attack enhances what strategists call "crisis stability." Minimizing the risks of a war beginning by pre-emption is extremely important, but is not the only goal of American strategy. Fortunately, not all policies that reenforce crisis stability contradict other security objectives; unfortunately, some difficult trade-offs exist.

If crisis stability were the only concern of American nuclear force planners, they would design an arsenal (if nuclear weapons were desired at all) that would be as invulnerable as possible, so that the Soviet Union could not believe American forces would be destroyed by a Soviet first strike. American planners would also want inaccurate missiles with very long flight times, so that Soviet leaders need never fear that their retaliatory forces would be destroyed in a surprise attack. Indeed, if the sole objective of American strategic forces was to reduce Soviet fears of pre-emption, the American arsenal might consist of only a small number of slow, invulnerable, and relatively inaccurate missiles. Such a force would minimize Soviet fears of the United States ever launching a pre-emptive strike and thereby would minimize Soviet incentives to strike first in a crisis.

Such a nuclear arsenal would, however, detract from other major American objectives. Having only the suicidal ability to destroy Soviet cities would likely reduce the credibility of retaliatory nuclear threats. It might thereby increase the likelihood of deterrence failing by attacks on allies or even on American nuclear forces. The need to maintain *credible* deterrence may, in this way, at least partly contradict the goal of crisis stability.

Some steps are unambiguously stabilizing. Reducing the vulnerability of American nuclear forces by putting some of them underwater or by otherwise making them mobile, for example, enhances crisis stability without diminishing the credibility of deterrence. The same thing can be said about reducing other vulnerabilities: improving American command, control, and communications systems ($C^3$), for example, would reduce Soviet incentives for striking first, but would not decrease deterrence.

Trade-offs may exist about American targeting of Soviet military forces. An American ability to attack Soviet forces may reduce crisis stability by increasing Soviet fears of pre-emptive attack; but such an American "counter-force" capability may also enhance the credibility of an American retaliatory threat that is not suicidal in nature.

American strategists disagree on how much the Soviet forces should be targeted and on which type of forces should be targeted. Some strategists believe American interests are best served by a large force capable of attacking Soviet missile silos and other forces; others favor some counter-force capability to enhance the credibility of deterrence, but not so much as to endanger crisis stability objectives; and still others believe the U.S. should have minimal counter-force capabilities, or none at all.

## IF DETERRENCE FAILS

Although the United States does not want to fight a nuclear war, it may be interested in nuclear forces with war-fighting capabilities for three reasons. First, as has been mentioned, some war-fighting capabilities may aid deterrence because weapons that would be usable only against cities would not enhance deterrence of some kinds of aggression. Second, if deterrence fails, it may be in the American interest to keep a limited war as limited as possible. Third, as long as there is a possibility of war, the United States is interested in the outcome: any nuclear war would be terrible, but some might be much worse than others. Some, but not all, American strategists place great importance on nuclear forces capable of reducing the destruction to the United States and its allies that would occur in such horrible circumstances.

What are American objectives if deterrence fails? What kinds of forces might improve our chances of achieving these goals? What trade-offs exist? Are the forces required for war-fighting missions counter-productive?

*War-fighting and war-winning.* There is much controversy over the idea of "winning a nuclear war," and much of it is a normal human reaction to the outrageous implausibility of the idea. Any major nuclear exchange between the United States and the Soviet Union would be disastrous. Both sides would be far worse off than they were before the exchange. One side, however, might be considerably worse off than the other. It has been estimated, for example, that with current forces and doctrines an all-out nuclear exchange aimed at military and economic targets could kill up to 155–165 million people in the United States and up to 64–100 million people in the Soviet Union.[1] In such a case, the Soviet Union would have suffered less than the United States. Only those with a taste for morbid metaphysics will devote much time to debating in what sense the Soviet Union could be said to have "won" such an exchange. The critical need is to prevent it from happening.

To do this, the U.S. government has tried to ensure that under no circumstances will the Soviet leaders conclude that they could fight and "win" a nuclear war, by their definition of winning. The problem is that we do not know what they would consider acceptable costs to "win" a nuclear war. Nor, in fact, do they. Their willingness to risk casualties in the tens of millions will depend on what they think their alternatives are. If the alternative were the disintegration of the Soviet Union, they probably would be willing to suffer such casualties. The Soviet government and people suffered 20 million deaths to prevent the Nazis from taking over their country. Soviet leaders might also be willing to risk the loss of many millions of their citizens if, as a result, they could be certain to emerge as the unquestioned primary military power in the world and the U.S. was reduced to a regional North American role.

It would be unwise for the U.S. to assume otherwise. Consequently, American strategy has been to have some nuclear war-fighting capability. In recent years, administrations have wanted sufficient capability to deny to the Soviet leadership any victory they might consider worthwhile. Administrations have disagreed on the level and nature of the forces necessary to achieve this goal, but all have recognized that some war-fighting capability is necessary not to win a nuclear war but to deter one.

*Damage limitation.* This is the objective of trying to limit, as much as possible, the destruction to the United States and its allies that would occur if deterrence failed.

How can the damage of war be reduced? Two general possibilities exist.

The first is possessing nuclear weaponry capable of destroying Soviet missiles and bombs before they would be launched. The ultimate threat to civilian punishment might serve as a foundation of deterrence, but if war occurred punishment attacks would serve little useful purpose. Indeed, as long as American cities were not harmed, attacks against Soviet cities would probably be very counterproductive, only increasing Soviet incentives to destroy American cities. In war, as the strategist Bernard Brodie once noted, the enemy's military forces, "insofar as [they] can be reached and destroyed, [are] certainly the first and most important target system. There is in fact no other target system worth comparable consideration."[2]

Indeed, since 1961 Soviet military forces have been the primary target of U.S. nuclear forces. One should not, however, ignore the reduced possibility of damage limitation and the trade-offs involved, given the large numbers of nuclear weapons in the Soviet arsenal today. The possibility is reduced because American attacks against Soviet nuclear forces cannot reduce damage from Soviet counter-attacks to an acceptable level; the same is true for the Soviets. The trade-off comes from the inescapable problem that one man's damage limitation, at a certain point, becomes another man's feared first strike. An American ability to attack all Soviet military forces might greatly increase Soviet incentives for a pre-emptive attack. Soviet missiles are also generally deployed close to populated areas, and the Soviets could well interpret an American damage-limiting attack as a major damage-creating attack. Thus a major question remains: What counterforce capabilities enhance security and what kinds may actually increase the likelihood of war?

The second approach to damage limitation is defensive measures. Air defenses, ballistic missile defensives, and civil defense can cut down on the destruction of nuclear war; consequently, the Soviets have consistently devoted substantial resources to defensive purposes. They have invested billions of rubles in the construction of an air defense system which has greatly reduced the potential effectiveness of U.S. bombers. They took the lead in deploying an anti-ballistic missile system. They agreed to stringent limitations on ABM systems in the SALT I Treaty, but have continued the one system permitted by the treaty around Moscow and have maintained a high level of research and development in this area. They have, finally, invested considerable effort in the creation of a civil defense organization, headed by a general equivalent to the commanders of the army, navy, and strategic rocket forces. It is estimated that they have built hardened shelters for 10%–20% of their urban work force and have plans, in the event of crisis, to evacuate the remaining non-essential personnel from their cities.

Russia has been vulnerable to attack for centuries and the Soviet Union has been vulnerable to substantial U.S. nuclear attack for 35 years. The U.S. experience has been different, and defense systems have never been popular here. Even if a defense system could be 90% effective, horrendous damage would still result from a nuclear attack. This has led American policy to emphasize the prevention of nuclear war by the threat of nuclear retaliation. Given the changing strategic balance between the United States and the Soviet Union, however, increasing attention is being given to whether the U.S. should devote more attention than it has to air, ABM, and civil defenses. All three figure in the strategic forces program proposed by President Reagan in the fall of 1981.

*Escalation control.* If war begins between the Soviet Union and the United States, it would be in the American interest to deny the Soviets any advantages gained from Soviet decisions to escalate the fighting. Escalation is impervious to intricate control, but efforts to control it must be made.

Two escalation control policies have been discussed by strategists. The first is to have "escalation matching" capabilities: forces that can fight a war at whatever level the enemy chose to fight. The hope is that this ability would deter the Soviets from expanding a war if deterrence failed. The other policy, "escalation dominance," refers to having superiority at every possible level of combat. Because such superiority would shift the burden of risk of escalation onto the Soviets if they began a war, it is hoped that escalation dominance would keep wars limited, if they occur, and would also minimize their likelihood.

Preventing the enormous leap from conventional warfare to the first use of nuclear weapons is the first and most important step in escalation control. This is a clear, unambiguous firebreak. Millions of people have been killed in conventional wars since 1945, but no one has been killed in nuclear wars. If nuclear weapons are used again, it will be a memorable—and tragic—day in the history of the human race. Reluctance to cross that firebreak is, and undoubtedly will continue to be, a major constraint on any responsible political leader.

Such willingness is, however, assumed by current NATO strategy. Once the conventional-nuclear line is passed, moreover, the other steps on the escalation ladder become much more likely. It would then be very hard to arrive at an implicit or explicit understanding on where to draw the line. American strategy has distinguished among battlefield, theater, and strategic nuclear weapons and between counter-force and counter-value targeting. Soviet strategy, by and large, does not emphasize these distinctions. Even if the distinctions are recognized, there can be important differences on how a weapon is classified. To a Soviet a U.S. "theater" missile fired from West Germany at the Soviet Union is a strategic weapon because it hit the Soviet Union.

Control of wartime violence, conventional or nuclear, requires that the political leaders on both sides know what is happening in the conflict, that they be able to issue orders to their military commanders, and that they be able to communicate with each other. The technical facilities that enable them to do these things are called $C^3I$: command, control, communications, and intelligence. They include intelligence satellites, communications satellites, transmission facilities, ground relay stations, headquarters networks, and a variety of other sensitive and complex electronics systems. The systems must reach from the national command headquarters—for the United States, the White House, an airborne command plane, or an underground command post outside Washington—throughout the world down to battalion commanders confronting Soviet forces on the German border. The $C^3I$ systems are highly vulnerable to enemy attack. At present, it would be almost impossible for U.S. national authorities to exercise effective escalation control over U.S. tactical nuclear forces in Europe and very difficult for them to exercise such control over U.S. strategic nuclear forces. This is one of the most serious deficiencies in the U.S. military setup, and both the Carter and the Reagan administrations have made dealing with it a top priority.

## WAR TERMINATION

If deterrence fails and nuclear weapons are used in warfare, it might still be possible to terminate hostilities rapidly, before escalation to total war occurred. Any negotiated settlement of a nuclear war would have two prerequisites: the technical capability to communicate with the enemy leadership and the continued existence of that leadership. It is not certain that either would exist after any but the most limited nuclear exchange.

The ability of American leaders to communicate with the Soviet leaders in wartime would be dependent upon fragile communications links such as the so-called "hot line" between Washington and Moscow. These communications links, however, might be destroyed by the collateral effects of even a limited nuclear war. Despite the hot line's importance, no special measures have been made to ensure that it would work after the nuclear war began.

There is a severe trade-off between efforts to limit damage in a nuclear war, which might include massive attacks on the enemy leadership, and efforts to terminate a war by negotiation, which would require someone to negotiate with. Currently, both the Soviet and the American command and control systems are extremely vulnerable to enemy attack: between 50 and 100 well-placed nuclear weapons might be able to "decapitate" a nuclear power, ensuring that leadership control of enemy forces would be impaired and creating at least some possibility that little retaliation would occur. Both superpowers appear to include the other side's command and control systems as early war targets. These plans reflect an all-or-nothing approach to damage limitation, for an attempt to limit retaliation by "decapitating" the enemy might well result in an uncontrolled, spasm response rather than no response at all.

Strategists disagree over whether and when enemy leadership should be attacked in a nuclear war. Some individuals believe that, once a nuclear war begins, the opportunity for negotiations is past and that all command and control targets should be quickly destroyed. Others believe that the enemy command system should be spared in order to limit damage by bringing war to a negotiated halt. Many strategists argue for a policy combining these two approaches: if deterrence fails, Soviet tactical military command centers should be attacked, but the overall political leadership should not be attacked in order to allow efforts to negotiate an end to hostilities.

## DIPLOMATIC SUPPORT

Frederick the Great once remarked that diplomacy without military armaments is like music without instruments. His point, that military power influences the course of diplomatic disagreements, is as true today as it was in the 18th century. But exactly how military power affects diplomacy is difficult to determine.

While nuclear weapons have not been used since 1945, nuclear threats have been, in times of crisis, by the U.S. and the USSR. It is impossible to know how crisis behavior was influenced by these threats, for two reasons. First, we know little about the methods or motivation behind Soviet decisions. Second, conventional forces also influence the outcome of a dispute. Even if it appears that one government has backed away from actions during a crisis because of another's nuclear threats, the change may be due to the balance of conventional forces, to important compromises between the countries, to the "balance of resolve" between the governments, or to differences in the importance of what is at stake to the two sides.

Given these unavoidable ambiguities in dissecting crises, any lessons about the political effects of nuclear weapons can only be stated tentatively. Still, it appears that as the Soviet Union has expanded its nuclear arsenal the U.S. has been less able to resort to nuclear warnings in times of crisis. One study has noted that there were 19 international incidents between 1945 and 1973 in which military forces with "a role in U.S. plans for strategic nuclear war" were utilized in such a way "that a nuclear signal of some type could be inferred." Of these cases of nuclear "signaling," 17 took place in 1945–65 and only 2 since then. There have been none since 1973, by which time the Soviet Union had achieved strategic parity with the United States.[3] During its years of nuclear superiority, the U.S. did not attempt to exploit its unique destructive capability to roll back Soviet power. When it felt major interests to be at stake, however, it did wage nuclear diplomacy, and on most of these occasions the U.S. secured all or most of the goals it sought. Why this was true is debatable, but with the emergence of nuclear parity, the U.S. has been much more reluctant to use nuclear threats in support of its diplomacy.

Since the Second World War the Soviet Union has not used nuclear threats in support of its diplomacy to the same degree as the United States. For much of this period, of course, Soviet forces were much weaker than American forces, and Soviet leaders were careful to avoid direct military confrontation with the United States. They were not always so restrained, however, with other countries. Kremlin leaders showed films of Soviet H-bomb tests to Yugoslav president Tito and to the Shah of Iran on the eve of important negotiations with them.[4] At other times, the Soviets attempted to make it appear that they were practicing nuclear diplomacy when they were not. In the Suez crisis of 1956, for example, Soviet premier Bulganin threatened Britain and France with Soviet missiles after the Soviets were sure that the United States had gotten them to agree to withdraw their forces from Egypt. Apparently the 1962 Cuban missile crisis was the only time when the Soviets raised the alert level of their strategic forces during a crisis. The Soviet border conflict with China is the only time when the Soviets made meaningful verbal threats involving their nuclear weapons while the crisis was unresolved.[5] As was generally true of American nuclear threats, the Soviet threat in this case was followed by accommodating action by their opponent.

As a result of the period of American nuclear superiority, extended deterrence is often thought of as a peculiarly American policy. The growth of the Soviet strategic arsenal and the emergence of strategic parity, however, could make it more likely that the Soviets will use their nuclear forces to influence the outcome of crises. They could attempt to practice their own form of extended deterrence, using their strategic forces to deter the U.S. from using its conventional forces to protect American interests in the Third World. Then U.S. strategic forces would presumably be called upon to play a counter-deterrent role: that is, deterring the Soviet Union from using its nuclear forces to deter the U.S. from using its conventional forces. This potential additional function for U.S. strategic forces underlines the importance of maintaining a situation of strategic parity between the United States and the Soviet Union.

The Reagan administration says U.S. strategic forces should also ensure "the margin of safety necessary for our security." It is unclear whether this has any practical meaning in terms of the nuclear balance that the administration conceives desirable and possible to maintain. All recent administrations, however, and many strategists agree that U.S. foreign policy requires that U.S. strategic forces have overall capabilities that are perceived as roughly equal to Soviet capabilities. The U.S. is the premier global power and the leader of a far-flung network of allied and associated countries dependent upon it for their security. While there is no agreed-upon definition of "parity," all American administrations have believed that failure to maintain at least rough strategic parity with the Soviet Union would be incompatible with the overall role of the U.S. in the world at large, would produce uncertainty, alarm, and possibly defection on the part of U.S. allies, and would encourage Soviet expansion and adventurism.

## ARMS CONTROL

The United States and the Soviet Union share certain common interests in attempting to reduce the risks and the costs of their nuclear arms competition. The decisions the U.S. makes on nuclear weapons should support U.S. arms control objectives or should be made with a clear understanding of the trade-offs that exist between arms control and the other major policy objectives discussed in this chapter.

Nuclear weapons decisions can complicate efforts to achieve arms control. The U.S. decision in the late 1960s to MIRV U.S. land-based and submarine-based ballistic missiles, for example, led to a major expansion in the number of American strategic nuclear warheads. MIRVing by the Soviets, in turn, made the U.S. land-based ICBM force potentially vulnerable to a Soviet first strike and hence could diminish crisis stability in any future confrontation between the two superpowers. Now the U.S. is proceeding with the development and deployment of air- and sea-based cruise missiles. Cruise missiles contribute to arms control and crisis stability in that they are slow, air-breathing vehicles, useful only for a second strike against Soviet strategic forces. They complicate arms control in that they are small and therefore easily concealed. It is almost impossible to distinguish between cruise missiles armed with nuclear weapons and those armed with conventional weapons. The negotiation of arms control agreements takes time, and the development of technology can run ahead of the ability of arms control negotiators to come up with effective means of identifying, counting, and limiting weapons.

But nuclear weapons policy can have a positive effect on arms control. It can create or threaten to create "bargaining chips": weapons systems the Soviets do not want the U.S. to have and which they will make major concessions to prevent from entering the U.S. arsenal. In 1972, as we have seen, the development by the U.S. of a superior ABM system played a significant role in inducing the Soviets to sign the treaty drastically limiting such systems. In the "two-track" NATO decision in December 1979, the threat of deployment of U.S. missiles to Europe has served as a bargaining chip to induce the Soviets to negotiate seriously over theater nuclear arms limitation in Europe. During 1981 and 1982, as that prospective deployment came progressively closer to reality, the Soviets began to adopt more forthcoming positions in the negotiations. The record suggests that while no nuclear weapon has been built exclusively or primarily as a bargaining chip, nuclear weapons policy decisions can, in the right circumstances, serve a useful purpose in arms control negotiations. In other circumstances they can complicate negotiations, or have no effect on such arms control efforts.

## FORTUNATE UNCERTAINTY

What do we want from our nuclear forces?

We want basic deterrence, extended deterrence, crisis stability, war-fighting and damage limitation capability, escalation control, war termination capability, foreign policy support, counter-deterrence, and arms control!

Each purpose imposes requirements on the nuclear forces. And most can be achieved only in part. Basic deterrence might require only a few hundred invulnerable strategic missiles. Extended deterrence might require many more strategic missiles plus theater nuclear capabilities in Europe.

Crisis stability is enhanced by invulnerable forces that cannot seriously damage the other side's forces. Damage limitation demands precisely the capability to impose such damage and also effective defenses. Escalation control requires parity or superiority at each rung of the ladder: battlefield weapons, theater weapons, strategic weapons. Foreign policy requires real and perceived equivalence with Soviet forces. Arms control traditionally has demanded weapons that can be easily identified and counted but not located and targeted by the other side, plus weapons that may induce accommodation and compromise.

Designing nuclear forces to meet all these requirements is no easy task, to say the least. There is no consensus among American strategists, just as there is no agreement among concerned citizens, about how best to pursue these diverse objectives.

This lack of consensus is not altogether unfortunate. Indeed, it is worth remembering that as long as nuclear deterrence succeeds, nuclear strategy will, by fortunate necessity, take place in a kind of twilight. It is impossible *to know* exactly how deterrence works, how it might fail, or how far it can be extended. It is impossible *to know* whether deterrence, once war began, could be reinstated. Such uncertainty produces prudence in political leaders; disagreement among strategists is also a product of ever present uncertainty.

The United States cannot ignore the difficult dilemma presented by the usability paradox: the United States requires, we believe, nuclear weapons that are usable, but not *too* usable. They should be usable enough to convince the Soviets that there is a real risk that the United States would retaliate under circumstances where the government has said it will do so. Forces should be usable enough that a president never lacks nuclear options between suicidal all-out responses and no nuclear retaliation at all. But forces should not be so usable that they would be launched when we do not want them to be used. American nuclear forces should not have a "hair trigger," nor should they force the Soviet Union to place its forces on a hair trigger.

## HOW MUCH AND WHAT KIND?

There is room for debate over the proper mix of strategic objectives and the nuclear forces necessary to achieve them. Two central, interrelated issues are the overall size and the nature of the U.S. nuclear arsenal.

Does the U.S. need almost 2,000 strategic launchers and almost 10,000 strategic warheads? Should it have more? Could the U.S. be just as safe, or safer, with many fewer?

Does the U.S. need a triad of ICBMs, SLBMs, and bombers? Should U.S. weapons be able to destroy all, some, or none of the Soviet nuclear arsenal?

Some strategists argue that U.S. nuclear forces are far larger than is necessary for U.S. security. They believe in what can be called the "minimum deterrence" standard: a relatively small number of nuclear weapons, if they cannot be destroyed by a Soviet first strike, would suffice to ensure that Soviet aggression would be unlikely to occur. This is the logic behind the French nuclear force. It has never been large enough to destroy all of the Soviet Union or all of its military forces in a retaliatory strike, but by destroying some Soviet cities, it could severely punish an aggressor. The French government hopes this potential punishment will be enough to dissuade the Soviets from attacking France. Some Americans think a similar force would be adequate for the U.S.

A second, somewhat similar standard is called "assured destruction": the ability of the United States to destroy, even after having been attacked first, a substantial portion of the Soviet Union's industry and population. This view is based on the assumption that the United States does not have to equal the Soviet Union in nuclear capabilities and that within broad limits enough is enough. In 1965, Secretary of Defense Robert McNamara set the "assured destruction" level at one-third of the Soviet population and two-thirds of Soviet industrial capacity. If nuclear forces able to inflict this level of punishment could be maintained, it has been argued, deterrence would be sustained. Secretary McNamara estimated that perhaps 400–500 strategic launchers would be enough for this objective.

Maintaining nuclear deterrence, if this approach were followed, would be easier in terms of number and kinds of nuclear forces required. It would be more difficult, today, because of credibility problems: such an approach might not ensure that the Soviets would believe American forces would actually be used, especially for any purpose beyond basic deterrence.

Both standards could be met with an American nuclear force significantly smaller than the Soviet nuclear arsenal as long as, and only as long as, a certain number of nuclear weapons would be able to retaliate even if the Soviet Union attacked the United States first. Thus both "minimum deterrence" and "assured destruction" standards could be met without quantitative competition in arms building with the Russians. The question "How much is enough?" could be answered, "Only as many weapons as necessary to ensure that Soviet cities could be destroyed in a retaliatory attack."

In terms of the purposes that Americans want their nuclear weapons to serve, "minimum deterrent" or "assured destruction" forces probably would deter a Soviet attack on American cities. They would be less likely to serve the purposes of extended deterrence. If they were invulnerable to Soviet attack they would contribute to crisis stability. They would not, however, give the U.S. capabilities to fight a nuclear war, to limit damage to itself, or to control escalation. Nor would they provide support for American foreign policy, reassure American allies, or prevent Soviet nuclear coercion. They might or might not be compatible with arms control measures, but they would not furnish "bargaining chips" to induce concessions from the Soviets.

There are three major difficulties in basing deterrence primarily on the ultimate threat to Soviet population centers. First, complete reliance on such a threat can become a self-fulfilling prophecy. Strategists stressing deterrence through punishment often believe that if a nuclear war begins in a limited way—for example, if nuclear weapons are used to try to stop a Soviet conventional attack against NATO—the fighting between the superpowers will inevitably escalate to a full-scale nuclear exchange. This may or may not be true. But, although unhardened military targets could be destroyed by inaccurate missiles, if the American nuclear arsenal was only capable of attacking Soviet cities, then any nuclear response to Soviet aggression would automatically bring on such a holocaust.

The second difficulty is the opposite side of the coin. If the United States became involved in a conventional conflict with the Soviets or was attacked in a less than total fashion by Soviet nuclear forces, it is possible that the American president would choose not to retaliate. As long as American cities were "held hostage" to the Soviet atomic arsenal, an American government might decide to back down. Here is the "credibility" problem: would the Soviets anticipate this, and would it reduce the effectiveness of the American deterrent? The answer is not known. But successive American administrations have sought to avoid making threats that are blatantly unbelievable.

The third difficulty revolves around moral considerations. Many Americans—covering the spectrum from left-wing activists to Catholic bishops to former Secretary of State Henry Kissinger—have argued that a nuclear strategy designed to attack the cities of the Soviet Union, even in retaliation, is immoral. While some individuals argue that such a threat holds the best chance of maintaining nuclear deterrence, and is therefore the least immoral strategy available, most strategists believe that some ability to resort to "limited nuclear options" is necessary to make deterrence credible.

At the other end of the scale from "minimum

deterrence" and "assured destruction" forces would be nuclear forces shaped primarily to serve the purposes of war-fighting, damage limitation, and escalation control. Given the size of the Soviet strategic forces, any effort to realize these goals fully would require a major expansion of the American strategic forces, with a huge investment in the development and deployment of ABM systems, air defenses, and civil defense. It would require the expansion of the U.S. land-based missile force considerably beyond what has been proposed by either the Carter or the Reagan administrations in order to have the capability to destroy most of the Soviet strategic forces in a first strike. It would also require much larger theater nuclear forces in order to ensure U.S. control of escalation.

Forces such as these—if obtainable—would not only enable the United States to fight a nuclear war with the prospect of less destruction and more success, but would also serve the purposes of basic and extended deterrence. They would, however, undermine stability in crises and make arms control difficult if not impossible. They would not necessarily make any significant contribution to American foreign policy generally. They would undoubtedly cause alarm among U.S. allies, as well as among the Soviets, and very probably among substantial sections of the American public. They would be extremely expensive. All in all, we conclude that the uncertain benefits from such an effort to re-establish American nuclear supremacy would not appear to be worth the assured costs and risks.

What types of nuclear capabilities should the United States have? Since the early 1960s, for example, the U.S. has maintained a strategic triad of ICBMs, SLBMs, and bombers. The Carter and Reagan administrations committed themselves to the maintenance of this triad and advocated programs to modernize each of its legs. Some strategists, however, argue that all three legs are no longer necessary or desirable. Land-based missiles, they say, will inevitably be vulnerable to a first strike and hence will threaten crisis stability and arms control objectives. The supporters of land-based missiles, on the other hand, point to their reliability, accuracy, and ease of command and control. They are, it is said, necessary if the U.S. is to have some capability to limit damage to itself by attacking Soviet strategic forces and to threaten limited nuclear strikes against Soviet targets.

## CONCLUSION

How much is enough? What numbers and what types of American nuclear weapons will best serve the various objectives of nuclear policy?

We have provided our views in the next chapter on current nuclear issues. It is important to remember, however, that there is no definitive arsenal size or composition that will uniquely serve all the goals of American security. A variety of possible forces of different size and different types might suffice. We believe that the American nuclear policy should maintain *rough parity* with the Soviet Union. It is undesirable and possibly disastrous for American nuclear forces to be significantly weaker than Soviet forces; it is unnecessary and probably impossible for them to be significantly stronger than Soviet forces.

Reasonable people can, and do, disagree about what numbers and what kinds of forces are needed to maintain such rough parity. But reasonable people should not disagree about one thing: the horrible nature of nuclear war. Nuclear weapons are enormously destructive. Once war with such weapons begins, it will be extremely difficult to control.

Nuclear strategists, in the United States and the Soviet Union, are responsible for thinking about every possibility, however difficult or unlikely. With their cold language and pristine logic it can sometimes seem that they ignore the horrible nature of these weapons. Nuclear statesmen, however, are responsible for maintaining the security of their nations. They rarely forget how horrible a nuclear war could be. For statesmen in the nuclear age the ultimate threat—that conventional or limited use of nuclear weapons might escalate—is always uncertain but always profound. It is this ultimate fear that has produced prudence in the minds of American and Soviet leaders.

## Notes

1. Secretary of Defense Harold Brown, Annual Report Fiscal Year 1982, p. 37. If the U.S. deliberately targeted population, it could kill millions more Russians.

2. Bernard Brodie, *Strategy in the Missile Age* (Princeton, N.J.: Princeton University, 1965), p. 402.

3. Barry Blechman and Stephen S. Kaplan, *Force Without War* (Washington, D.C.: Brookings Institution, 1978).

4. Veljko Mićunović, *Moscow Diary* (Garden City, N.Y.: Doubleday, 1980), p. 93.

5. Stephen S. Kaplan et al., *Diplomacy of Power: Soviet Armed Forces as a Political Instrument* (Washington, D.C.: Brookings Institution, 1981), pp. 54–56, 669–70.

# PART III

## What Can Be Done?

# 8

# Choosing Weapons: What Are the Alternatives?

Nuclear forces are shaped by national goals, military requirements, technological advancements, economic realities, and political processes. There are differences between West and East in each of these areas, but none contrast as sharply as those in the realm of political processes. Most nuclear weapons policy decisions in the Western democracies are made explicitly, openly, and with increasingly broad public discussions of alternative views. This is the antithesis of the secretive and closed policy-making processes characteristic of the Soviet Union. Thus the following discussion of contemporary nuclear issues is restricted substantially to an examination of debates within the West on impending nuclear weapons decisions facing the West. We don't know the nature, substance, or significance of corresponding debates within the Soviet Union, nor even whether such debates occur on an appreciable scale.

Few nuclear issues are entirely new. For example, decisions on whether—and, if so, how—to modernize nuclear forces are before us always. New threats emerge or are anticipated, deployed weapons become obsolescent, and new technologies provide new opportunities. The basic nature of the problems changes little with time, but the alternative solutions available are modified continuously by changes in the military, technological, economic, and political environments.

What factors should be considered while analyzing a nuclear weapons issue and selecting a preferred course of action? There is no universally accepted "checklist," but even the most rudimentary list would include the short- and long-term effects of alternative courses of action (1) on the likelihood of war; (2) on the consequences of war should it occur; (3) on the economic cost of maintaining an adequate military posture; (4) on the political implications of maintaining that posture; and (5) on negotiated arms control.

---

**Checklist for
Nuclear Weapons Issues**

Consider the short- and long-term effects of alternative courses of action on:

1. *Likelihood of war*
   Basic deterrence
   Extended deterrence
   Crisis stability

2. *Consequences of war*
   War-fighting capability
   Damage limitation
   Escalation control

3. *Economic costs*
   Program costs
   Associated costs

4. *Political implications*
   Domestic implications
   Diplomatic implications

5. *Negotiated arms control*
   Compliance with existing agreements
   Prospects for future agreements

Ten specific contemporary issues are addressed below, in four categories: European theater nuclear forces, strategic nuclear forces, command and control, and defense against nuclear attack. The European theater issues involve whether the United States should deploy on European soil new missiles capable of reaching targets in the Soviet Union, and whether NATO should renounce first use of nuclear weapons in a European conflict; strategic force issues involve the vulnerability of land-based ICBMs to surprise attack, ICBM and SLBM modernization, bomber modernization, and the deployment of long-range cruise missiles; command and control issues involve plans for upgrading the earth- and space-based components of the command, control, communications, and intelligence network required to support the use of strategic nuclear forces in war, and plans for developing an operational anti-satellite capability; and the defense issues involve active defense against ballistic missiles, and civil defense. Only those "checklist" factors which appear to be affected significantly will be explicitly discussed.

## NATO NUCLEAR ISSUES

By 1955 the United States had deployed nuclear weapons in Western Europe to balance Soviet superiority in conventional forces. Today some 6,000 nuclear warheads are stored at about 70 European locations and can be dispersed in time of crisis to 200–300 sites. These warheads equip Lance and Pershing I short-range ballistic missiles, a variety of dual purpose aircraft, land mines, and, until recently, anti-aircraft missiles. Several NATO allies, including the Federal Republic of Germany, operate nuclear-capable delivery systems, but the United States maintains custody of the nuclear warheads. These systems can only be used with both American and allied consent, under a "dual key" arrangement. Other weapons are under American control alone. All but the oldest weapons have multi-step electronic locks called "permissive action links" (PALs), intended to foil accidental or unauthorized use.

From the perspective of NATO, the theater nuclear balance was satisfactory through the late 1970s. Both sides had nuclear-capable aircraft—NATO's were newer and better, the USSR's more numerous. Both sides had thousands of battlefield nuclear weapons, from land mines to artillery shells. The Soviets had, in addition, roughly 600 large warheads on their old SS-4 and SS-5 land-based missiles (the same types that existed during the 1962 Cuban missile crisis). To compensate (at least on paper) for this Soviet advantage in intermediate-range missiles for theater use, NATO's commander had (and still has) about 400 Poseidon warheads (which count as strategic weapons) on submarines assigned to him.

By 1977 the Soviets had begun to deploy the SS-20 missile and the Backfire bomber, maintaining that both were overdue modernization programs. NATO sees these deployments as new elements that tip the balance in Moscow's favor, partly because the new systems are much more capable in range, payload, accuracy, and survivability than the ones they replaced, and partly because the USSR has not retired older systems as fast as the new ones have become operational.

## THE TWO-TRACK DECISION: DEPLOYMENT AND NEGOTIATION

In December 1979, after extensive debate within the alliance, NATO announced a "two-track" decision on long-range theater nuclear forces. The first track was a decision to deploy 108 Pershing II ballistic missiles (replacing shorter-range Pershing I missiles on a one-for-one basis) and 464 ground-launched cruise missiles (GLCMs); the second track was a commitment to pursue simultaneously negotiations aimed at limiting theater nuclear forces.

The 108 Pershing IIs would be deployed in West Germany, and the 464 GLCMs in Great Britain (160), Italy (112), West Germany (96), Belgium (48), and the Netherlands (48). Implementation of the deployment decision has come to be viewed by many as a test of NATO's internal cohesion and "resolve" to do what is needed to deter direct Soviet attack and subtler processes of coercion.

The Soviet Union has taken a decidedly dim view of the pending NATO deployments. The Pershing II is designed to be more accurate than the current generations of ICBMs and SLBMs. The Soviets claim that the range of this missile is greater than the United States asserts, and that it could reach Moscow from West Germany in less than ten minutes. Thus, the Soviets say, it could be upon much of Soviet central command and control just about as fast as Soviet detection systems could sound a warning, and would pose a severe risk of surprise attack. GLCMs are much slower, but almost as accurate, and capable of attacking targets in the vicinity of Moscow in about two hours. Since neither the Pershings nor the GLCMs would be limited by the SALT II Treaty, Moscow views these deployments in Europe as an American effort to circumvent that agreement.

NATO could have chosen to base its new missile forces at sea, aboard surface ships or submarines. Sea basing has some technical drawbacks (communications, for example), but (especially if submarine-based) would have been less vulnerable to pre-emptive attack than the approach NATO chose. But because U.S. willingness to place long-range missiles on European soil was seen by some in Europe as a token of continued American commitment to its security, allied willingness to accept the missiles became a similar token of resolve to face the common foe.

As a result, NATO plans to deploy long-range nuclear missiles that both threaten Soviet territory and are open to Soviet attack. The Pershings and GLCMs will be mobile and can be evacuated from their peacetime shelters in crisis. But both missiles travel with large convoys of support vehicles, which would make rather visible and very soft targets for Soviet weapons—conventional or nuclear. Thus the debate over the survivability of NATO nuclear forces is unlikely to be stilled if and when the new missiles are deployed.

The arms control negotiations mandated by the second track of the NATO decision opened in October 1980. Known as the Intermediate-range Nuclear Force (INF) talks, these bilateral U.S.-USSR negotiations face substantial obstacles. Three key questions must be addressed: What kinds of weapons should be counted? Whose weapons should count? And who should do the counting? First, are there to be constraints on missile launchers, missiles, warheads, aircraft-deliverable nuclear weapons, sea-based systems, or some combination of these? Which specific systems? Second, should the bilateral talks encompass only Soviet and American weapons, or include British and French nuclear forces in some way? And last, the two sides need to reach agreement on the current levels of deployments—a matter which is complicated by the difficulty of monitoring deployments of mobile systems.

Both parties have set forth proposals in the INF talks, ranging from a Soviet opening offer to freeze deployments of SS-20s in Europe in return for a NATO commitment not to deploy Pershing II and GLCMs, to the American opening position of a "zero option," under which NATO would forgo its planned missile deployments if the Soviet Union would dismantle all of its SS-4s, SS-5s, and SS-20s. Compromises also have been discussed. At the time of writing, it remains to be seen whether agreement can be reached and, if it cannot, whether NATO's nuclear modernization program can move forward on a single track.

We view the NATO modernization decision as an attempt to solve the credibility problem of the American nuclear guarantee by means of an American technical solution. This attempt has created many problems. Yet to disengage from the decision now would be to incur high political costs among and within the NATO nations. The purpose of the planned deployment is twofold: to respond to the SS-20s targeted on Western Europe, and to demonstrate America's political commitment to its European allies. If these objectives can be met without missile deployments, we would be satisfied. Our highest hope is for an INF agreement which would preclude the need for any new missiles, but that is unlikely. More realistically, we might hope for an agreement which permits some of the currently planned deployment in exchange for reductions on the Soviet side. Even if no INF agreement is reached, a deployment of far fewer than 572 missiles could conceivably serve the purpose: maintaining the cohesion of the alliance and deterring of Soviet aggression. The exact numbers would be decided among the NATO governments. Finally, we recognize that the political and military context on which we base these views can, and undoubtedly will, change; consequently, the need for modernization of NATO's nuclear forces must be reassessed continuously.

## NO FIRST USE

The extension of America's nuclear umbrella to the European members of NATO is not without complications. Some Europeans fear that the United States might not engage in nuclear war to defend European interests, but they also fear that, if the U.S. were willing to "go nuclear," the ensuing nuclear war might be confined geographically to Europe. What these Europeans want is a U.S. willing not only to engage in a nuclear war on their behalf, but a U.S. willing to initiate a global nuclear war to serve European interests. Allied security, in their eyes, is seen to rest upon the prospect of any European war escalating rapidly and more or less uncontrollably to a worldwide nuclear holocaust, a prospect which, presumably, would continue to deter Soviet aggression in Europe.

But what if this extended deterrence should fail? What if Soviet conventional forces do move into Western Europe? Should NATO initiate nuclear war if it is unable to repulse the Soviet attack by non-nuclear means? In other words, should NATO be prepared to use nuclear weapons first? NATO's answer has always been yes.

First use has its roots in NATO's traditional inferiority to the Warsaw Pact in conventional forces (and a concomitant allied reluctance to increase defense spending to rectify the imbalance). First-generation NATO nuclear weapons were for direct, battlefield use against invading Pact forces. However, in hypothetical situations desperate enough to call for the use of battlefield nuclear weapons, the would-be user's positions could well be overrun long before authority to retrieve, load, and fire those weapons would be granted and communicated by NATO's political leadership.

Advocates of a doctrine of "no first use" also consider it probable that NATO's first use of nuclear weapons would engender a Soviet response in kind, or worse. Opponents contend that adoption of a *declaratory policy* of no first use, if credible, would amount to an invitation to the Warsaw Pact to invade Western Europe with conventional forces, and that peacetime pledges of no first use could hardly be relied upon once a war began. Many Europeans would oppose no first use even if conventional forces were strengthened. After all, conventional deterrence in Europe has failed catastrophically twice in this century, with world wars as a result.

The issue of whether NATO could afford an *operational doctrine* based on no first use, declaratory policy notwithstanding, hinges on assessments of the two sides' conventional force capabilities. Some defense analysts conclude that NATO could repulse a "bolt from the blue" conventional attack without recourse to nuclear weapons. Others, apparently examining the same data, argue that NATO could hardly resort too quickly to nuclear use.

Most analysts agree that, if the Warsaw Pact is to win a war in Europe, it would have to win it quickly. The Pact's political control structure is thought to be too brittle to withstand an inconclusive (or unsuccessful) conflict; supply lines to West Germany would be long; and the Pact's weapon systems have limited field endurance. The prospect of a stalemate in a conventional war, in this view, should be enough to deter such a Soviet assault.

If NATO capabilities are up to the task of conventional defense, then the requirement for nuclear first use options is much diminished, and nuclear weapons committed to Europe's defense can assume a role more like the one currently played by central strategic systems—deterrence of nuclear war alone. If, on the other hand, NATO's capabilities are inadequate for conventional defense, adoption of no first use could be dangerous. Major improvements in NATO conventional forces could reduce its reliance on nuclear weapons and thereby enhance conventional deterrence. Yet, because relative conventional capabilities cannot be fully tested short of actual war, a no first use policy would be the result more of political considerations than of military ones. The burden of persuasion rightly falls on the proponents of this fundamental change in NATO's doctrine. We are not yet persuaded.

## OFFENSIVE STRATEGIC FORCE ISSUES

American (and, to some extent, Soviet) strategic forces of the 1990s and beyond will be shaped by decisions made in the next few years. Particularly important issues arise in connection with ICBM vulnerability, ICBM and bomber modernization, and cruise missiles.

### ICBM VULNERABILITY

In the late 1950s, in anticipation of Soviet deployment of intercontinental missiles, strategic analysts became concerned with the susceptibility of U.S. strategic forces to sudden missile attack. This concern led, in the early 1960s, to a policy of keeping some of the intercontinental bombers armed and in the air at all times. (This practice was discontinued in 1969 after several serious accidents, and to cut costs.) The vulnerability concern also led to basing ICBMs in concrete silos able to withstand a nearby nuclear blast. Soviet ICBMs of the 1960s had accuracies of not better than a mile at maximum range, so the chance of destroying a U.S. silo of that period, even with a 5-megaton warhead, was only about 1 in 4. As Soviet missile accuracies improved, silos were further hardened. Vulnerability to attack began to grow in the 1970s, however, as the Soviets deployed much more accurate multiple-warhead missiles. Numbers and accuracies of Soviet ICBM warheads are sufficient to allow the USSR, in theory (though, many believe, not in practice), to destroy 85%–90% of the U.S. land-based missile force.

That is not the same as a "disarming first strike." The U.S. would retain thousands of nuclear warheads on bombers and submarines capable of retaliating against Soviet targets. Some believe, however, that the mere existence of such "silo-busting" capability, even if theoretical, could give the USSR additional political leverage against the U.S., or against its allies.

Hedging against the risk, U.S. leaders for the better part of a decade have been searching for ways to improve the survivability of land-based missiles. Among the approaches explored have been arms control, launch-on-warning, new basing modes, and active defense. (Active defense—that is, the destruction of attacking missile warheads in flight—receives expanded treatment as a separate issue later in this chapter.)

Attempts to solve the ICBM vulnerability problem by means of negotiated arms control agreements have been notably unsuccessful. (It is worth noting, however, that the ABM Treaty essentially guarantees that surviving retaliatory missiles will be able to reach their targets.) To reduce substantially the threat to U.S. ICBMs posed by Soviet forces, especially by their MIRVed ICBMs, would require very deep cuts in the numbers of Soviet missiles and severe limits on the numbers of warheads per missile, and possibly also constraints on missile accuracy. Agreement on such drastic measures is not likely to be reached in the foreseeable future.

The Soviets would hardly be tempted to attack U.S. ICBMs if they knew that the American missiles would be launched before the Soviet warheads arrived at their targets. Such a launch-on-warning strategy is technically feasible, but risky, because missiles, once launched, cannot be recalled. The obvious danger lies in the possibility that a false alarm, due perhaps to a faulty radar signal or a garbled electronic communication, could result in the unintended initiation of a nuclear war. But, of course, the Soviets could never be sure that the U.S. would not launch on warning.

Dozens of new basing schemes designed to improve ICBM survivability have been considered and rejected. Concrete and steel silos could be "super-hardened" and made more resistant to the effects of nuclear explosions, but they would remain vulnerable to attack by highly accurate missiles. ICBMs could be deployed on mobile launchers on the ground or in the air, and moved continuously over a large geographical area; however, it is unlikely that such systems would be politically acceptable in the United States in peacetime. Concealment and deception could contribute to the survivability of ICBMs, for if the Soviets didn't know where the U.S. ICBM launchers were, they couldn't target them. (Of course, under such conditions they would also have difficulty verifying compliance with any arms control agreement which limited the numbers of ICBM launchers.)

The Multiple Protective Shelter (MPS) system proposed by President Carter made use of both mobility and deception. Some 200 ICBMs on ground-mobile launchers would have been shuttled at random among 4,600 concrete shelters. To attack all of the missiles, the USSR would have to attack all of the shelters; that would use a number of Soviet missile warheads far greater than the number of American warheads destroyed. The number of shelter systems was chosen with the expectation that SALT II would be ratified. Without such an arms control agreement limiting the number of Soviet missile warheads, MPS would be far less attractive, for the United States would be forced to proliferate expensive shelters and missiles to match new warheads added to the Soviet arsenal. The Reagan administration canceled the MPS program soon after it came into office, and proposed to place some new missiles in modified and super-hardened Minuteman silos while the search for a better basing mode continued. Congress rejected the notion of deploying new ICBMs in fixed silos, maintaining that the system would be defeated by improvements in Soviet missile accuracy.

Late in 1982 the administration came up with still another basing concept known as "closely spaced basing" or "dense pack." In this scheme, 100 missiles would be placed in super-hardened silos less than half a mile apart. In theory, any full-scale Soviet attack on the base would do more damage to itself than it would to the sheltered missiles; early-arriving warheads would create a maelstrom of heat, dust, and debris that would at least deflect, and possibly destroy, following warheads. Critics argued that a relatively small number of high-yield weapons (5 megatons or more) might put the field out of operation either by digging up the silos or by burying them under tens of feet of rubble. Proponents acknowledged that the initial 100-missile, 100-silo array might need augmentation as Soviet capabilities evolve, with additional silos or perhaps active defenses. Congressional reaction to President Reagan's initial dense-pack proposal was no more favorable than it was to his modified Minuteman silos. The search for a satisfactory basing mode continues.

The search may be fruitless; it may be that no politically acceptable land-based force can remain invulnerable to attack by a large number of accurate nuclear warheads. Some, who consider this outcome likely, argue that the United States should do away with its increasingly vulnerable ICBMs because they invite pre-emptive attack in time of crisis, and that America should rely for deterrence on SLBMs, bombers, and cruise missiles. Others argue that, even if the ICBMs are vulnerable in theory, they should be retained because they complicate a Soviet first strike, increase the uncertainty of the outcome, and serve as important symbols of military power. The ICBM proponents emphasize in particular the unique ability of ICBMs to perform reliable, prompt attacks in a controlled manner against a variety of targets, including hardened ones. Bombers and cruise missiles, because of their long flight times to their targets, cannot attack as promptly as can ballistic missiles; and the SLBM force has neither the accuracy of ICBMs nor the reliable communications links. (The SLBM accuracy deficiency is scheduled to be remedied by the end of the decade, but the communications disadvantage would be difficult to overcome.)

We conclude that a high priority should be assigned to establishing a reliable and secure system for communicating with the submarine missile force. So long as that capability remains in question, we judge the arguments favoring retention of land-based ICBMs—even a theoretically vulnerable force of ICBMs—to outweigh the arguments against it.

## ICBM AND SLBM MODERNIZATION

In principle, the ICBM basing question does not need to be coupled with any particular missile. If a satisfactory basing scheme is found, current ICBMs can be redeployed or a new missile can be deployed or there can be some combination of the two. In fact, however, all the basing modes seriously considered have been designed for one particular missile: the MX. It is three times as heavy as the current Minuteman III, would deliver ten warheads rather than three, and would do so with greater accuracy.

Addition of the MX to the U.S. strategic arsenal would

increase America's ability to launch prompt attacks (and, if based survivably, prompt counter-attacks) against hardened targets, including Soviet missile silos. Some argue that this characteristic would enhance deterrence and, therefore, that the MX should be deployed. Others believe that deployment of the MX would undermine crisis stability, for it both threatens Soviet ICBMs and is itself an attractive target for them. Many in the latter group would prefer to see ICBM modernization take the form of small single-warhead missiles, in numbers perhaps even larger than the number of ICBMs currently deployed.

Yet another factor to be considered in judging whether to proceed with the MX is its potential as a "bargaining chip" in arms control negotiations. If, indeed, this missile would pose a significant threat to Soviet forces, then the Soviets should be prepared to pay an arms control price to prevent its deployment. If, on the other hand, MX deployment would be unattractive economically and/or contrary to the American interest in crisis stability, then its value as a bargaining chip would be questionable or even negative.

There is merit in the arguments on both sides of the MX debate. Some of us would terminate the MX program; some would also begin development of a small single-warhead missile. Others favor the development of the small missile and, at the same time, would deploy the MX in modified Minuteman silos unless or until either a much more survivable basing mode appears or the MX is "bargained away" in reaching an arms control agreement. In the final analysis, constraining the counter-silo threat through arms control may be an essential component of (though not by itself sufficient for) any satisfactory resolution of the ICBM vulnerability and ICBM modernization issues.

Many of the arguments for and against the MX ICBM apply also to the next generation of SLBMs. America's D-5 missile, now in development and scheduled for deployment on Trident submarines in the late 1980s, would carry 8–10 warheads capable of destroying hardened targets, including ICBM silos. Unlike the MX, however, the Trident submarine is not vulnerable to a Soviet first strike and there is no significant dispute over the survivability of missiles on Trident submarines at sea. A disadvantage of SLBMs compared to ICBMs lies in the relative difficulty of communicating promptly with submarines.

Our views on the D-5 program parallel our views on the MX. A case can be made that, because the D-5 would undermine crisis stability by threatening Soviet ICBM missile silos, the program should be terminated. Most of us, however, support deployment of D-5 on Trident submarines.

## BOMBER MODERNIZATION

Even before the first B-52s rolled off the assembly line in the mid-1950s, the U.S. Air Force was planning its next generation of manned bombers. The first successor, the B-70, was canceled by the Kennedy administration. Though capable of flying at 2,000 miles per hour, the high-altitude B-70 would have been an easy target for Soviet air defenses.

Its successor was the Advanced Manned Strategic Aircraft, a design that evolved in the early 1970s into the B-1. The first B-1 flew in 1974. Three years later it was canceled by the Carter administration in favor of accelerated development of cruise missiles and (secret) development of the "Stealth" bomber—a plane that was to be largely invisible to radar and infrared detection. Still later, the B-1, modified to make it harder to detect on radar, and about five times as expensive, was revived by the Reagan administration. One hundred are scheduled to be built, with the first one operational in mid-decade.

There are strong arguments for retaining a modern fleet of long-range penetrating bombers. Manned aircraft have some unique attributes. They are the only strategic delivery systems with which we have had actual combat experience; they have been, and could again be, used in non-nuclear roles; they have human minds aboard, and therefore are well equipped to assess damage and to select targets of opportunity; and, perhaps most important, even if "launched on warning" of a Soviet attack, manned bombers can be recalled. Special encoded messages must be sent by the National Command Authority and received by the flight crew before the aircraft can deliver armed nuclear weapons. The system is designed to "fail safe";

i.e., failure to send or receive the message results in abortion of the mission. This is unlike the case of ballistic missiles which, once launched, travel inexorably toward their targets, and cannot be recalled.

The B-1 is intended as a penetrating bomber, but it may not be able to evade Soviet air defenses past the end of the decade. After that, it would be assigned the role of cruise missile carrier and the penetrating role would go to the Stealth aircraft. The combined cost of these systems has caused critics of the manned bomber to question the need for any modernization at all once the B-52 finally reaches the end of its useful life. (Later models will finally be retired in the 1990s, after 30 years of service.)

In light of these considerations, augmented by a strong preference for robust and redundant deterrent forces, we conclude that the United States should retain a fleet of nuclear-capable long-range manned bombers; however, we view procurement of the B-1 as an unnecessary expenditure. We believe that B-52s, augmented by air-launched cruise missiles, could fulfill the needs for manned bombers until the generation of aircraft beyond the B-1 (probably the Stealth aircraft) becomes available.

## CRUISE MISSILES

Cruise missiles are essentially unmanned aircraft with self-contained guidance systems. They can be launched from the ground, from ships at or under the sea, and from manned aircraft. The earliest cruise missile was the German V-1 "buzz bomb" used against Great Britain in the final years of the Second World War. It was slow and inaccurate, and served primarily as a terror weapon.

By the mid-1950s both the United States and the Soviet Union had deployed somewhat more capable cruise missiles, some armed with nuclear weapons. The U.S. even had an intercontinental cruise missile, the Snark, a subsonic, high-altitude vehicle whose accuracy was measured in miles. It was made obsolete soon after it was deployed by the advent of the faster, equally accurate, and harder-to-counter ICBMs. In fact, ballistic missiles generally replaced cruise missiles in all U.S. forces—tactical and strategic—by the late 1960s.

Soon after the signature of SALT I, however, the cruise missile staged a comeback. Miniature electronics and advanced engine technology made it possible to build a small, accurate, hard-to-detect missile that could carry a nuclear warhead 1,500 miles or more—far enough to hit most targets inside the USSR if launched from near its borders. Some analysts argue that its rebirth was due largely to SALT; that the cruise was seen as a bargaining chip that traded on the U.S. advantage in military technology. The Soviets were (and are) thought to be five to ten years behind the U.S. in advanced cruise technology. Others, however, saw the cruise as a realistic answer to the nagging question of bomber modernization. One of those was President Jimmy Carter. When he canceled the B-1 bomber in 1977, he accelerated the development of air-launched cruise missiles.

The Reagan administration restored the B-1, and kept the cruise missile as well, planning for the deployment of several thousand air-launched missiles (most of which are to employ the Stealth technologies) in addition to the 464 ground-launched versions slated for deployment in Europe, and several thousand more to be deployed with the U.S. Navy. Some of these naval missiles would be nuclear-armed and some conventionally armed. The two types of missiles look the same to an outside observer.

This is one of the problems with cruise missiles: their potential impact on arms control. To date, strategic arms control agreements have relied heavily on quantitative limits: counting launch vehicles (bombers and ballistic missile submarines) and missile launchers (for ICBMs and SLBMs). The ability of each party to verify independently that the other party is keeping to the limits has been a key ingredient in SALT/START. Modern cruise missiles are small enough (about 18 feet long and 2 feet wide with wings folded) to be hidden and launched from almost anywhere. That is one reason why the Soviet Union insisted on some limits on ground- and sea-launched cruise missiles in Salt II—even though the protocol covering them was of more limited duration than the main treaty—and why they continue to seek such limits. If and when the USSR develops the technology for comparably sophisticated missiles—and they are seeking it—this will become a problem for the

U.S. (The U.S. discovered Soviet missiles in Cuba in 1962, for example, because their deployment areas were large and well defined; systems the size of cruise missiles might not be as readily detectable.)

Air- and sea-launched versions can be controlled indirectly via control of their launch vehicles (bombers and ships). The cruise missile has some clear advantages from the standpoint of crisis stability. The relatively slow speed of a cruise missile makes it more useful as a retaliatory device than as a first-strike weapon.

We conclude that the contributions of air-launched cruise missiles (ALCMs) to deterrence and crisis stability outweigh the potential costs to negotiated arms control. However, on the question of whether to deploy sea-launched cruise missiles (SLCMs) on submarines and surface ships, we believe that the arms control costs are likely to outweigh the strategic benefits. Thus we believe that ALCMs should be deployed on some U.S. long-range bombers and that, unless an arms control agreement imposing verifiable constraints on SLCMs and their modes of deployment are achieved. The U.S. should not take the lead in deploying modern SLCMs.

## COMMAND AND CONTROL ISSUES

The most secure deterrent forces in the world would be of no use to a country whose leadership could not control them or receive timely intelligence of an enemy's actions. Today the command and control systems of both the United States and the Soviet Union are much more vulnerable to attack than are the respective strategic forces (despite continuing efforts by the Soviets to improve the survivability of their command and control systems).[1] For the United States, two specific issues related to command and control are the vulnerability of the U.S. command and control network, and the development of anti-satellite capabilities.

### MODERNIZATION

The minimum requirements for a command and control system are for it to provide receipt of sufficient warning to permit evacuation of the president to a secure command post; communication and execution of war orders during and immediately after the initial attack; and maintenance of command and control weeks and months after an attack ("endurance").

The president must be informed of a nuclear attack within two or three minutes of first detection of incoming missiles. Submarine-launched missiles may take as little as ten minutes from first warning to impact, depending on how far offshore the submarine is and how far inland its target is. If the president is in Washington, only 50 miles from the Atlantic coast, he may have only ten minutes in which to call and board a helicopter, fly to Andrews Air Force Base, board a specially equipped airplane which can serve as a command post, take off, and fly beyond lethal radius of the warheads targeted on Washington. Exercises indicate that, even under the best of circumstances, the president may not be able to escape.

If the Soviets attack the command and control network, most ground-based installations would cease operations no later than the 30-minute mark (the approximate flight time of an ICBM). The endurance of bombers and airborne command posts, less vulnerable to attack than their ground-based counterparts, is also limited. They can be refueled (if tanker aircraft and their bases are still operational), but mechanical considerations require them to land after about three days.

The missile submarines at sea could remain there until they ran out of food for the crew. At that point their commanders would face some uncomfortable choices. They could approach the surface (risking detection) and listen for orders in the U.S. fleet broadcasts, or listen for other high-frequency (shortwave) broadcasts to determine whether the war was continuing. They could put a supply party ashore at night in some southern hemisphere port to restock. Or they could carry out pre-planned attacks on the assumption that the U.S. had been destroyed, and that any extra damage they might do to the USSR would be well deserved.

On land, the batteries in current ICBM silos would provide only a few days of power for launching the missiles. Batteries can be modernized, but without communications with the outside world, launch control commanders would be in much the same predicament as their sea-based colleagues, with the added worry of being a visible target for renewed attacks.

The vulnerability of command and control systems casts doubt upon the ability of either superpower to conduct a measured nuclear exchange and, in time of crisis, may encourage early and massive use of nuclear forces in the expectation that later use may be impossible. Accurate intercontinental missiles mean that every fixed command post and jet-capable airfield could (and probably would) be attacked sooner or later in a war. The surest backup system would appear to be high-altitude satellites in conjunction with ground-based transmitters and receivers small enough to mount on trucks (or perhaps seaplanes) for mobility and thus better prospects for long-term survival. The designs of U.S. military satellites are evolving to meet these demands, but anti-satellite (ASAT) weaponry is evolving too.

We share the view held almost unanimously by students and practitioners of defense policy that modernization of the U.S. strategic command and control network should be among this nation's top defense priorities. The system must be robust enough to assure that no Soviet leader can have confidence in his ability to deliver a "knockout blow." Even with a modernized network, however, one cannot be confident that nuclear war, once begun, will be "limited" in any meaningful way. But nuclear war might begin and, if it does, we will want to have the communications means available to bring it to a halt as rapidly as possible. Despite such efforts, it would remain overwhelmingly likely that not fighting a nuclear war would be an outcome far preferable to fighting one.

## ANTI-SATELLITE (ASAT) WARFARE

In September 1982, 25 years after the launch of Sputnik I, the U.S. Air Force established a Space Command, the first organizational unit at that level devoted exclusively to the operational use of space. The Soviet Union has had a counterpart organization, a branch of national air defense, since the mid-1960s. Both countries have active programs to develop ASAT. The Soviets have been testing a low-altitude ASAT system since 1967 and is now credited with an operational capability to damage satellites as much as 1,500 miles up. The Soviet interceptor typically orbits the earth once or twice after launch before it is in position to attack its target.

The United States is developing an ASAT system which employs a rocket fired from a high-flying aircraft. The rocket does not enter orbit, but flies directly to its target. The American system is slated to be operational about 1986.

A good deal of effort is being devoted by the U.S. to devising military satellites that are resistant to attack by nuclear or conventional means. Unfortunately, such features add significantly to the complexity, cost, and weight of a satellite.

Two principal arguments are offered in support of a vigorous American ASAT program. The air force maintains that to forgo development and deployment of offensive and defensive capabilities in space would be to cede the "high ground" to the Soviets, along with all of the advantages accruing from such a position. The navy argues that Soviet ocean surveillance satellites would pose a direct wartime danger to aircraft carrier battle groups. Carriers' positions could be noted by satellite and the information passed on to Soviet aircraft and submarines beyond visual range of the carriers and their defensive screens. Cruise missile attacks could follow.

The Soviets, no doubt, have similar rationales for similar capabilities. An additional incentive may be found in the nascent Chinese military space program. China is not a party to many arms control agreements; it does not belong, for example, to the 1967 Outer Space Treaty that bans nuclear weapons in orbit. So long as the Chinese do not forswear such weapons, the USSR may be reluctant to forswear capabilities to shoot them down.

Thus far, negotiations to limit the development or testing of ASAT systems have not produced tangible results. Without an ASAT agreement, threats to valuable military space satellites providing reconnaissance, communications, and other vital services will increase, and the cost of protecting satellites against those threats will increase proportionally. Military reliance on and interest in the use of space is unlikely to diminish during this decade.

We conclude that the security of the United States would be enhanced far more by the ensured survival of its space systems than by its ability to destroy Soviet satellites. Accordingly, while we support the U.S. ASAT program, we assign high priority to negotiations aimed at inhibiting ASAT capability and we will view the U.S. program as having been most effective if negotiations lead to its, and the Soviet ASAT program's, termination.

## DEFENSE AGAINST NUCLEAR ATTACK

Discussions of the prospects for meaningful defense against nuclear attack usually focus on ballistic missile defense and civil defense.

### BALLISTIC MISSILE DEFENSE

The Anti-Ballistic Missile (ABM) Treaty of 1972 imposes severe constraints on Soviet and American development, testing, and deployment of ABM systems. (The terms "anti-ballistic missile" (ABM) and "ballistic missile defense" (BMD) are used interchangeably to describe systems for defense against ballistic missiles.) As the ICBM vulnerability issue has grown in prominence, so has interest in ABM as one way to reduce that vulnerability. In October 1981 President Reagan specified ABM as one MX basing option to be studied, and in mid-1982 the Department of Defense inaugurated a comprehensive study of missile defense. The ABM Treaty (as modified by a subsequent protocol) confines deployments of ABM systems by each side to a single site. The Soviet Union has its site at Moscow and is modernizing the system components in a manner consistent with the treaty. The United States had an ABM system deployed at its Grand Forks, North Dakota, ICBM base, but it was shut down in 1976 by order of Congress. The demise of the Grand Forks ABM installation was justified primarily on economic grounds; it was claimed that continued operation of the system was not worth the cost.

Following ratification of the ABM Treaty, America's ABM research and development program declined sharply, both absolutely and relative to the essentially constant Soviet effort. In recent years the U.S. program has been directed toward development of less vulnerable and more effective systems. ABM technology has advanced over the past decade, but so has the offensive missile technology it is intended to counter, and the advantage remains with the offense. ABM alone cannot yet solve the ICBM vulnerability problem, nor can it provide meaningful protection of other targets against determined Soviet attack.

Even if an effective ABM technology were available, the question remains whether it would be in the United States' interest to withdraw from the ABM Treaty or to seek to modify it to permit more extensive deployments. First among the relevant considerations is that whatever termination or modification of the treaty would allow the U.S. to do, it would allow the Soviets to do. While the survivability of American ICBMs would be enhanced, the ability of those ICBMs (and of the SLBMs) to penetrate to their targets would be degraded by the expanded Soviet ABM network. And an ABM system would be more effective against a retaliatory attack than against a larger and better-coordinated first strike. Second, seeking a revised agreement would entail some risk of emerging from the negotiations with something very different from our preferred outcome. Third, any change which would permit the Soviets to deploy an expanded ABM system could threaten the utility of the independent deterrent forces of our British and French allies. Finally, opening the door to competition in ABM could lead to an all-out strategic arms race, including both defensive systems and the offensive weapons needed to overwhelm them.

We believe that the ABM Treaty remains very much in the interest of the United States (and of the Soviet Union as well), and that no action should be taken to modify or withdraw from it. At the same time, the U.S. should maintain a vigorous ABM research and development program (consistent with the treaty) to keep pace with Soviet progress in this field. Maintaining a balance of potential ABM capabilities is, ironically, the surest way of keeping the treaty in force, for then neither side can find advantage in terminating the agreement.

## CIVIL DEFENSE

Passive measures to protect the population against nuclear attack—civil defense—have never had strong support from the American people and rarely from their government. Early civil defense programs concentrated on providing urban populations with shelters for protection against radioactive fallout, but they could not (and still cannot) offer protection against direct nuclear attack. Recent proposals focus on urban evacuation and population dispersal.

The Soviet Union has for decades maintained a substantial civil defense effort. This program now provides blast-resistant shelters for over 100,000 leaders and plans by 1985 to provide shelters for up to one-fourth of the urban population. Given warning time of three to seven days, the remaining urban population could be evacuated to rural areas.

Proponents of civil defense maintain that it can contribute in important ways to deterrence, to crisis management, and to survival. First, it would strengthen basic and extended deterrence by enhancing the credibility of America's threats of nuclear retaliation, and by conveying to the Soviets and the NATO allies the seriousness of America's commitment. Second, the proponents argue, civil defense would contribute to crisis management by reducing the possibility that the Soviets could in effect blackmail the United States. What would happen if the Soviets began to evacuate their cities in a time of crisis and the United States did not have a comparable capability? U.S. leaders could be faced with a choice of either starting a nuclear war or bargaining from a weak position where most of the U.S. population, but a smaller proportion of the Soviet population, could be held hostage to nuclear annihilation. Third, a civil defense program can contribute to the survival of Americans if, despite all efforts, nuclear war should come. It is not possible to predict just how many lives would be saved, but it could be tens of millions.

Critics of civil defense argue that it would be ineffective and would increase the risk of nuclear war. They maintain that it would be ineffective because the American people dislike the idea and would resist its implementation; because even if the public cooperated, it would take days or weeks to evacuate the cities, and the Soviet Union would not have to wait the requisite period before launching a nuclear attack; and because the Soviets could choose to destroy facilities essential to the recovery of the society, such as ports, railroads, dams, oil refineries, power plants, and hospitals. Civil defense, the critics claim, would increase the likelihood of nuclear war in two ways: first, because any initiation of the evacuation of cities would be seen by the adversary as a clear sign of preparation for nuclear war and could provoke a pre-emptive attack; and second, because leaders who might come to believe (rightly or wrongly) that their populations no longer were hostage to attack by the other side would be more willing to take risks, including the risk of engaging in nuclear war.

All in all, the existence of a civil defense capability on one or both sides is unlikely to have a significant effect on the probability of nuclear war. Civil defense can only mitigate the terrible consequences if deterrence fails. No one can conclusively demonstrate that a particular civil defense program will or will not save lives. Obviously that depends on not only the nature of the program but also the scope and nature of the nuclear attack. In some circumstances civil defense might save lives; in others it would not. Civil defense is, in this sense, like seat belts on an airplane. In some crashes they save lives; in other accidents everyone on board is killed despite the seat belts.

The key issue is the economic and social costs involved, not the likelihood of war itself. The range of our views reflects sharply contrasting assessments of the contribution which civil defense might make to saving lives in a nuclear war. Some of us believe that the potential contribution to human survival justifies expenditure of modest sums—about 0.1% of what the U.S. spends on military defense—to provide some capability to evacuate urban areas. Others believe even this relatively small sum would be a waste of resources.

## THE RIGHT ANSWERS

At least one lesson can be derived from this brief examination of some contemporary nuclear issues: informed individuals can and often do disagree on what course of action to pursue. Occasionally their differences can be attributed to asymmetries in knowledge, but far more often they stem from differences in assumptions, perspectives, or values. Understanding and appreciating these differences may not always lead individuals to choose the same "right" answer, but it can help everyone to avoid choosing some of the "wrong" ones.

### Note

1. The command and control system is the means by which the president (or his Soviet counterpart) can use strategic nuclear forces. This system, which often is referred to as the strategic $C^3I$ system (where $C^3I$ stands for command, control, communications, and intelligence), includes sensors (such as ground-based radars and space-based telescopes) to detect an attack; command centers to evaluate the information; decision makers authorized to order the use of nuclear weapons; a communications network connecting these elements and the strategic nuclear forces; and intelligence resources to gather, analyze, and communicate information on the status of the adversary's war-making capabilities.

# 9

# Arms Control and Disarmament: What Can and Can't Be Done?

In a drama about the Trojan wars an ancient Greek hero returns from the horror of battle vowing never to fight again. But after his eloquent praise of pacifism, a drunken soldier stumbles on stage and begins to molest the hero's wife. Almost involuntarily, the hero's hand reaches for his sword. The scene is moving because it captures a basic dilemma: most people believe killing is horrible, but most people also believe there are some values worth fighting to defend. In an imperfect world, few people have been willing to adopt pure pacifism, which means the refusal to defend one's self, family, country, or allies from any kind of attack.

Those who are not pacifists must wrestle with many difficult choices about weapons, their existence, and their potential use. This has always been true. Warfare is as old as human history, and disarmament as a prescription for avoiding it dates back at least to biblical times. Though the implementation of disarmament has been rare, its basic premise—that war is not possible without weapons—is both simple and appealing. Once plowshares replace swords, war will end.

Regrettably, the premise is flawed. The supply of

188

weapons is not the sole or even the prime cause of war. Disarmament may remove the most destructive weapons, but others will be found. If firearms are denied, wars can be fought with knives and clubs. Nonetheless, knives and clubs do less damage than firearms and other modern weapons. This qualitative difference has led to many quests for disarmament, especially during the last hundred years.

## DISARMAMENT AND DISTRUST

Successful efforts at disarmament are extremely rare, but there have been some. An outstanding example was the reduction of naval forces on the Great Lakes during the 19th century. Naval battles in the War of 1812 against Great Britain proved the importance of naval control of the Lakes. Both sides threatened to build more ships in the period following the war. A treaty concluded in 1817, still in force today, limits navy ships to sizes smaller than the existing fleets. As a result the U.S. and British fleets were dismantled, the threat of a future war was removed, and a major step was taken on the road that has produced the longest, enduring demilitarized border in modern history.

One reason that successful disarmament efforts are rare is that they require a degree of political accommodation that is difficult to achieve. Unless some political trust exists, efforts to disarm prove fruitless. Such trust is difficult to build, but not impossible—witness the peaceful relations between France and Germany today in contrast with the past. But political accommodation and trust are built slowly and this makes complete disarmament—as contrasted with more limited arms control—a long-term rather than an immediate prospect.

Complete disarmament would require some form of world government to deter actions of one nation against another. In a disarmed world, without such a government armed with sufficient force to prevent conflict between or among nations, differences in beliefs and interests might easily lead to a renewal of war. But any world government capable of preventing world conflict could also become a world dictatorship. And given the differences in ideology, wealth, and nationalism that now exist in the world, most states are not likely to accept a centralized government unless they feel sure of controlling it or minimizing its intrusiveness. A weak central machinery would be ineffective. And even a strong one—assuming governments would agree to set it up—could still be faced with breakdown. It is worth remembering that the central government of the United States fell apart in the mid-19th century, leading to a horrible civil war. Such a breakdown of authority in a world government would not only lead to bitter power struggles for domination of the world government in order to advance one or another national group, but could also lead to massive warfare. Individual nations would rearm. And those who could, would race to make nuclear weapons.

Disarmament would leap into the unknown; each state would accept it only if the dangers it feared could be ended or if it thought that the danger of nuclear holocaust outweighed the risks involved in nuclear disarmament. Despite the present costs of national military forces and arms competition, despite the limited gains which the threat to use force now brings, and despite the enormous risks such uses may entail, most nations still see a clear national advantage in having such forces. They provide the possibilities of deterring aggression and of projecting political influence. Disarmament would not necessarily ensure a state's position in the international contest between states. It would not necessarily ensure a state's security. Nor would disarmament guarantee that the funds saved from weapons would necessarily be devoted to raising the living standards of poor peoples. As a result, governments, even in this dangerous nuclear world, have preferred a combination of arms, self-restraint, and arms control to complete disarmament.

Ironically, while complete disarmament may be a worthy long-term goal, trying to achieve it before the requisite political conditions exist could actually increase the prospects of war. If the political pre-conditions of trust and consensus are missing, complete disarmament is inherently unstable. In a disarmed world, the first nation to acquire a few arms would be able to influence events to a much greater extent than it could in a heavily armed world. Nuclear weapons greatly magnify this effect.

On a cold January day in 1977, a little boy listened to President Carter aspire in his inaugural speech to remove nuclear weapons from the face of the earth. "Daddy, do you think he really means it?" the boy asked. "Yes," his father replied. After a moment's thought the boy responded. "Daddy, don't you think we should hide at least one?" The boy had a point. While mistrust exists, there will be strong temptation to hedge one's bets. Moreover, nuclear weapons can be easily hidden or quickly reinvented. At high numbers, even hidden bombs do not matter. But if the numbers are few and political mistrust persists, rumors of hidden bombs or fears of their reinvention by any number of nations could lead to the worst kind of nuclear arms race—a crash program of rearmament with few of the safety features that are built into existing weapons.

## ARMS CONTROL

Therefore, when the consequences and risks of complete world disarmament are examined it appears that it does not guarantee peace and security if attempted before the political conditions are right. But nuclear arms races do not guarantee peace and security either. Instead they can guarantee enormous destruction if war occurs either by design, or more likely through accident, miscalculation, or misunderstanding. With no safe port in complete nuclear disarmament or in unrestricted competition, mankind has been compelled to seek safety by using arms control to lower the risks that nuclear weapons impose on peace and security.

"Arms control" has to a large extent replaced "disarmament" in the specialist's vocabulary since about 1960, but as long as disarmament is not taken to mean complete disarmament, the terms overlap. Arms control includes a wider range of actions than the removal of arms. For example, it includes steps that improve stability and help avoid accidents. Some "arms control" agreements reduce armaments; but not all do.

A common criticism of arms control and disarmament is that they mistake the symptoms for the disease. Since the origins of conflict do not reside in the weapons, its cure should not be sought in their restraint. But this is

## Existing Arms Control Agreements

|  |  | Signed | Parties |
|---|---|---|---|
| *Mass destruction weapons:* | | | |
| Geneva Protocol | Chemical weapons | 1925 | 115 |
| Biological Weapons Convention | Bans production/use | 1972 | 84 |
| SALT I ABM Treaty | [See p. 94] | 1972 | U.S./USSR |
| SALT I Interim Agreement | Observed though lapsed [see p. 94] | 1972 | U.S./USSR |
| SALT II Agreement | Tacitly observed but unratified [see p. 94] | 1979 | U.S./USSR |
| *Nuclear weapons testing:* | | | |
| Limited Test-Ban Treaty | Bans atmospheric, underwater, outer-space nuclear tests | 1963 | 108 |
| Threshold Test-Ban Treaty | Bans underground nuclear U.S./USSR tests over 150 kilotons. Tacitly observed but unratified | 1974 | U.S./USSR |
| Peaceful Nuclear Explosions Treaty | Bans. Tacitly observed but unratified | 1976 | U.S./USSR |
| *Weapons proliferation:* | | | |
| Antarctic Treaty | Demilitarization | 1959 | 22 |
| Outer-Space Treaty | Bans placing of mass destruction weapons in orbit | 1967 | 76 |
| Treaty of Tlatelolco | Bans nuclear weapons in Latin America/Caribbean | 1967 | 23 |
| Nuclear Non-Proliferation Treaty | Limits spread of nuclear weapons | 1968 | 115 |
| Seabed Arms Control Treaty | Bans placing of weapons of mass destruction on the ocean floor | 1971 | 66 |
| *Other:* | | | |
| Hot-Line Agreement/ Modernization | Crisis communications | 1963/71 | U.S./USSR |
| Accidents Measures Agreement; Prevention of Nuclear War Agreement | Reduction of probability of accidental nuclear war | 1971; 1973 | U.S./USSR |
| Environmental Modification Agreement | Bans use of some environmental warfare techniques | 1977 | 27 |

SOURCE: *Strategic Survey, 1981–82* (London: IISS, 1982), p. 123.

only a partial truth. The easy recourse to weapons in times of stress or panic does increase the likelihood of their use. This problem is ever so much larger in the Nuclear Age.

The parallel can be seen with handguns. Clearly they are not the sole or even the primary cause of murders, but where they are not generally available to the adult population, there are fewer murders, as in Britain, Japan, and the Soviet Union. Where guns are widely available, as in the United States, and much more so in Lebanon, murder is considerably more common. In daily life or international politics the proper control of arms, whether they are symptoms or not, can lower the risk of their being used.

Arms control alone is not enough. It is also important to attack the sources of conflicts. The ultimate hope for peace clearly lies with improving international relations to the point where conflict does not threaten to erupt into war and reconciliation replaces aggression. Whether the world eventually reaches this goal or not may depend on the combination of arms control with effective deterrence over the next decades.

## DIFFICULTIES CONFRONTING ARMS CONTROL

During the past three decades the military establishments of the United States and the Soviet Union have become, by most counts, the most powerful and most expensive institutions ever created. It is no wonder that they are difficult to change. Such enormous bureaucracies often resist the changes that arms control initiatives attempt to introduce. The Arms Control and Disarmament Agency of the U.S. government is funded at an annual cost of less than the cost of the least expensive fighter aircraft! Ideally, arms control and security policy should go hand in hand. But in reality many arms control initiatives do not survive the raised eyebrows of the defense community and defense decisions may therefore ignore their arms control implications.

This uneven situation would ordinarily suppress most arms control initiatives were it not for heads of governments. It is chiefly by this route that arms control has had a role.

Even so, its role is precarious and vulnerable to the changing views of successive administrations. Nevertheless, at least in democracies, polls show recurrent public support for efforts at arms control. When presidents ignore these opinions, they do so to their own political peril.

Another difficulty encountered by arms control is the unusual U.S. constitutional clause on the ratification of treaties. The United States alone among industrialized Western countries requires a two-thirds majority in the Senate to ratify treaties. This means that a minority, one that often represents much less than one-third of U.S. voters and one motivated by diverse interests, can block ratification. The role of arms control would have been much greater in the last decade if ratification required only a majority vote.

These examples, which do not exhaust the list, illustrate why arms control is often harder to accomplish than it would first appear. Two more problems deserve special attention: conflicting views about Soviet conceptions of arms control and the special limits that may be set by verification.

## SOVIET ARMS CONTROL POLICY

Arms control negotiations have been a constant ingredient of Soviet-American relations for a quarter of a century. There is ample evidence that the Soviet Union, like the United States, has been motivated by an interest in preserving and managing the strategic relationship. Not only does this make for diminished risks and greater effectiveness in both sides' military planning, but it has also helped establish the Soviet Union's claim to co-equal status with the United States. As might be expected in a country which has steadily increased its military spending for two decades and where the defense programs are insulated from fluctuating public attitudes, Soviet arms control policy has been tightly integrated with Soviet military policy.

The substance of the Soviet Union's arms control positions can be summarized as follows. Until about 1960 the Soviet Union was in such an inferior position strategically that it resisted Western arms control initiatives for the understandable reason that agreements would freeze them in perpetual inferiority. However, they camouflaged this negative position by campaigns for general and complete disarmament and offers to ban weapons first and work out verification later. Nevertheless, from 1959 through the 1960s a number of agreements were negotiated that prohibited nuclear deployments in Antarctica, space, and the seabed, banned nuclear tests in the atmosphere, and created a Non-Proliferation Treaty. With the approach to parity in the 1970s it became possible to open up negotiations in the domain of central strategic forces.

The Soviet approach was limited by their concept of deterrence, which emphasizes that whichever side can deliver the greatest blow first is likely to remain in a dominant position thereafter. This explains the Soviet preoccupation with land-based, highly controlled, large ICBMs rather than bombers. Hence a main Soviet arms control objective has been to retain these forces and to ensure their modernization. They have resisted American efforts to use arms control to encourage greater Soviet reliance on their submarines (which they have regarded as an area of American advantage). At the same time, they have stressed a number of measures which do not reduce their central forces, such as a series of bans and limitations on new weapons or weapons in the planning stage. The successful treaty limiting anti-ballistic missiles defenses was of this sort.

Another Soviet preoccupation has been with the concept of equality. Not only has the symbol of equality with the U.S. been important to them, but they have argued that "equal security" requires more than an equal number of weapons. They use the term to justify claims of compensation for geographical handicaps, for nuclear weapons in Europe, and for British, French, and Chinese nuclear forces. They are less open to U.S. claims that they have a geographical advantage because of their proximity to Europe. This complicates efforts to negotiate reductions that maintain rough "parity."

The Soviets, like the U.S., often use arms control proposals as propaganda weapons; with no effective public opinion at home, this is far easier for them to manage than for democracies. The extent to which the Soviet Union publicizes its role in negotiations seems to tell something about the seriousness with which it wants a compromise agreement. The negotiations of SALT I and SALT II were generally carried out with considerable privacy until the late stages. This seems to apply to the START negotiations as well. However, the INF negotiations have been carried out in public view almost from the beginning. One of the Soviet objectives in these negotiations is to split Western Europe from the United States and thereby halt or limit the deployment of intermediate-range forces. But if this tactic fails, an agreement may be possible.

What does the Soviet record tell us about the outlook for future arms control agreements? The picture is mixed. On the one hand, the proposals of the Reagan administration would cut deeply into the Soviet land-based missiles. These forces have been sacrosanct in the past. The "deep cuts" approach runs counter to the Soviet penchant and tradition for slow increments of change. In a period of political transition, Soviet leaders often find it especially hard to move in radical directions. The new Soviet leader, Yuri Andropov, is a product of this system and is beholden to military support in attaining his current position of leadership. Not surprisingly, the Soviets have only offered proposals for more modest reductions and restrictions on new systems of interest to the U.S.

On the other hand, changes do occur in international politics. There are several possible catalysts for change in the Soviet situation. Andropov came into office in 1982 at the age of 68. With only a few years to leave his mark, he may wish to move faster in arms control negotiations. More important, the new leader faces serious political and economic problems: a decreasing Soviet work force; minority pressures for larger roles; a chronically incompetent agricultural system; inadequate consumer goods production; unrest in Eastern Europe; and most of all, a shrinking growth rate that does not provide the base it once did for the Soviet military machine. Together, these pressures may induce a more active search for maintaining the military competition with the West at lower levels of risk and expenditure.

## VERIFYING ARMS CONTROL AGREEMENTS

Given the distrust between East and West, only arms control agreements that are verifiable are likely to be negotiated and ratified. How severe will this limitation be?

In the 1950s, the West routinely proposed, and the Soviet Union routinely rejected, measures to monitor arms control and disarmament agreements which involved on-site inspection, that is, provision for the physical inspection of a country's weapons and facilities by foreign experts. Until technology developed that permitted states to monitor one another at a distance, nuclear arms control was not possible. The absence of acceptable verification measures prevented the negotiation of limits on strategic weapons systems. When President Eisenhower proposed, in 1955, his Open Skies arrangement whereby the United States and the Soviet Union would exchange military blueprints and open one another's airspace to airborne reconnaissance the Russians rejected it, but in 1956 the U.S. began carrying out aerial reconnaissance photography anyway, using the U-2 aircraft. By January 1961, the first successful photo-reconnaissance satellite was launched. Such satellites have continually improved, and the level of detail gleaned by modern satellite scanners is, by all accounts, quite remarkable. In addition to photography, satellites have infra-red sensors (which work at night and through clouds) and listening devices for monitoring radio transmissions from Soviet missile tests.

The U.S. employs a variety of means, besides satellites, to determine the size of Soviet forces as well as verify Soviet compliance with arms control treaties, including large radars in the Aleutians, a space-tracking ship, line-of-sight radar stations around the Soviet periphery, and over-the-horizon radars. In combination, these systems provide detailed information on Soviet missile tests and weapons deployments. The Soviet Union has similar ships and satellites, which are collectively referred to as "national technical means" of verification.

But even such sophisticated measures as these cannot be all-seeing. There are aspects of the weapon systems production cycle that remain difficult to monitor by national technical means. The production of individual bombs, warheads, and missiles takes place in secrecy and production rates can only be inferred from scrutiny of what comes to the factories. If small changes in numbers of weapons are important, this process may be far too crude to be adequate.

It was the revolution in verification technology in the 1960s that made the more ambitious efforts of the Strategic Arms Limitation Talks possible. Of necessity the SALT process reflected the limitations of verification technology. Only delivery vehicles that were large enough to spot from space (for example, ICBM silos) or that, if mobile, could only operate from relatively few, known bases (heavy bombers and strategic submarines) could be verified. It was possible, however, to set limits on warheads and bombs, which were too small to be verified directly, by agreeing to somewhat arbitrary counting rules. A missile was counted as having the maximum number of warheads ever tested on that missile, rather than the actual number deployed (which might be much less). In this way verification was extended to what could not be seen.

While the Soviets have elaborate surveillance equipment, their interests in verification are less than those of the United States because of the very different nature of the two societies. The high level of reporting from American congressional hearings, media coverage, leaks to newspapers, and the likelihood that any violation of an agreement will find its way into newspapers make verification much easier for the Soviet Union. Hence exacting verification procedures are seen by the Soviets as something they "give" to the United States. At the same time, the Soviet Union is extremely secretive about military matters, a tradition with deep roots in the history of a frequently invaded Russian state. Many of the verification measures proposed by the U.S. look like espionage measures to the Soviets. Over the years, negotiations helped convince the Soviets that such procedures are not a cover for espionage but are an essential requirement for ratifiable arms control measures. Yet in each instance procedures must be justified in minute detail and negotiated in ways that minimize intrusiveness.

It should be remembered that the vast system of monitoring and intelligence collection that the United States must use for verification is needed whether arms control agreements exist or not. Indeed, arms control agreements, especially SALT II, have greatly increased our knowledge of the Soviet nuclear arsenal: both sides have promised not to interfere with each other's surveillance devices, and both have agreed that certain activities will not be concealed but will remain open to monitoring. Hence the verification of future agreements will have a broader foundation on which to build. Moreover, improvements in verification technology continue and it is reasonable to expect that capabilities that were not possible in the past will exist in the future.

When matters of national security are at stake, both the government and the public wish to know for certain whether agreements are being kept. But in daily life we know that we must live with some uncertainty. Verification of arms control agreements is no different; some risks are inevitable. But an untrammeled arms race also creates risks. Risks must be balanced and judgments made about adequacy. Verification must be adequate enough so that a Soviet violation of an agreement large enough to threaten our security could be detected in time for us to be able to make a sufficient response. Ironically, some of these judgments are easier to make at current high levels of weaponry than would be the case if there were deep reductions in numbers.

Much of the U.S. internal debate during the SALT II negotiations and ratification hearings focused on such judgments. Although the verification of some treaty provisions was seen to be less adequate than others, the trade-offs made between uncertainty and the importance of the item to be limited was generally agreed to be prudent.

Nevertheless, the new weaponry scheduled for deployment in this decade raises new problems. Cruise missiles will present a special challenge to verification. They are small and can be easily changed from conventional to nuclear warheads. The focus may have to be on restricting the ships and planes and geographical regions of their deployment. Close monitoring of both sides' production plants may also help. Mobile ICBMs will require special measures as well. As greater emphasis shifts to the number of warheads and the ability to reload missile launchers, further measures will be required. In each case difficult judgments of two sorts will have to be made: what kinds of violations have significant adverse consequences on American security, and what is the probability that such violations could be detected. If one insists on absolute certainty in verification, then very little can be verified and arms cannot be controlled. On the other hand, if verification procedures are absent or lax, cheating may occur and confidence will be lost in the other side's compliance. The task is to find the right middle ground.

Verification procedures in future agreements will be subject to even greater scrutiny for two reasons. First, the Soviet Union refused to cooperate with American efforts to discover if an outbreak of anthrax in a Soviet city was a violation of the Biological Weapons Convention of 1972. Second, there is increasing evidence of the use of poison gas by the Soviet forces in Afghanistan and by the military forces they support in Cambodia. In the latter case there is a technical loophole in that the countries allegedly under attack were not themselves parties to the Geneva Protocol that prohibits such use. Those conventions did not have the elaborate verification provisions and procedures that the SALT treaties have. Soviet actions have therefore reinforced the importance of having such provisions in any future arms control agreements.

Despite all of these difficulties, however, over the past 25 years there has been a gradual improvement in Soviet willingness to provide information, even to negotiate details of on-site inspections in the 1976 Threshold Test-Ban Treaty, and to permit the discussion of such requirements. It has been a slow process but it should not go unnoticed.

## THE ROLE OF PUBLIC OPINION

Arms control has tended to succeed in the United States in periods of significant public involvement and concern. The 1963 Test-Ban Treaty and the 1972 ABM Treaty both were achieved during such periods. One of the most interesting developments of the early 1980s was the remarkable rise of public interest and public protest in the area of nuclear policy. Failure of the U.S. to ratify SALT II, after a similar failure to ratify two treaties negotiated in 1976 to further limit nuclear tests, suggested to the public that arms control was not working, and that the principal diplomatic lever for controlling the arms competition was stuck. The 1980 election was filled with rhetoric about rearmament. Concern in Europe about these events and the plans to deploy new nuclear weapons helped to stimulate mass movements. A year-long series of pronouncements by the U.S. president and his secretaries of state and defense which reflected a preoccupation with improving U.S. nuclear war-fighting capability and a new level of hostility toward the Soviet Union followed. This was accompanied by rapidly increasing military budgets.

As budgets and rhetoric escalated, so did the memberships and the influence of public and professional groups opposed to nuclear war. Physicians' groups, some dating from the campaign against nuclear testing two decades earlier, were particularly effective in reminding Americans of the horrible human suffering and death that would accompany nuclear war. Because of this revival of public interest in arms control, the current nuclear freeze movement, the careful examination of the moral basis of nuclear policy by the U.S. Catholic bishops, and intensified support for arms control in the scientific and professional community came into being.

The nuclear freeze movement began in the spring of 1980 with a call for bilateral, verifiable freeze on the production, testing, and deployment of all nuclear weapons systems in the U.S. and the USSR. Its aim is to prevent further development or deployment of counterforce and other destabilizing weapons, and to stabilize the current balance so that reductions can go forward. Various freeze resolutions were supported by the electorates in eight (of nine) states where it appeared on the ballot in November 1982. Public opinion polls at the end of 1982 showed the freeze idea appealed to some three-quarters of the public if it is verifiable and would grant no significant advantage to the Soviet Union. The same polls showed overwhelming opposition to unilateral disarmament and considerable mistrust of the Soviet Union.[1]

Earlier freezes suggested by Presidents Johnson and

Carter did not have any obvious drawing power, nor have the various moratoria proposed by the Soviet Union. But with the combination of the seemingly bellicose pronouncements of the early Reagan administration and the belief that arms control was not being seriously pursued, the freeze movement took hold with the public. Considering the difficulty of any treaty of substance gaining the two-thirds Senate vote needed for ratification, this degree of public arousal may turn out to be an essential requirement for any future arms control agreement.

In Europe, the anti-nuclear opposition has focused on deployment of new NATO missiles and is strongest in northern Europe and among the Protestant churches. By contrast, in the U.S. the initiative from the religious sector has come from the Catholic bishops. This has taken the form of a well-planned, deliberate debate.

A further indication of the spread of concern is seen in the mobilization of support for arms control in the scientific community. Not only are activist scientists busy refining freeze proposals, but the establishment itself is involved. For the first time the National Academy of Sciences passed virtually unanimously a resolution urging intensified efforts at the negotiating table and adherence to the still unratified treaties. A carefully crafted statement by the presidents of scientific academies and other leading scientists on these matters was presented to Pope John Paul II in September 1982. It urged curbing "the development, production, testing and deployment of nuclear weapons systems and their reduction to substantially lower levels," claiming that "the sole purpose of nuclear weapons, as long as they exist, must be to deter nuclear war," and calling upon all nations "never to be the first to use nuclear weapons."

This brief overview cannot convey the full extent of the diversity and vigor of the new public engagement in nuclear policy. Like public involvements in the past, this one may be changed or move in new directions. But it seems likely that this new force will prove durable enough to affect government policies.

## THE FUTURE OF ARMS CONTROL

Although no arms control treaties of significance have been ratified during the last decade, the numerical growth of nuclear forces has been somewhat restrained compared to what it might have been, by limits in agreements (ratified or not), and by the retirement of aging weapons. From 1978 to 1982 numbers of strategic launchers actually decreased by about 1% for the Soviet Union and about 9% for the U.S. The total number of warheads and bombs deployed by the U.S. remained essentially constant during that period. The Soviet Union, completing its MIRV programs, did, however, increase its strategic warhead total by 60%, reducing the U.S. lead in that category.

The arms race in recent years has been not in terms of numbers, but in terms of technological improvements. Both sides, for example, have greatly improved the accuracy of their forces. More improvements are to come. If new arms control restraints are not negotiated, the next few years will see a breakout of new weaponry incorporating even more remarkable technological changes: new bombers, new ICBMs, new SLBMs, new cruise missiles mounted on bombers, trucks, ships, and submarines, the attainment of absolute accuracy, and anti-satellite weapons. Although many of these are planned replacements there will be an increase of about 25% in numbers by 1990 if no agreements are reached.

Arms control is an effort to bring stability to the nuclear weapons competition, and this stability has three dimensions by which arms control proposals can be judged. One is deterrence stability, which means the assurance that our forces are capable and credible enough to deter the Soviet Union from political adventures that could lead to war through miscalculation. A second dimension is arms race stability, or controlling the weapons buildup in the two countries so that the military relationship is more predictable and resources can be used for purposes other than weaponry. The third dimension is crisis stability, or creating forces of a type which provide no incentive for either side to launch a first strike in a time of crisis. In addition to these central criteria, arms control proposals

---

### Checklist for Arms Control Proposals

Consider the short- and long-run effects on:

1. *Deterrence stability*
   Is deterrence strengthened or weakened?

2. *Arms race stability*
   Is predictability increased and are resources saved?

3. *Crisis stability*
   Are incentives for nuclear use increased or decreased?

4. *Negotiability*
   Can agreement be expected in a reasonable time?

5. *Verification*
   Can adequate verification procedures be devised?

---

can be judged in terms of the negotiability and verification problems we have discussed earlier.

All too often people think of arms control simply as formal treaties for reducing existing weapons. But there are other aspects of arms control. Bargaining and agreements can be informal as well as formal. Agreements can affect future types of forces even if they do not reduce existing forces. And some arms control measures may be designed to build confidence or stability through improved communications rather than changes in forces. The range of possibilities for arms control can be usefully grouped under four headings, though there is overlap, and some components from different categories can be packaged together into interesting and complex proposals. At the risk of oversimplification, these four categories are reductions, freezes, force restructuring, and stabilizing measures.

*Reductions.* Reducing the number of existing weapons is probably the most common measure by which the public judges arms control. The reductions approach addresses the view, shared by many experts as well, that the nuclear arsenals of both sides have grown irresponsibly large, that a much smaller nuclear force would be adequate and cheaper. Moreover, some argue that such an abundance of weapons encourages further excursions in planning for nuclear war-fighting and drives the appetite for more weapons. The additional risks that result would be removed if substantial reductions were negotiated.

Reductions are, however, not as simple as they first look. The wrong kinds of reductions could hurt political stability or crisis stability unless the most destabilizing weapons were reduced first. It is also important that the critical deterrent purposes of the arsenal are not compromised, and that increased deployments of non-limited weapons do not compensate for the agreed-upon reductions.

The wrong kind of reductions could increase, not lessen, instability. For example, if single-warhead missiles were reduced in preference to MIRVed missiles, fears of pre-emption would increase. The danger of nuclear weapons lies in their use, rather than their existence. While high numbers may increase some statistical probability of use in an accidental or mechanical sense, and may encourage some exaggerated targeting plans by the military, they do not necessarily increase the probability that nuclear use would be initiated deliberately. On the contrary, low numbers may invite pre-emption or raise uncertainty about the perceived stability of the military balance and thus increase the probability of weapons actually being used.

Certain types of proportional cuts, such as cutting all existing categories by 50%, could also be destabilizing. It might be dangerous, for example, to cut the number of strategic submarines in half. Half of the remainder would then be in port, and fewer than ten submarines would have to be tracked and destroyed for a successful surprise attack against what is now the most invulnerable part of our force.

Another problem arises because the forces on the two sides differ so much that reductions in broad categories may affect one side quite differently from the other. Attempts to exploit such differences waste much negotiation time. Each side can be expected to urge reduction schemes that remove the weapons it most fears on the other side but permits retention of its own preferred weapons. Treated wisely, however, asymmetries can become the means of agreeing on important trade-offs that have to be made if negotiations are to succeed.

Another problem with the deep-reductions approach

is its focus. If all efforts were concentrated on such reductions, would other aspects of arms control be neglected? The danger is that the search for the perfect becomes the enemy of the good, and all arms control can be stalled or discredited. As a long-term device, the right kind of deep cuts proposal is sensible, but as the sole focus of arms control it may have substantial problems.

One can see in both the Soviet and the U.S. opening positions at the START negotiations some examples of the points just made. There are clear benefits in the reductions described in both proposals. The U.S. proposals, however, attempt to alter the balance between land-based and sea-based missiles within the Soviet forces. Although this is done in the interests of improved stability, it also requires changes the Soviet Union is unlikely to want to make unless compensated by substantial gains elsewhere in the treaty. Likewise, the U.S. proposal to postpone restrictions on bombers and cruise missiles, where much of the U.S. growth will take place, is unlikely to be attractive to the Soviets. The Soviets clearly wish to stop these developments through negotiation. Hence, they propose severe restrictions on cruise missile deployments, new bombers, and new submarines. On balance, however, there seems to be enough in common between the two positions to make a compromise possible.

In negotiating reductions in missiles, two new features are coming into prominence: rapid reload and mobility. Launchers for some new-generation missiles can be used more than once and thus can be reloaded and refired if more missiles are available in nearby storage. Consequently, arms control agreements would have to be worked out that would ban storage of extra missiles near the launcher. This was done for ICBMs in SALT II. The principal problem with mobile missiles is verification. The U.S. has taken the position that the side which proposes such deployments is obligated to devise an accompanying verification system satisfactory to the other side.

Finally, it should be noted that little progress has been made in working out verification procedures for aircraft other than the heavy bombers treated in SALT II. The smaller and more numerous the aircraft, the more difficult it is to monitor them. And for the very large numbers of aircraft whose sizes lie between medium-bomber and short-range tactical aircraft, there is the important additional problem that such aircraft can deliver both nuclear and conventional weapons. The same problem is likely to arise with cruise missiles. How does one tell the difference between a cruise missile carrying a nuclear warhead and one carrying conventional explosives? Some easily recognized external feature that distinguishes the differences between conventional and nuclear weapons may solve the problem in principle, but its negotiation will be difficult.

*Freezes.* Freezes present much the same verification problems as reduction schemes; therefore, the two approaches have much in common. SALT II was primarily a partial freeze agreement and the most time-consuming part of its negotiation was that relating to verification. In the current discussion of freezes, the importance of reaching an agreement in relatively short time has stimulated some to propose that what is initially frozen be simply the items covered in previous negotiations. This would include the strategic launchers of SALT II, a nuclear test ban, and possibly a ban on anti-satellite weapons.

Another approach[2] lies in taking the SALT II agreement as the starting point and modifying it to prohibit the deployment of the one new ballistic missile it allowed to each side, to carry out reductions over a number of years until 50% reductions have been achieved, to halt the deployment of all cruise missiles and Pershing II missiles in return for the elimination of the Soviet SS-4s, SS-5s, and SS-20s. This is a hybrid proposal, about half a freeze and half a reduction scheme.

The real challenge comes in finding ways to meet the demanding requirements of those freezes that have produced such large public followings: to freeze the production, testings, and deployment of all nuclear weapons systems on the two sides in a verifiable manner and to negotiate this quickly enough to have a decisive role in bringing the arms race to a stop.[3] Consider what this involves. It means devising and then negotiating verification procedures for weapons production, and the development, testing, production, and deployment of nearly a hundred kinds of weapons and delivery systems that make up the offensive and defensive forces at the strategic, intermediate, and battlefield levels on both sides. If stability is to be maintained in the long run, one would also have to freeze counter-measures to these weapons such as anti-submarine warfare capabilities and air defenses. And then for each weapon system one must decide what is to be allowed with respect to maintenance and modernization. Are replacements to be allowed? If so, can they be improved versions of the same weapons systems? What if the original factories and components no longer exist? How much improvement is to be allowed?

A comprehensive freeze or comprehensive reductions would require extensive and elaborate negotiations. Unless the arms control budgets of the superpowers were raised a hundredfold or more and many teams negotiated simultaneously and were convinced that both nations wanted this kind of agreement, one cannot imagine such agreements being negotiated in a few years. This is the challenge presented by those who advocate a negotiated comprehensive freeze or a comprehensive reduction regime.

It may be too easy, however, to undercut a comprehensive freeze proposal by driving it to its maximum interpretation. Much of the public would be satisfied with far less than a total freeze. It might be possible to freeze the most destabilizing weapons first, followed by less dangerous weapons. The verification problems for less than total freezes might be less difficult. And total bans of some new weapons may be simpler to verify than limits because only one sighting would be sufficient to prove a violation. However, in the end there would undoubtedly remain some systems that would require special verification measures inside the other country; such requirements would have to be met if the freeze were to be truly comprehensive.

There is a conflict, moreover, between two strongly held points of view among those concerned with these nuclear issues. One group wants a freeze to stop all technology and development as completely as possible. Others see a danger of disassembling the whole nuclear weapons research and development and production establishment. These people would see virtue in allowing certain developments to proceed in order to allow less vulnerable and more stable weapons to replace existing systems. For example, a freeze in 1959 would have stopped deployment of our invulnerable Polaris submarine-based missiles, and that would have made the 1960s *less* safe. On the other hand, a freeze in 1969 would have avoided the instability that was caused by the introduction of multiple independently targeted re-entry vehicles (MIRVs) on missiles in the 1970s.

It is an open question whether a freeze today would enhance crisis stability or not. Some threatening systems would be stopped, but a freeze could also prevent such developments as a new small single-warhead land-based missile that many experts believe is the best way to remedy the current problems created by MIRVs. Clearly there is a strong case for discriminating restraints on weapons technology rather than a total freeze.

One such limited freeze is a cap on the number of nuclear warheads—each side now deploys roughly 11,000 on systems with ranges over 1,000 miles—requiring that any warhead added to the two arsenals be compensated by at least an equal number withdrawn.[4] This would be consistent with the simplicity that is the great virtue of the freeze idea. It leads to a simple relevant list of what is to be frozen (strategic warheads); it might be quickly negotiated; and it would be verifiable by the already negotiated SALT rules and procedures being observed by both sides, coupled with negotiated procedures to verify warheads on cruise missiles and intermediate-range missiles. This would avoid the potentially dangerous approach of freezing the modernization of certain forces while letting their counter-measures run free. Moreover, it would lead quickly to more complex arms control negotiations without reducing Soviet incentives to bargain.

Freezes produce public enthusiasm, and if and when alternative schemes of arms control are devised, they may well have to meet this test of eliciting strong public support to ensure ratification. Even if it appears unlikely that a total freeze will be negotiated, serious efforts to achieve various partial freezes may offer a route to a less dangerous future.

*Force Restructuring.* If negotiations fail or proceed too slowly, an alternative approach is to seek simple agreements to change certain weapons on each side. The change could be one of several kinds: elimination, reduction, freeze, or replacement with new weapons less threatening to the other side. For example, the U.S. might propose, as it did several years ago, not to deploy the MX missile if the Soviet Union were to eliminate some proportion of its MIRVed ICBM force. Or, as the Soviet Union has already proposed, the construction and deployment of large ballistic missile submarines could be stopped on both sides. If several such trades could be made in separate agreements, the effect would equal that of most proposed negotiations of a more comprehensive sort.

The most ambitious proposal in this direction seeks to solve one of the most hotly debated problems confronting the two sides: the vulnerability of the land-based missiles. This proposal would provide a schedule by which current land-based missiles would be replaced by much smaller mobile missiles. The schedule of replacements would be coordinated so that neither side reaps a temporary advantage. The key feature of this proposal is that missiles of this small size can carry only one warhead, and not a very large one. The consequence would be that over a period of 10 to 15 years all the MIRVed land-based missiles on both sides would be replaced with single-warhead missiles. Thus the land-based forces on both sides would no longer be vulnerable to a first strike by the other side.

Of course it follows from the earlier section on Soviet arms control policy that this trade-off may be unattractive to the Soviet Union because of its larger investment in and commitment to land-based missiles. Consequently it may be necessary to allow two or even three new missiles for each MIRVed land-based missile destroyed. In any event, the result would be not only a dramatic reduction in the numbers of warheads but a vast decrease in the vulnerability of the land-based force, a feature that may become increasingly attractive to the Soviet government.

*Stabilizing Measures.* These measures aim not so much to diminish or restructure nuclear forces as to introduce ways to make their use less likely. The aim of these measures is to reduce the chance of accidents that might lead to war, to bolster crisis stability, to ban certain weapons and tests, and to build confidence in the East-West strategic relationship by introducing a much higher level of communication and dialogue. A few examples will illustrate this approach.

An agreement for both sides to abandon the development of weapons in space, either for satellite destruction or ballistic missile defense, would profoundly improve all three kinds of stability over the next few decades. Satellites have become increasingly central to early warning and to the command and control of nuclear forces. An attack on these systems would so threaten to blind the other side that it would be considered an act of war requiring immediate retaliation. Hence stopping work toward this capability would be mutually reassuring. The possibility of building space stations from which ballistic missiles might be destroyed shortly after launch is discussed elsewhere. The costs of such schemes might make them politically impossible and their vulnerability would make them militarily unreliable. Still, unless agreement is reached to prohibit them, development is likely to proceed on each side.

Stability would also be promoted by agreements to prohibit the close approach of submarines to each other's coasts. Such forward deployment puts bomber bases at special risk because it reduces warning time of an attack below that required for bombers to become airborne. Such an agreement would also reduce the risks of a "decapitation" strike by giving more time for political leaders to evacuate in time of war. Another stabilizing measure would be an agreement on defining ocean sanctuaries for submarines carrying nuclear missiles, thereby reducing the likelihood of accident or misunderstanding in a crisis.

Another measure, already proposed at START, would be to agree on extensive notification of planned missile tests so that there would be no ambiguity when launches were observed. Bans or limits on flight tests (or nuclear tests) can help to reassure both sides that the pace of modernization of weapons is limited. It could reduce the confidence of any government considering striking first in a crisis.

Stabilizing measures and force restructuring suggestions might be best handled by separately organized and continuing talks involving, for example, staffs of the Joint Chiefs and their Soviet counterparts as well as representatives from the other parts of government usually involved.[5] Such a continuing forum could also attempt to resolve other important matters such as naval incidents, the meaning of ambiguous intelligence, misunderstandings arising from changes in force deployments that might occur in places like Poland and the Caribbean, and technological developments that it may be in the mutual interest of both sides not to pursue.

Moving even further in this direction, the establishment of a joint crisis management center, suggested by Senators Nunn and Jackson, deserves serious examination.[6] They have proposed that the hot line be supplemented by a jointly manned crisis center where all information relevant to a developing crisis would be examined and discussed within permitted limits. Even more radical developments might be possible, such as establishing linked teleconferencing centers in both capitals, again jointly manned, which would be ready for use by high-level government officials whenever needed. Such a joint crisis management center could attract top-level government personnel.

A number of initiatives to build further confidence could also be tested and perhaps brought into operation through the technique of reciprocal restraint. For example, one side could announce that it would hold its nuclear submarines back a certain distance from the other's shores as long as the other side reciprocated, or that it would restrain its development of certain weapons so long as the other side did so. In short, even if formal and comprehensive arms control fails or proceeds slowly, there is much else that can be done outside such proceedings by means of separate steps. And there is nothing to prevent such measures from being explored while formal negotiations are proceeding.

## CONCLUSION

When a country is faced with a military threat, there is a strong impetus to match that threat. But an equally valid response is to try to constrain the threat. Arms control is an effort to constrain the Soviet military threat. If pursued wisely it can save money as well as enhance our security. It should be seen as a part of a national security policy that is as important as the defense budget. The two are not alternatives. They are partners in the pursuit of stability and security.

There are many paths by which arms control can contribute to stability and security. Although reductions and freezes have captured the most attention, partial agreements, informal approaches, and stabilizing measures can be of equal importance in averting nuclear war. Most important, if properly applied, these various approaches can be complementary rather than competitive with each other.

Viewed this way, arms control has accomplished more in the past two decades than is sometimes realized by those who point to the absence of deep reductions. Certain areas and technologies (for example, anti-ballistic missile systems) have been "fenced off" from competition. As we will discuss in the next chapter, a system has been set up to slow the spread of nuclear weapons to additional countries. Limits on existing arsenals may have helped to keep weapons and expenditures below what they otherwise might have been. And most important, the beginnings of a process of communication and cooperation have been established between the two major nuclear adversaries and it has weathered very difficult times.

At the same time, there are limits to what arms control can accomplish. It cannot be totally separated from the political problems in U.S.-Soviet relations. Even if both sides avoid the tactical temptation of linking progress on arms control to behavior in other political and economic matters, complete separation is impossible, particularly in democratic politics. Thus arms control will to some extent be limited by the overall condition of relations with the Soviet Union. In the long run, as we will argue in Chapter 11, arms control must be accompanied by some improvement in U.S.-Soviet relations if humanity is to cope with its nuclear predicament.

## Notes

1. Lou Harris Associates Polls.

2. Federation of American Scientists, *Public Interest Report,* 36, 1, January, 1983.

3. R. Forsberg, *Scientific American,* 247, 5, November 1982.

4. J. M. Lodal, "Finishing START," *Foreign Policy,* No. 48, Fall 1982; J. S. Nye, "Needing a Simpler Freeze Proposal," *Boston Globe,* November 8, 1982.

5. J. S. Nye, "Restarting Arms Control," *Foreign Policy,* No. 47, Summer 1982.

6. Henry M. Jackson, "Nuclear War and the Hot Line," *Wall Street Journal,* September 3, 1982.

# 10

# Nuclear Proliferation: Can the Spread of Nuclear Weapons Be Controlled?

Can anything be done to prevent nuclear weapons from spreading, or "proliferating," to other countries? Imagine a future in which dozens of governments possess nuclear weapons. Would war be more likely? Could nuclear peace be maintained in such a world?

These questions are not just theoretical. The technology for building nuclear weapons is forty years old now, and already well within the grasp of many nations throughout the world. Given that fact, what is surprising is not that nuclear weapons have spread, but that so many states have chosen not to build nuclear arsenals.

Fortunately, such pessimistic predictions have so far proved inaccurate. In 1963 President Kennedy envisioned a world in the 1970s with 15 to 25 nuclear weapon states, presenting "the greatest possible danger." The number of governments possessing nuclear weapons has, in fact, grown much more slowly. The United States built the first atomic bomb in 1945, followed by the Soviet Union in 1949, Great Britain in 1952, France in 1960, and the People's Republic of China in 1964. A decade passed before another state tested a nuclear device. In May 1974 the Indian government detonated what it called a "peaceful

215

nuclear explosion." But today's peaceful nuclear explosion may turn out tomorrow to have been an actual nuclear weapons test.

Since 1974 no more countries have openly exploded nuclear devices, but the situation could change rapidly in the future. No one knows for certain who will get the bomb next, or when. But countries such as Pakistan and South Africa are poised at the nuclear threshold. Most observers believe that Israel has secretly built weapons or could do so at very short notice. Many other states are not far behind. The pessimism expressed by President Kennedy could, therefore, soon prove justified, if steps are not taken to control the spread of nuclear weaponry.

What can be done to minimize the risks of nuclear proliferation? Any effort to control the spread of nuclear weapons must take into account the two factors that contribute to a government's decision to build a nuclear force: the technical capability and the political or military desire to do so. Many nations that have the capability today do not have the motivation to produce atomic weapons. Many states that appear to have sufficient motivation currently lack the necessary technological capabilities. Non-proliferation policy should seek to continue this situation, as much as possible, for as long as possible.

## WHY DOES NUCLEAR PROLIFERATION MATTER?

Some individuals believe that we should not try to control the spread of nuclear weapons. After all, they argue, if nuclear weapons have produced prudence between the two antagonistic superpowers, could they not do the same for other nations? Perhaps the proliferation of nuclear weapons would create a series of peaceful regional balances of power: Argentina and Brazil could deter each other with nuclear arsenals; India and Pakistan could maintain nuclear peace on the Asian subcontinent; South Africa and Nigeria could balance each other's power in Africa. Strategists who envision such a world believe that nuclear proliferation is not a dangerous process. Just as the risk of nuclear war since 1945 reduced the incidence of conventional war in Western Europe, they argue, so the risk of nuclear war might reduce the incidence of conventional war worldwide. Such individuals see a world of nuclear powers that act like porcupines: each would be so prickly that no one would dare attack it.

Nuclear proliferation has also been justified on other grounds. Some individuals in developing countries have criticized the superpowers for monopolizing nuclear weapons. They say that the United States and the Soviet Union are racist and elitist because they trust themselves but not others with nuclear weapons. Furthermore, the superpowers seem to be unable to break their habit of adding to their own nuclear arsenal. If more countries were to acquire nuclear weapons they could reduce superpower domination by their enhanced military strength.

These arguments in favor of nuclear proliferation are extremely mistaken. Nuclear proliferation is far more likely to hurt than to help international stability. One can oppose proliferation without being either elitist or racist. One should oppose it because it is dangerous.

It is true that the Soviet Union and the United States have thus far avoided war with each other and that the existence of nuclear weapons has contributed to prudence in superpower relations. But this situation would be repeated elsewhere *only if* the political and military conditions that enhance nuclear stability between the superpowers also existed elsewhere. This is not often the case.

A key ingredient is the political stability of the governments controlling the weapons. Yet statistics show a much higher incidence of governmental breakdown through military coups and civil wars in many of the areas where these weapons might spread. Revolutions, civil wars, and coups may increase the likelihood of nuclear weapons being used. This is doubly dangerous if combined with impulsive leaders such as Uganda's former president Idi Amin and Libya's current leader Muammar al-Qaddafi.

The other missing ingredient is strategic stability. The mere presence of nuclear weapons has not created a stable "balance of terror" between the Soviets and the Americans. Rather, as previously noted, it is the assured second-strike capability—the ability to strike back even if an opponent launches a nuclear attack—which enhances deterrence. New nuclear weapons states, however, may be unable to

build enough invulnerable nuclear weapons to be confident of such an assured second-strike capability. On the
contrary, their early weapons are likely to be large cumber-
some ones located on land rather than on submarines.
Such a small vulnerable nuclear force may increase the
risk of pre-emptive attack by frightened neighbors.

A third problem is that few of the new nuclear powers could develop the elaborate system of command and
control, special safety devices (discussed in Chapter 3) or
mutual arms verification (including satellites) which have
reduced the risks of war between the superpowers. If a
crisis or a conventional war broke out between two new
nuclear powers, there would be greater incentives to launch
pre-emptive nuclear strikes, and greater risks of unauthorized or accidental nuclear use.

Opposition to nuclear proliferation is therefore not
simply a question of either elitism or racism. Nuclear
peace has been kept between the superpowers because of
a particular set of conditions. There may be some regional
situations with similar conditions, but far more appear to
be different. Under these circumstances, no country should
press its luck. The concern behind non-proliferation efforts is that as more countries develop nuclear weapons,
the probability of their use somewhere increases.

## SHOULD AMERICANS CARE?

Even accepting the idea that nuclear proliferation is
bad, would it hurt the United States if a couple of far-
away countries used crude nuclear devices on each other?
Such horrible results may even do some good, some have
argued, in dissuading other countries from taking the
road to destruction.

Such an attitude is not only callous; it is also politically
misguided. It hearkens back to a deep-rooted American
sense of being isolated from the troubles of the rest of the
world. But today American security and economic interests are global; widespread nuclear proliferation would
definitely affect everyone. Nuclear proliferation, which
could increase the risk of conventional wars in some region
escalating to nuclear wars, would be disastrous to American interests in that region and beyond. American forces

might be involved in such a conflict, for instance, in the Middle East, if one of the combatants were our ally. It is even possible that the United States could be intentionally dragged into a mortal conflict not of its own making, as in the "catalytic war" scenario of Chapter 3 where a third party disguises its attack on American forces as a Soviet attack. Nuclear proliferation would also increase the likelihood of nuclear terrorism either through terrorists being given a weapon by a government that supported their cause or by theft. In none of these cases would the results of proliferation be anything but dangerous for Americans.

## HOW AND WHY

Will more states build nuclear weapons in the future? Probably. There is a kernel of truth in the cliché that "the horse is out of the barn." But how many horses are wandering about makes a big difference. To design policies which can minimize the danger, one must first understand how nuclear weapons technology has spread as far as it has and why some nations want, or don't want, nuclear weapons.

The "how" of nuclear proliferation is straightforward. The general technology for building a fission explosive is well known. (The knowledge of how to build hydrogen bombs is less widespread.) Undergraduates at Princeton and MIT have drafted roughly feasible atomic weapon designs, drawing only from unclassified documents. Over time, foreign governments could certainly train or hire skilled scientists and engineers. If all went according to their plans, it might cost only about two hundred million dollars to build a nuclear weapon over a six-to-ten-year period. Such a sum could be fitted into many countries' defense budgets.

Building the technological infrastructure and getting a high number of good scientists and engineers are more difficult than the monetary costs. For example, India began its nuclear program three decades ago, and it has involved more than ten thousand people at the professional level. In contrast, Libya, which is reported to have been seeking a nuclear weapons capacity for slightly over a decade, has not yet succeeded. The country does not lack money, but has only a few hundred professionals in its nuclear programs.

The most difficult step in making a nuclear weapon is obtaining sufficient nuclear explosive material. The two materials commonly used to manufacture weapons—uranium-235 and plutonium-239—are not readily available. Natural uranium contains only 0.7% uranium-235. To be usable in weapons, it must be "enriched" in its uranium-235 content to at least 40% and usually over 90%. Such enrichment plants are difficult and costly to build. Plutonium-239 is found only in trace amounts in nature. Quantities needed for bombs are created through nuclear "alchemy" in reactors where natural uranium is bombarded by neutrons. The common form of uranium, namely, uranium-238, "captures" a neutron and is transformed into weapons-usable plutonium-239, which must then be separated chemically from the residual uranium and radioactive materials in the spent reactor fuel by a method called "reprocessing." Reprocessing plants are also relatively expensive and difficult to operate safely. Because of the special role which enrichment and reprocessing play in weapons manufacture, it is not surprising that there has been special international concern about the transfer of these technologies.

The 1974 Indian explosion of a "peaceful" nuclear device used plutonium from a research reactor supplied by Canada. Various nations developed plans for commercial use of plutonium fuels. Korea and Pakistan arranged to import allegedly commercial reprocessing plants from Europe for what later turned out to be nuclear explosives programs. South Africa and Pakistan built their own uranium enrichment plants cloaked under heavy veils of secrecy, the former using a partly indigenous process and the latter based on plans stolen from the Netherlands. Eventually, governments with a reasonable technical infrastructure that are strongly committed to get hold of weapons-grade uranium or plutonium will probably be able to do so, though the process may take considerably longer than they initially expect. And while sophisticated delivery systems such as submarines or missiles take time and technology to develop, some delivery systems such as advanced fighter-bombers can be bought "off the shelf" or received in military aid packages.

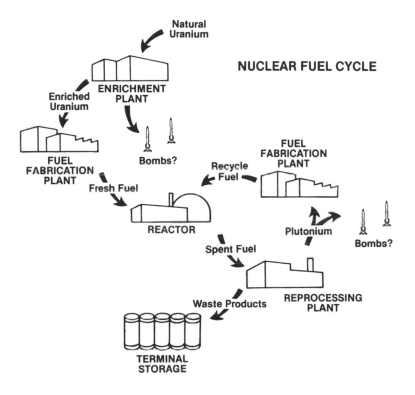

The "why" of nuclear proliferation is more complex, and since, in the long run, governments cannot be stopped from becoming able to go nuclear, it is critically important to understand why they would. After all, there are probably some thirty to forty states throughout the world that could have the capability to construct nuclear weapons but have chosen not to try. The main reason is not difficult to understand: these governments believe that their security is better maintained *without* nuclear forces. In many cases this is because such states are, in part, protected by American military power. Ironically, in some cases, it is the existence of nuclear weapons which reduces the incentive for the spread of nuclear weapons (see box). In other cases, the security threats faced by these states can more easily be met with conventional forces.

## NUCLEAR WEAPONS CAPABILITY WITHIN THIS CENTURY

| Possession: | Little Motivation: | Some Motivation: | High Motivation: |
|---|---|---|---|
| United States | Australia | Argentina | Iraq |
| Soviet Union | Austria | Brazil | Libya |
| Great Britain | Belgium | Chile | Pakistan |
| France | Canada | South Korea | South Africa |
| China | Czechoslovakia | Taiwan | |
| India | Denmark | | |
| Israel (?) | East Germany | | |
| | Egypt | | |
| | Finland | | |
| | Iran | | |
| | Italy | | |
| | Japan | | |
| | Mexico | | |
| | Netherlands | | |
| | Norway | | |
| | Poland | | |
| | Romania | | |
| | Saudi Arabia | | |
| | Spain | | |
| | Sweden | | |
| | Switzerland | | |
| | West Germany | | |
| | Yugoslavia | | |

In the case of nations who lack nuclear weapons, but have the motivation to build them, security threats are not so readily met. Such states fall under three general categories: pariah states, which feel threatened by a large group of hostile neighbors; weak states, which are confronted by a large neighbor, with or without nuclear weapons, and feel that their own nuclear force is the only way to enhance their security; and radical states, which think nuclear forces would support their revolutionary cause. Unfortunately, a number of perceived advantages exist for those states to acquire nuclear weapons: the ability to deter an adversary's aggression, to obtain coercive power or political influence through the threat of nuclear weapons, or to enhance national prestige.

Nuclear programs that have weapons potential also have their drawbacks. They may become military targets, as the Iraqi government painfully learned when on June 7, 1981, Israeli jets bombed its research reactor (designed to use weapons-grade uranium) into a pile of rubble. Nuclear weapons programs may alienate friends as well as frighten enemies. For example, President Carter, under congressional mandate, froze military and economic aid to the Pakistanis when their nuclear efforts came to light. And India found its civilian nuclear program somewhat disrupted by curtailment of outside support after 1974.

Thus a nuclear weapons program, even if desired by a government, can bring both advantages and disadvantages to their promoters. Non-proliferation policy can seek to reduce the motivations for states to go nuclear, when it is possible, through enhancing their security in other ways. For example, the threat of losing American security guarantees helped to persuade South Korea and Taiwan to give up incipient nuclear weapons programs in the 1970s. Threats of sanctions can also create disincentives to creating nuclear weapons. A non-proliferation policy must have two legs: technological controls to buy time and diplomatic measures to reduce incentives.

## DOES THE RATE OF NUCLEAR PROLIFERATION MATTER?

Perhaps it makes no difference whether the twentieth nuclear weapon state joins the ranks in 2000 or 2020. It is more reasonable, however, to expect that the rate is important. If the rate can be slowed, there are better chances of managing the destabilizing effects and the prospects of nuclear use. For every extra year in which an additional country does *not* have nuclear weapons, there is at least some reduction in the likelihood of nuclear war. The rate of proliferation will probably help to influence neighboring governments. If one government sees all of its neighbors going nuclear in rapid succession, it, too, will be more likely to want to obtain nuclear weapons. Otherwise, it risks being surrounded by neighbors whose demands it might be unable to resist.

Such a regional scramble for nuclear weapons would be especially dangerous, because governments fearful of being frozen into inferiority may react drastically in self-defense. The incentives for pre-emptive attacks might increase dramatically. Nations building forces in haste may build less secure or more accident-prone weapons. Controlling the rate of proliferation can help avoid such a scramble.

Fortunately, as we have seen, although building nuclear weapons is not the most difficult of tasks, it is not the easiest either. Most of the countries considered most interested in nuclear weapons still rely on the advanced nations for supplying key technological components. The Pakistanis smuggled blueprints out of the Netherlands and used front companies to buy machinery under false pretenses for their uranium enrichment program. The governments of North America, Europe, and Japan succeeded in slowing this illicit commerce. Since the late 1970s restraint by suppliers has been more effective because suppliers of nuclear technology have agreed to follow common guidelines. Such cooperation helps to weaken the old trick of pitting competing nuclear suppliers against one another until one gives in and sells a dangerous technology for the sake of winning a profitable contract.

Controlling the rate of proliferation requires more than merely preventing nuclear explosions. "Proliferation" consists of more than a single nuclear explosion. It can be thought of as a staircase, with many steps leading up to and then beyond a first nuclear test. The first explosion is the politically important one. Militarily, however, a single crude explosive device does little. To be turned into a weapon, the explosive must first be made small enough to be delivered, and must second be installed in a delivery vehicle. Even after fission weapons are built, the development of thermonuclear weapons can still be slowed. In some cases it may be possible to negotiate "halts" or "plateaus" among regional rivals rather than allow an unrestrained regional nuclear arms race. Such efforts can be important, since the difference between having a crude fission device and a modern nuclear arsenal is as stark as the difference between having an airplane and having an air force.

Thinking about proliferation as a staircase rather than a cliff helps suggest policies for nations at various levels of nuclear development. Governments need not (and should not) wait until a nuclear explosive test is imminent before trying to discourage a government from taking that irreversible step, nor should they give up the effort once a test has occurred. Policy should be designed to keep nuclear programs well below the "first-test" landing and, if a test occurs, to keep them below the "weaponized" landing. It is worth noting that for nearly a decade India did not venture beyond its first test of a fission explosive.

## WHAT HAS BEEN DONE?

Efforts to restrain the spread of nuclear weapons began in 1946 when the United States presented the Baruch Plan in the United Nations. Its failure ushered in a "closed-door" era, during which the United States maintained strict secrecy in the hopes of maintaining its monopoly over nuclear technology. Even our wartime allies and Manhattan Project collaborators were excluded. This effort failed, as the Soviets in 1949 and the British in 1953 detonated nuclear explosives. Apparently, the secret could not be kept.

Subsequently, the United States reversed its closed-door policy. In December 1953 President Eisenhower inaugurated the Atoms for Peace program which directed American nuclear export policy for the next twenty years. Atoms for Peace pledged U.S. assistance in promoting nuclear technology to all those nations which promised, in return, not to use that assistance for military purposes. The idea was to trade technological assistance in non-critical areas for the development of international norms and institutions to help maintain that distinction. It spawned the International Atomic Energy Agency (IAEA) in 1957, which administers a system of safeguards to over 600 nuclear facilities. These safeguards, which consist of automatic monitors, surveillance cameras, and regular visits by inspectors, are designed to detect whether any dangerous nuclear material has been diverted from peaceful uses, so that pressure can be brought to bear on the offending government before it can use the diverted material in a nuclear explosive.

The 1974 Indian nuclear test illustrated the dangers of applying the Atoms for Peace program in too simple-minded a manner. The Indians had used "peaceful" nuclear assistance from Canada and the United States to produce the plutonium for their "peaceful" nuclear device. The facilities had not been safeguarded, and the Atoms for Peace agreements with India had been loosely written to permit "peaceful uses" without excluding "peaceful explosions." The Indians made full use of the legal loophole and could hardly be compelled to unlearn nuclear technology in the aftermath. The Indian test made suppliers more conscious of the fact that weapons and peaceful technology could not be perfectly insulated from each other.

The result was the establishment of the Nuclear Suppliers Group, which published new guidelines for nuclear commerce in January 1978. Its 15 members—including Canada, France, Great Britain, Japan, the Soviet Union, the United States, and West Germany—agreed henceforth to exercise restraint in exporting enrichment and reprocessing technology, to safeguard all exports, to consult in cases that might require sanctions, and generally to try to isolate commercial competition for nuclear exports from non-proliferation requirements. In broad outline, the guidelines have worked well, though difference of interpretation in gray areas still occur. The United States tends to lead in urging restraint of nuclear trade. Some Europeans, on the other hand, argue that cooperation with the non-nuclear weapon states helps reduce the political incentives for proliferation, and futile efforts to restrict *all* technology transfers would provoke rather than prevent nuclear weapons spread by weakening support for the Non-Proliferation Treaty (NPT).

That treaty is the centerpiece of postwar non-proliferation efforts. The NPT was signed in 1968 and entered into force in 1970. The non-nuclear weapon states undertake not to transfer or receive any nuclear weapons (Articles I and II), and to submit all their source or special fissionable material to IAEA safeguards (Article III); the nuclear weapons states promise "the fullest possible exchange" of nuclear technology (Article IV), provision of the potential benefits from any peaceful applications of nuclear explosions (Article V), and good-faith negotiations on effective arms control and disarmament measures (Article VI). With 115 members, the NPT enjoys widespread support, but several significant holdouts remain: Argentina, Brazil, China, France, India, Israel, Pakistan, South Africa, and Spain.

Some of the holdouts condemn the treaty's discrimination between the nuclear haves and the have-nots, and believe that ratification of the treaty surrenders valuable bargaining leverage in return for few tangible benefits. Nuclear suppliers' concerns over the dangers of sensitive nuclear technology exports have dampened their vigor in implementing Article IV. Peaceful nuclear explosions are now considered indistinguishable from weapons tests and devoid of practical utility, which reduces the value of Article V. And other parties complain that the U.S. and Soviet Union have not lived up to Article VI by harnessing their strategic arsenals. Nevertheless, the NPT has succeeded in reinforcing the global presumption that proliferation is bad, and that its perpetrators must pay the political costs involved in flouting international consensus. In a world of sovereign states this is no small achievement, and is certainly a necessary, if not a sufficient, basis for a policy of slowing nuclear spread.

## CURRENT POLICY ISSUES

In considering how to deal with today's non-proliferation problems, it is important to keep the issue in perspective. Non-proliferation is not a foreign policy. It is one objective of a foreign policy, which must be weighed against conflicting objectives in order to achieve as much as possible, in a disorderly world. The attention given to proliferation in the late 1970s raised its priority for many governments. This priority has been diminished somewhat under the Reagan administration. While the administration has followed the main lines of policy established in the mid-1970s, it has been something like a train that follows the main tracks, but with little steam in the engine and subject to minor derailments. The emphasis on East-West conflict led to neglect of some areas of non-proliferation cooperation with the Soviet Union. It is worth noting that historically self-interest has frequently led the rival superpowers to cooperate in slowing the spread of nuclear weapons.

## SECURITY ASSISTANCE AND PROLIFERATION

If governments desire nuclear weapons to enhance their security, American military assistance or alliance policy might reduce the incentives to go nuclear. This has certainly been crucial in the case of some major allies, as well as for South Korea and Taiwan. But it is difficult to extend security guarantees to all countries—witness South Africa. And the use of conventional military assistance to meet security concerns—as in the Pakistan case—runs the risk that the country will eventually take the carrot offered and then run in a nuclear direction anyway, and perhaps even use the conventional weapons as delivery systems. Security guarantees and assistance will remain vital components of an effective non-proliferation policy, but they alone will not be sufficient or easy to apply.

## NUCLEAR ENERGY AND WEAPON PROLIFERATION

Abolishing nuclear energy and nuclear exports would not solve proliferation problems because there are other paths to the making of bombs. Moreover, a totally restrictive policy on nuclear exports would rend the fabric of international institutions (the IAEA and NPT) purchased at some expense through the Atoms for Peace approach. Also, threat of loss of nuclear supply can provide important leverage over non-nuclear weapon states who might be tempted to transgress by crossing the line between peaceful and weapons uses.

At the same time, the lessons of the Indian explosion in May 1974 should not be forgotten. Important steps remain to be taken, such as technical improvement of IAEA safeguards, full-scope safeguards (which means refusal to ship technology and materials to countries with *any* unsafeguarded facilities, whether imported or indigenously developed), special arrangements for managing plutonium and highly enriched uranium, and international provisions for the storage of spent nuclear fuel, which contains plutonium.

## NUCLEAR PROLIFERATION AND ARMS CONTROL

The spread of nuclear weapons to more states is sometimes called horizontal proliferation, while the increase of nuclear weapons within an existing nuclear arsenal is called vertical proliferation. Defense specialists in the developing world have insisted that horizontal and vertical proliferation are linked, and that the failure of the Americans and Soviets to restrain their own nuclear arsenals dooms to failure all efforts to stop horizontal proliferation.

This view is too simplistic. The decision to obtain or not to obtain nuclear weapons is critically important to all governments and is made through careful consideration of how nuclear weapons will affect national security. This depends far more on delicate regional balances of power or security guarantees than upon whether the United States and the Soviet Union sign a new arms control agreement.

Nevertheless, arms control can significantly help nonproliferation. To profess indifference to the superpower nuclear arms relationship, in particular the U.S.-Soviet negotiations, can weaken non-proliferation in two ways. First, a disdain for the arms control institutions and concerns expressed by non-weapon states can exacerbate the claim by less developed countries that the nuclear powers discriminate against them. And considerations of prestige and discrimination are part of the incentives to go nuclear for some countries. Second, nuclear doctrines and deployments that stress the usefulness of nuclear weapons for war-fighting may increase the credibility of deterrence under certain circumstances, but they also tend to make nuclear weapons look more attractive to others. If states that have deliberately eschewed nuclear weapons see them treated increasingly like conventional defensive weapons, they may one day reconsider the decision to forgo them.

## REGIONAL AGREEMENTS

Diplomacy at the regional level deserves special effort, since that is the level where incentives and disincentives are strongest. Regional agreements can reinforce the NPT and IAEA regime. For example, the 1967 Treaty of Tlatelolco established a Nuclear Weapon-Free Zone in Latin America. Brazil refused to sign the NPT, on the grounds that it is discriminatory, but ratified the Treaty of Tlatelolco. The only two holdouts are Argentina and Cuba; the former promised to ratify Tlatelolco but still has not.

In regions such as South Asia or the Mideast where states have crept close to or across the first explosion threshold, a non-explosion or "no-further explosions" zone might be useful. Hostility within each region creates enormous political obstacles. But perhaps these could be overcome. For example, it might be possible to generalize the existing Israeli statement that they will not be the first to introduce nuclear weapons into the Mideast. Such an agreement would be difficult to achieve and might require input from and cooperation between the two superpowers, but it is not impossible.

## SANCTIONS AGAINST PROLIFERATORS

From time to time, punishment of governments that do violate IAEA safeguards or test nuclear weapons has been urged, in the belief that a harsh international reaction could convince other would-be proliferators that they would lose more than they would gain by following suit. The IAEA safeguard system is like a burglar alarm. If the alarm works but the policymakers do not react, it has little effect as a deterrent in the future. This kind of situation tempts nuclear exporters to seek commercial advantage, and each superpower to seek political advantage, by reacting mildly to any new state that builds nuclear weapons. For instance, neither the Americans nor the Soviets took major steps against India in 1974, although subsequent responses by Canada and others did seriously slow the Indian nuclear program. While sanctions cannot be absolute (since other diplomatic interests will persist), they can be used to show that proliferation is costly and to deter further steps up the proliferation staircase. Given technological spread, proliferation will be more feasible over time. It is critical that proliferation be seen as politically costly.

## CONCLUSION

Nuclear proliferation has not proceeded as rapidly as President Kennedy predicted. The reason, in many cases, is not that governments could not acquire nuclear weapons, but that they chose to remain non-nuclear. The continuation of this fortunate situation should be encouraged. In other cases, states lack the technological infrastructure and material. This too can be prolonged.

Though proliferation is only one part of the overall problem of living with nuclear weapons, it is a part that will always be with us. There will always be someone, whether a political leader or terrorist or both, who would gladly use nuclear weapons to threaten the destruction of his adversaries. Any mishap could be catastrophic. Complacency in non-proliferation policy is dangerous.

Governments must constantly be vigilant if they wish to minimize the rate of the spread of nuclear weapons. A steady policy should try to persuade governments at every step of the nuclear staircase from ascending to more dangerous ones. A complacent policy will be reduced to frantic efforts at "crisis management" as nations come close to the nuclear threshold.

The problem of proliferation is therefore a long-range problem which demands long-range vision and constant effort. There is a temptation to downplay the importance of non-proliferation policy because its impact is not always dramatic and it is often expensive in the short run. Such temptations must be resisted if the world is to continue living with nuclear weapons. And living with nuclear weapons, as will be discussed in the following final chapter, is the only real alternative to future disaster.

# 11

# Living with Nuclear Weapons: Is There a Choice?

This book began by recalling a myth from ancient Greece: the story of Prometheus, whose crime was giving fire to mankind and whose punishment was a life of dread. Since 1945 humanity has existed, like Prometheus, with recurrent fear of atomic fire. Yet if we are to continue living in the nuclear world another character from Greek mythology must also be our model. This is Sisyphus, whom the gods ordered to push a block of stone up a mountainside. Whenever he approached the summit, he was forced back by the weight of the stone. But each time Sisyphus began his task anew, an enduring effort to attain an unattainable goal.

Like Sisyphus, modern man continually pursues an unreachable objective—absolute security—only to find the weight of political rivalries, conflicting interests, and opposing ideologies pushing back against him. Perfect security is a goal that can never be achieved; it can only be approached. But persisting in the effort is important because it is only through such actions that the likelihood of war can be reduced, even if the possibility of war cannot be banished altogether.

Preceding chapters have discussed current nuclear issues and suggested alternative policies that may contribute to the unending pursuit of security in the nuclear world. An approach combining arms control when possible and arms improvement when necessary is a useful guide, but is also only a short-term vision. This chapter is about a longer-term question: Can humanity continue living with nuclear weapons? And if so, how?

## IS NUCLEAR WAR INEVITABLE?

An "absolute" vision of the nuclear future exists today. This vision is becoming more widespread and counsels that a nuclear holocaust is incvitable unless complete nuclear disarmament is achieved. This prediction is not of a world of enduring efforts to achieve security, but rather an either/or future: either complete success or complete failure; either global peace and disarmament or global nuclear holocaust.

Jonathan Schell, in *The Fate of the Earth*, has most eloquently preached this either/or philosophy:

> If we are honest with ourselves we have to admit that unless we rid ourselves of our nuclear arsenals a holocaust not only *might* occur but *will* occur—if not today, then tomorrow; if not this year, then the next. We have come to live on borrowed time: every year of continued human life on earth is a borrowed year, every day a borrowed day.[1]

This either/or vision is appealing, but misleading. It is appealing because it calls for action. And action is necessary. It is misleading because the future is not limited to a choice between nuclear holocaust and universal disarmament.

It is conceivable to defend predictions such as C. P. Snow's that nuclear war was certain within ten years, on the grounds that such warnings will be justified if war takes place in a hundred years.[2] But the difference between a decade and a century makes all the difference in the world when it comes to dealing with our nuclear predicament. Over a century, profound changes that reduce the risk of nuclear war are possible, partly as the result of deliberate, concerted actions. And ironically, as

---

**C. P. Snow's 1960 Prediction:**

We are faced with an either/or and we haven't much time. . . . The *either* is acceptance of a restriction of nuclear armaments. . . . The *or* is not a risk but a certainty. It is this: there is no agreement on tests. The nuclear arms race between the United States and the Soviet Union not only continues but accelerates. Other countries join in. Within, at most, six years China and six other states have a stock of nuclear bombs. Within, at the most, ten years, some of those bombs are going to go off. . . . That is a certainty. . . .

SOURCE: C. P. Snow, "Risk of Disaster or a Certainty," reprinted in, *New York Times,* August 17, 1981.

---

we argued in Chapter 9, some efforts to force profound changes within a decade could actually increase the prospect of nuclear use by encouraging miscalculations.

The either/or mentality can also lead to a false sense of despair, with very unfortunate consequences. Belief that nuclear war is inevitable can counsel a resignation or fatalism which would divert energy from practical political steps and thus make war more likely.

Modest steps matter. In the short run, we can take steps to reduce the probability of nuclear war, while gradually trying to improve international relations. And a future made up of short runs which improve by 1% a year would mean a dramatically different world within our children's lifetimes.

We do not belittle the central question raised by the either/or approach: Is nuclear war inevitable in a world of deterrence? The answer depends on two other questions: How long are we talking about? What else is going to happen?

Since humans are neither perfect nor perfectly rational, it would be foolish to deny that there is some chance of deterrence failing—perhaps along one of the scenarios traced in Chapter 3. Even if that chance were low, it would eventually occur if the situation went on long enough. Eventually even the most skillful juggler is likely to drop a ball. But if there is enough time, the situation can be changed; the juggling game can be cautiously brought to an end. Or to alter the metaphor, if two people who strongly dislike each other are locked in a small room and armed only with hand grenades, it is not inevitable that they blow each other up; they may eventually learn how to live together.

As we argued in Chapter 9, nuclear disarmament may be an appropriate goal for the long term, but its successful achievement depends upon political preconditions and trust that can only be built slowly. Conventional weapons would still exist and the danger of conventional war might be increased if nuclear disarmament came too quickly. Moreover, premature disarmament in the absence of such political preconditions could enhance the risks of renewed nuclear arms races and wars. But if there is enough time—that is, if we continually take steps to reduce the risk of nuclear war—then the situation may change.

The nuclear dilemma is serious, the most serious danger mankind faces. But there is no reason to assume that absolute solutions—either holocaust or disarmament—are the only answers mankind is capable of developing. History shows that many important events have occurred in international relations over long periods of time. War is not the inevitable result of a rivalry between two nations. It has not been so in the past and need not be so in the future. It is especially misleading to focus on current dangers of war and to think that the technical and political environment of the future will remain unchanged while the future probability of war increases. Other factors that influence the likelihood of war can change too. Many future worlds are possible. The point is perhaps best understood by examining what factors might affect the prospects for peace in the future. We will, therefore, discuss what one can reasonably expect to happen in the next four decades. Are the trends mainly encouraging, or discouraging?

## WHAT COULD HAPPEN BY 2020?
## HOPES AND FEARS

The world has seen many changes in the years since the atomic bomb was invented. What could occur in the next four decades other than holocaust or disarmament? Forty years ago, we and the Soviets were allies. Forty years forward, it is not farfetched to imagine a less hostile relationship between us than now exists. Forty years back, there were no nuclear ballistic missiles. Forty years forward could see new technologies of defense against them. New alliances may form; countries may change; new institutions may be developed; loyalties may gradually evolve beyond the national level. Or change may come from a shocking event such as a nuclear accident or war in a remote region.

Extreme modesty is, of course, necessary whenever making long-range forecasts: the likelihood of the developments described below cannot be estimated with any degree of certainty. Two things *are* certain, however. First, our actions can influence the prospects of specified events occurring. Second, it is not just an isolated development but rather the conjunction of several that can influence the likelihood of war. In other words, even minor progress, if it occurs in several of the areas described below, can reduce the risks of war. Progress in one area can also improve progress in other areas.

The possible developments described below are provided as suggestions, not as the only possibilities or as certainties. They are given as reasons for rejecting despair, not as excuses for complacency. For indeed, complacency will diminish even the limited hopes for the future.

### TRENDS IN ARMS AND ARMS CONTROL

Two very important developments in nuclear weaponry could occur by 2020. The system of nuclear deterrence, which has since 1945 depended on the threat of retaliation, might in the future be based on defensive weaponry. Arms control, which has had limited, although still important, success thus far in the nuclear age might have more significant influence in the future.

The difficulties that have plagued efforts to build a defense against nuclear weapons in the past will continue to exist in the future. But unforeseen technological advances might possibly increase the prospects of what strategists call a "defense-dominated" nuclear system. There is little reason to expect such a technological switch from offense to defense, but it is not out of the question.

In such a world the consequences of a breakdown of deterrence might be less catastrophic than in the current world of near total mutual vulnerability. And, depending on the technology used, the incentives for increased arms racing might be diminished. That is the good news with respect to defensive systems. The bad news is that the degree to which such an evolution in nuclear deterrence would reduce the likelihood of war is not clear.

Potential "destabilizing" effects of a defense-dominated system would depend in part on how the superpowers got there: if the Soviet Union developed a workable defensive system before the United States, for example, American officials would fear that Soviet incentives to avoid nuclear war would be diminished. A defense-dominated world might also be less stable depending on how perfect defense systems were believed to be. In such a world, there might be heightened incentives for surprise attack, or for efforts to develop new, more decisive offensive systems. On the other hand, if governments were absolutely certain that nuclear attack or retaliation was impossible in all circumstances, might this not increase the likelihood of other, conventional conflicts?

In the United States today, overall disappointment in the process of arms control is expressed far more often than is an appreciation of its limited successes. As we saw in Chapter 9, while arms control has not led to deep reductions, it has helped to increase transparency and communication and thus to limit some of the worst-case assumptions that the two sides otherwise might have made. It has also produced some modest but useful agreements. It would be misleading to minimize the potential progress in this area over the next forty years. As in the recent past, negotiated arms control between the superpowers in the future will not end their profound political rivalry. But as in the past, arms control can have important effects in reducing destabilizing technology, producing predictability in arms programs, and even in saving money. In the long run incremental progress is incrementally more important.

Indeed, as discussed earlier, the common view of an ever escalating nuclear arms race in the post-1945 era is not entirely accurate. To give two important examples, there are today a clear restriction on anti-ballistic missile systems and a tacitly agreed-upon ceiling on Soviet and American offensive strategic nuclear weaponry, albeit a ceiling which remains in an unratified treaty. Arms control in the future should neither be expected to solve all problems nor be ignored. The degree to which it can help produce stability will, at least in large part, depend upon the political relations between the United States and the Soviet Union.

## TRENDS IN U.S.-SOVIET RELATIONS

Soviet-American relations have had their ups and downs. Wartime alliance was followed by a Cold War hostility in which the two sides barely communicated in the early 1950s. In the early 1970s we witnessed a gradual relaxation which came to fruition as "détente." Now we're involved in a return to hostility, which grew out of the continued expansion of Soviet defense spending and events such as the invasion of Afghanistan.

In view of recent tensions, some observers have spoken of a new Cold War. But U.S.-Soviet relations today are quite different from what they were at the height of the Cold War. Both sides are living not only by the ABM Treaty but largely by the unratified SALT II Treaty. New arms control talks have been launched. Despite embargoes, trade continues, as do tourism and scientific exchanges. The degree of communication in the relationship is much greater than during the Cold War era.

Another important change has occured over the past four decades. Through trial and error the superpowers have developed some prudent practices for handling crises.

Both sides continue to avoid direct clash of forces; each has avoided the use of nuclear weapons, and observes some restraint in the other side's sphere of dominant influence. Some crises have been deliberately provoked (over Berlin, from 1948 to 1961) or have arisen from a regional conflict, but they have been managed without war or humiliation. Others have been avoided, often because one or the other superpower chose not to treat an event as a challenge. In addition to arms talks, the two sides have agreed not to interfere with each other's satellite surveillance, and meet regularly to discuss their observance of existing agreements, as well as other subjects, such as slowing nuclear spread. There is still a long way to go, but as we saw in Chapter 9, a variety of suggestions have been made for enhancing such stabilizing practices.

There is also a prospect of gradual change in the Soviet Union over the next forty years. As previously stated, American understanding of the Soviet Union is unfortunately limited. The combination of Communist ideology and Russian history has produced a society which is closed and secretive. There is not the rich web of formal and informal contacts we enjoy with other societies, and, as we have said in Chapter 2, this makes the Soviet Union something of a "black box" to us. The U.S. has repeatedly been surprised by Soviet moves—in southern and eastern Africa, into Afghanistan—and often either underestimated their efforts (as in the realm of nuclear arms, in the 1960s) or exaggerated their significance (as at the time of the Korean War).

On the other hand, the United States has also confused the Soviet Union by our extraordinary openness and cacophony of views. Such confusion and misreading of intentions can lead to miscalculation. For example, Stalin was probably surprised by our response in Korea shortly after we had declared the area outside our defense perimeter; Khrushchev may have been taken aback by the strength of our reaction to the missiles in Cuba; and Brezhnev may not have expected our grain embargo to follow the 1980 invasion of Afghanistan when our reactions to the initial Communist coup in 1978 were so relaxed. Had the Soviets understood American politics better, they might have foreseen how a number of their actions in the 1970s could contribute to the undermining of détente.

There is no consensus among Western observers of the Soviet Union over the prospects for future evolution in the Soviet system or even on how to interpret the changes that have taken place in the past few decades. Some Americans believe that the "mellowing of Soviet power" which George Kennan described as the objective of containment in 1947 has to some extent taken place. Others argue that the Soviet leadership has changed its aspirations only in less significant ways.

Most observers would agree, however, that over the past forty years there has been progress, albeit glacial and uneven, on a different dimension—the degree of Soviet openness and communication with the outside world. Andropov's Soviet Union is very different from the country that Stalin ruled until 1953. The Soviet economy is less autarkic, there are more exchanges with the West, and there is a better awareness of American politics. When Stalin did not like the predictions of his Institute of World Economy, he abolished it. Studies of the outside world were cast in a rigid ideological mold. Today there are more Soviets in influential positions with a greater sense of the reality of the outside world. This need not make them more benign in their intentions toward us, but it may help to reduce the prospects of miscalculation. The prospect of gradually improving transparency and communication—to open rays of light into the black box—is also a reasonable expectation over the next forty years.

In addition, the U.S. may work for gradual improvements in its policy toward the Soviet Union by trying to give clearer and more consistent signals and by avoiding the past excesses of optimism and pessimism that have so characterized its policy. Americans may come to realize that they will have to live with a Soviet society they dislike for a long time, and that they will not be able to change that society quickly, if at all. The problem is one to be managed and gradually improved, not quickly solved. The growing domestic problems in the Soviet empire—economic and political crises both inside the USSR and in Eastern Europe—are often cited today as reason for hope in the future. This may be true, but the international effects of such developments are not either necessarily or uniformly positive. American enthusiasm for the eventual breakup of the Soviet empire may come to be tempered by the memory of the fatal role the decline of Austria-Hungary played in 1914.

In short, improved Soviet-American relations are critical to efforts to reduce the probability of deterrence breaking down. Particularly important, as we saw in Chapter 3, are steps to improve transparency and communication in order to avoid war by miscalculation. The Western world's ability to change the Soviet Union is limited, but change does occur, even if at a slow pace. It is not likely that Soviet-American relations forty years from now will be like British-American relations today, but it is not unreasonable to believe that they can be much better than they are at present.

## WORRIES AND DILEMMAS

As we said earlier, these possible improvements should not encourage complacency, for they depend on our efforts. And some stark reasons for concern still remain. These concerns have emerged from the evolution of nuclear weapons and current political problems. They will not go away by themselves.

The lessons of the past are both gloomy and only partly relevant. Chances for peace, in earlier times, came about in regional areas of peace and security, in balance-of-power systems, and in empires. But as we saw in Chapter 2, the conditions that made balance-of-power systems possible and effective are missing. A world empire could only be established through war. And regional areas of peace are never more than oases; today the Soviet-American contest always tends to intrude, and to disrupt them.

The superpowers face two formidable dilemmas. On the one hand, if deterrence is entirely successful in averting any resort to nuclear weapons, won't nations feel more confident again about launching conventional wars? But if in order to deter these one tries to lower the nuclear threshold—to take measures that suggest a plausible early use of nuclear weapons—won't such measures be dangerous (and scare one's own population or allies)? On the other hand, once nuclear weapons have been used, what are the possibilities of control? A limited and selective use may appear controllable, but what if it fails to stop an opponent: does one then accept defeat rather than escalate?

Moreover, the superpowers are not the only players in the game. Over the next forty years, more states are bound to acquire nuclear weaponry—though how many is far from certain. Some regional rivals may learn prudence; but life in a nuclear-armed crowd is a foreboding future. Many observers feel that the highest probability of nuclear weapons being used in coming decades will be among insecure regional states with weak political and technical systems for commanding and controlling their new nuclear weapons. Optimists argue that the shock of such nuclear use could well precipitate major progress toward more rigorous control of nuclear weaponry among the superpowers. Pessimists merely see the forty-year taboo on nuclear use broken with few positive lessons learned and a danger of the superpowers becoming involved.

Such uncertainties and dilemmas suggest three views of possible futures in the next four decades. The "ideal" one envisages a future much like the recent past: no direct military clashes between the superpowers, a very slow spread of nuclear capabilities, serious progress in arms control, and a reduction in world violence. Even in this most optimistic view of a world where the uses of force are kept limited or avoided altogether, the causes of conflict among states are never eradicated or resolved. Thus the risk of new violence, and of superpower involvement, never entirely dies. A gloomier view envisages a gradual weakening of the restraints on war, a rapid spread of nuclear weaponry, lesser states resorting to violence more freely, and a grave risk of war between the superpowers arising out of a serious crisis. An intermediate view predicts continuing nuclear deterrence, some nuclear spread, and some arms control as well as an increase in the risk of Third World nuclear wars or conventional confrontation between the superpowers.

No one knows which of these visions of the future is true. What is certain is that our actions can shape the future, can make it more secure or more dangerous. Nuclear war is not inevitable; nor, unfortunately, are the steps necessary to reduce humanity's nuclear dangers. The steps must be taken; they will not be achieved without effort.

## WHAT SHOULD BE DONE?

Precisely because the worst could happen, and the best requires deliberate efforts, one must ask what should be done, in a world that is not going to "reinvent politics" or abolish states or soon disarm them, in order to avoid a nuclear holocaust. One can look at the problem in two ways—what are our moral imperatives, and what should be our political objectives—as long as we remember that in international affairs as in all other areas of human action, ethical action and practical action are really inseparable: ethical rules must take political realities into account, and practical action always has moral implications and effects.

### MORAL CONSTRAINTS ON STRATEGY

Strategy and morality are often considered to be antithetical, as in the common phrase "All's fair in love and war." But few individuals, when they repeat this aphorism, actually mean what they are saying: that any dishonesty is fair in romance and any kind of violence is justified in warfare. What is really meant is that moral standards are made more difficult—and therefore are followed less often and often less strictly—when extreme competition rules. But people still apply moral standards when thinking about such problems. Even people who say "All's fair" think and feel "This is not right" when their moral standards are ignored or flaunted.

Moral considerations matter in strategic debates primarily because nuclear strategy involves the fate of millions of innocent people. In addition, in a democracy, public perceptions of the ethical soundness of a government policy or strategy can turn public support away from government actions, in peacetime or in war. Public support is always the acid test of a democracy's behavior in international relations.

Certain moral standards are part of what we are trying to secure when we talk about national security. We expect our government to behave morally as much as possible as much of the time as possible. We also expect the government to protect our lives and our property, and if this goal can only be achieved through what we think of as immoral actions, then a dilemma exists.

It is never easy to decide between two moral objectives that are in conflict. It is important to recognize this sort of conflict whenever it arises, even if it cannot be resolved. Ignoring the conflict does not make it go away.

It is often argued, for example, that the real problem in the Nuclear Age is the existence of sovereign states. If one could get rid of national sovereignty, then one could get rid of these horrible weapons.

That may be correct, but what this cold phrase "national sovereignty" really means is independence, the moral right of individuals to choose their own form of government and their preferred way of life. Preserving such rights is a moral objective and should be stated as such. The claim that "national sovereignty" is the problem is therefore misleading. Securing national sovereignty is a moral goal worth pursuing; indeed all nations pursue it. But the protection of our sovereignty by nuclear weapons must not place other innocent people at high risk. This sets limits on what is justifiable in nuclear strategy.

The dilemma is that policies and strategies deemed necessary to achieve the moral objective of security might not be consistent with the moral goal of trying to act in a way that respects the right of many innocent people to survive. The question is, therefore, What kinds of military actions are ethical in wartime and what kinds of strategies are ethical in peace? Have nuclear weapons shattered any hope for moral behavior?

## THREE MORAL DILEMMAS

As long as nations have fought wars efforts have been made to place moral restraints on the violence unleashed. Medieval writers on the subject sought to encourage what they called a just-war theory. Justice in warfare required several conditions: a good cause (for example, self-defense rather than aggression); some proportion between the ends sought and the means used; and keeping the distinction between civilians and combatants, between innocent by-standers and soldiers fighting a war. Nations at war have never been able to follow this moral distinction with com-plete success, but many have tried. The history of warfare contains many stories of statesmen, generals, even com-mon foot soldiers attempting to spare civilian lives even in the midst of fighting. Such actions are efforts to maintain a sense of the moral world even in the hell of war.

Have nuclear weapons made such efforts futile and destroyed the just-war tradition?

Not completely, although they have shaken some of its assumptions. Aggression can still be condemned, and in principle one can conceive of small-scale use of very low-yield nuclear weapons which would do less destruc-tion than conventional bombs (thus meeting the criterion of proportion), and allow discrimination between enemy soldiers and civilians. The key question, however, is whether the violence would remain at that level. Once the nuclear threshold has been crossed, will conflict escalate to large-scale nuclear war where the distinction between civilians and soldiers is lost in blind ferocity, and all sense of proportion is obliterated? No one knows. And therefore, however just the cause involved, unintended consequences could transform a limited nuclear use into a highly im-moral action. Certainly it is hard to envisage any circum-stances in which a nuclear war that would destroy the societies in conflict would be morally justifiable.

The Catholic bishops of the United States are address-ing these issues. One of the dilemmas they have discussed is whether it can ever be moral to initiate the use of nuclear weapons, even if a conventional war is being lost. If one believes that escalation is unlikely to be controlled and that a full-scale nuclear exchange would be immoral, can initiating the use of nuclear weapons ever be morally justified?

The dilemma arises because it is not known whether, in a conventional war, the use of nuclear weapons in an extremely limited fashion, to destroy a Soviet radar site for example (see Chapter 3) would be more likely to lead to nuclear escalation or to stop the conventional war. If initiating the use of nuclear weapons led to escalation, the action would have been immoral. But if it led to a quick end of the conventional war in Europe, might not the action be seen as moral? Perhaps. But every effort would have to be made to keep close control of the risks (i.e., small weapons; no delegation of authority to dispersed military units; continual communications with the Soviet Union; a clear idea of how to terminate the conflict, etc.). Even then, given the enormous cost of the unintended consequences, and the uncertainty about reaching the intended ones (a quick de-escalation or end of violence), such an action could only be a last resort. What morality and prudence dictate is "no early use" of nuclear weapons a policy and strategy, and a highly selective and limited use if it should come to that; indeed, morality and prudence suggest that were deterrence to fail, one should have the means to carry out an alternative, non-nuclear strategy.

This brings us to the second dilemma that the bishops have raised: Can it be right to have nuclear forces and a targeting doctrine that deliberately aim at civilians? The bishops believe not. Many others differ over this issue. Some have argued that assured destruction is an immoral doctrine because it rests on the deterrent threat of disproportionate damage to civilians and industry. The American government does not aim its weapons at the Soviet population per se, and ever since the 1950s our doctrine has in practice involved military targets. But many people also powerfully argue that counter-force targeting is immoral because it makes nuclear weapons seem more usable, and requires ever more war-fighting capabilities: there is no limit on the number of targets and weapons, thus the insatiable needs of the nuclear arsenal will compete with other moral claims on the resources of our society. Moreover, destruction of large parts of civilian society is an unavoidable part of any large-scale strategic nuclear war.

Targeting certainly raises an important moral issue. But it is not the theology of "counter-force versus counter-city." The issue is whether our strategy and arsenal can reduce the prospect of war in a time of crisis. Since the moral claims for deterrence rest on averting large-scale nuclear war, the truly immoral behavior is to have nuclear force and doctrines that invite pre-emptive attack by one's opponent or by oneself. For example, a force that is highly lethal and highly vulnerable at the same time will tempt a political leader to "use it or lose it" at a time of crisis. Even an invulnerable but complete counter-silo capability may incite one's opponent to use his vulnerable missiles against some enemy targets before the missiles are lost. Morality is not just about choices at a time of crisis; it can also be about averting terrible choices at a time of crisis. The crucial moral question about force posture and targeting doctrine therefore is: How can our current actions ensure that even in a deep crisis no general on either side can persuasively argue that it is imperative to launch his nation's strategic forces because they might otherwise be lost?

A third dilemma raised by the bishops' letter concerns neither the use nor the specific targets of nuclear weapons, but the morality of deterrence itself. It can be called the "intentions versus consequences" dilemma: Is it justifiable to threaten a nuclear attack that might destroy innocent civilians if the intention is to deter nuclear war altogether? Even if the consequences of the threat are moral—if deterrence works, in other words—is making the threat itself morally acceptable? Some theologians who stress the importance of intent believe it is not, and that therefore the whole notion of nuclear deterrence is morally unsound. They argue that it is wrong to threaten what it is wrong to do. Others would place more stress on consequences. For example, we may believe it is wrong to kill another person, but believe it moral to threaten to kill someone who is about to attack our children if such a threat would deter the act.

Most people judge the morality of actions on their intentions and their consequences. Moreover, in deterrence our intentions are not to do evil. Our threat is intended to avoid both the horrible outcome of nuclear war and aggressive behavior by the other side. Our intent in making the threat is not immoral, and the consequences depend in part upon the intentions of the other side. On the contrary, to remove the threat altogether—because it is evil to threaten to kill entire populations, or to threaten to attack military targets with weapons that are likely to be neither discriminating nor controllable—might indeed have disastrous moral effects, if it incites one's adversary to take greater risks, and thereby made war more likely.

While we differ with some details raised by the bishops' arguments about nuclear weapons, we are sympathetic to their overall conclusion that nuclear deterrence is morally tolerable as long as there is no acceptable alternative means to prevent a feared action and the intent is to avert the greater evil of nuclear war. We agree with the bishops that nuclear deterrence is only conditionally moral; the condition being that we make genuine efforts to reduce dependence on nuclear deterrence over the long run. To resort to nuclear deterrence in order to protect low stakes is a morally and politically nasty bluff. To resort to nuclear deterrence to protect *high* stakes makes political and moral sense only if the credibility of the threat is enhanced by the availability of non-nuclear weapons, which may make the actual execution of the threat unnecessary.

Those who disagree with this position would argue that deterrence implies some risk of nuclear war, and that nothing is worth nuclear war, particularly if it would end life on earth. This might be obvious if a breakdown of deterrence would really end life on earth. Trust in the existence of future generations pervades our daily life. We seek to preserve the environment, to save money, to raise children properly, all the time assuming that life will continue to exist. But a nuclear war between the superpowers today would most likely not end all human life on earth. A critical moral goal should be to avoid passing that awful threshold.

Of course that is not enough. The current inventory of 50,000 weapons could wreak indescribable devastation. Even if its use would not end human life, it would destroy the human society we now know and cherish. But that does not mean one could not imagine a moral use of nuclear weapons. Suppose a nuclear war were limited, and the alternative was to succumb to a Hitler-type domination of the world in which tens of millions of innocent people would be exterminated without war. Many people would think such a war worth fighting. Fortunately, that is not our current situation.

Even if one believes that nothing is worth fighting nuclear war, it does not follow that nothing is worth the risk of nuclear war. Imagine, for the purposes of argument, a tiny risk of a nuclear war occurring in the first place, and only a small risk of it escalating to a large scale if it did break out. But imagine that the threat of that risk helped to prevent large-scale conventional war that would cost tens of millions of innocent lives as occurred in the Second World War. Would it be immoral to rely on a small risk of nuclear war to avoid the higher probability of large-scale conventional war? We think not—so long as efforts are made to keep the risks as low as possible, and so long as one realizes that this is only an interim solution. A complacency that led one to relax about the dangers of relying on nuclear deterrence could become the source of great immorality. But so also would a utopianism which could raise both nuclear and conventional risks.

In short, nuclear deterrence can be tolerated, but never liked. Deterrence can be seen as a necessary evil. Because it is necessary, one cannot abandon it carelessly; because it is evil, one must strive to rely on it less.

How might this be done? Steps to reduce dependence on nuclear deterrence will necessarily involve both arms control and gradual efforts to transform political relationships. We are thus led back to political imperatives.

## POLITICAL IMPERATIVES: THE WEAPONS

Living with nuclear and with conventional weapons will require deliberate efforts to make sure that in a crisis, the existence of certain weapons, or the presence of armed forces, does not tempt a party to attack, or set in motion a mechanism that leaves little leeway for diplomacy, or make a restoration of peace more difficult if war breaks out. Literally, it is true that only people, or states, cause conflicts, and that weapons do not. But weapons tempt: people or states with certain arms can do far more harm, and have greater opportunities to do harm, than people or states without such weapons.

In the long run, insofar as nuclear weapons are concerned, what each superpower[3] needs for the deterrence of nuclear or major conventional attacks on itself and its main allies is the capacity for assured destruction (which requires a moderate number of survivable but not particularly accurate weapons) and a *limited* capacity for actual warfare. A complete counter-force capability would be disastrous for crisis stability if it consisted of vulnerable forces; and even a complete invulnerable counter-force capability might incite the opponent to strike first in order to use his vulnerable weapons.

This means that, in the long run, there is a political imperative to stabilize the arms race by avoiding the endless production and deployment of counter-force weapons. Such a stabilization would entail considerable reductions in numbers. It would also require an improvement in controls and communications, as well as measures limiting the development of anti-satellite systems.

These objectives should be pursued by a mix of unilateral and negotiated measures. Any unilateral actions should avoid significantly reducing crisis stability. Some weapons, such as some short-range battlefield nuclear weapons, might be withdrawn after consultations with our allies but not necessarily after negotiations with the Soviets. In negotiations, efforts can be made not only to achieve reductions, but also to enhance communications and develop confidence-building measures.

Nuclear reductions and a strengthening of crisis stability risk, as we know, making the world safe for conventional war—a danger in itself, with the additional risk that such a war may not remain conventional if the superpowers are involved. Controls on conventional weapons have rarely been achieved. Many states believe conventional weapons, unlike nuclear weapons, can be safely used for political gain. Thus, one can no longer separate a consideration of the arms from a discussion of the underlying political issues that may provoke a resort to war.

## POLITICAL IMPERATIVES: THE SUPERPOWERS

Wars arise out of concrete issues or generalized fears. In order to reduce the latter and to allow specific conflicts either to be resolved or to develop without war, four imperatives must be heeded.

The first applies to each superpower, and particularly to the U.S. Each must define its national interests in a way that is limited and flexible. All national interests are not equally vital. To act as if any move made by one's opponent, or made by an ally of one's opponent (or made by a third party, but benefiting one's opponent) is automatically a threat to a vital interest is a recipe for overcommitment, inevitable external failures, domestic frustrations, and dangerous confrontations. We have to learn that every Soviet success or advance is neither irreversible nor an American defeat, and that some setbacks are secondary and can be offset by more important progress elsewhere.

The second imperative concerns Soviet-American relations. Any foreign government's ability to change the Soviet system is very limited, and it is impossible to know whether such attempts would make matters better or worse. The U.S. government must therefore concentrate on the Soviets' external behavior and try to affect it by a combination of a number of policies. One consists of keeping the risks and costs of aggressive Soviet moves high: this is why nuclear deterrence, within the limits of morality and prudence suggested above, must be preserved and why credible regional conventional balances (that would rely, whenever possible, on local forces) must be either maintained or built up.

Another policy consists of preventive political and economic diplomacy. Such a policy would attempt to deprive the Soviets of opportunities for expansion by directly addressing problems of social injustice, political oppression, ethnic antagonism, or regional conflicts which Moscow could exploit.

A further policy consists of what might be called détente without illusions, or a balance of power policy with cooperation. This policy would be aimed not at making

Moscow accept American concepts of political stability, but at affecting the intensity with which, and the places where, the Soviets play their own game. It would entail a certain amount of cooperation in areas such as arms control, including cooperation against nuclear proliferation. This approach would encourage most economic, scientific, and cultural exchanges and would also encourage political agreements in areas where both sides have interests and clients, and where conflicts cannot be resolved without the participation of both. A balance of power and cooperation policy would require greater efforts not only at managing crises when they occur, but at preventing them. General agreements on rules may not be possible, but at least mutual communications aimed at defining clearly the limits of what is tolerable, or on the contrary unacceptable, to each side should be encouraged. Moreover, engagement is not only important for short-run problems; it can contribute to increasing transparency and communication over a longer period.

The third imperative affects more than the superpowers and their allies. Precisely because local crises—within or between states—always offer temptation and opportunities for superpower involvement, it will be essential to improve what can be called the conflict resolution machinery available for dealing with such crises. Too many disputes have been left unresolved, sometimes because they are intractable, sometimes because the most brutally effective way used to resolve them in the past—force—no longer works well. Attempts at a solution are, however, the only way of avoiding periodic outbursts of violence or external intrusions in domestic conflicts. These attempts, to be effective, will have to include the more important powers of a given region as well as have the support of the superpowers.

The fourth imperative is to strengthen regional and international organizations and agreements on international rules and procedures for dealing with global problems. Arms control, especially if its scope expands, non-proliferation, the handling of economic issues—from energy to the oceans, from the world monetary system to trade or satellite communications—and the resolution of political conflicts will require institutions for management, enforcement, inspection, adjudication, and arbitration. Increasingly, some granting of powers to a variety of international agencies will become necessary if the world is to live without either a world government or a resort to war as a routine.

## CONCLUSION: AVOIDING ATOMIC ESCAPISM

Where American citizens should stand on the range of moral, political, and strategic dilemmas forced upon us by nuclear weapons must be determined by each individual after careful thought and according to his or her values, judgments, and assumptions. Different individuals will resolve such dilemmas in different ways. But if the answers are to have meaning, they must honestly address the true dilemmas of the Nuclear Age, and not merely ignore them.

Atomic escapism must be avoided. One form of escapism is to believe that nuclear weapons will go away. They will not. Because they will not, mankind must learn to live with them if we are to live at all. The other form of escapism is to think that nuclear weapons can be treated like other military weapons in history. They cannot. And because they are different, humanity must live with them carefully, vigilantly, gingerly, always displaying the utmost caution.

Escapism of either sort presents a falsely attractive world. Avoiding the discomforting dilemmas of nuclear deterrence, however, can be dangerous. If escapism leads to an American nuclear policy that ignores the requirements of deterrence or the requirements of crisis stability, it will not contribute to security. Such escapism may make us feel more comfortable; it will not make us more secure.

The approach to the nuclear dilemma presented in this book is not a comfortable approach, but that is because the nuclear world is not a comfortable world. It is not comfortable because nuclear weapons are enormously destructive, because the Soviet Union and the United States have many conflicting interests, and finally, because man himself is a fallible creature.

In 1934 T. S. Eliot criticized human beings because they:

constantly try to escape
From the darkness outside and within
By dreaming of systems so perfect that no one will need
   to be good.[4]

The darkness outside and within remains. There is no foolproof escape. There is no system so perfect that humanity will be forever safe from the threat of nuclear weapons. Imperfect mortals will still have to be good.

Like Adam and Eve, we have eaten of the tree of knowledge and have been cast into a world where we can never be perfectly secure. This is not, however, a cause for discouragement; for mankind has throughout history lived in a permanent search for security. This quest can and must continue. Humanity's nuclear future need not end in holocaust.

This will be the case only if the men and women of this planet make it so. The truly important steps out of our nuclear dilemma are not imagined leaps into mythical worlds of perfect security. They are not quests for the impossible: a recreation of previous American nuclear supremacy or an early abolition of nuclear weaponry. The most important actions are the modest but real steps toward improved safety that can be taken now. Without them, the future will come without hope. But with such steps, human progress can continue.

This is not a call for "politics as usual." In the foreseeable future, governments will continue to have competing interests, opposing ideologies, and alternative visions of mankind's destiny. And competition in its many forms will continue between the East and the West. But it is possible, and indeed necessary, that such competition will exist with more restraint and more cooperation than has been the case. Even if this happens, however, nobody should be complacent about nuclear deterrence.

Therefore, citizens in free countries must insist that they and their political leaders honestly face the dilemmas of the Nuclear Age. Any form of atomic escapism is a dead end. Living with nuclear weapons is our only hope. It requires that we persevere in reducing the likelihood of war even though we cannot remove the possibility altogether. This challenge will be both demanding and unending, but we need not perish if practical steps continue to be taken. Surely there is no greater test of the human spirit.

## Notes

1. Jonathan Schell, *The Fate of the Earth* (New York: Knopf, 1982), pp. 163–64.

2. Thomas Powers, *Thinking About the Next War* (New York: Knopf, 1982), p. 17.

3. The issue of nuclear proliferation has been dealt with in Chapter 8.

4. T. S. Eliot, *The Rock* (New York: Harcourt, Brace, 1934), p. 42.

# Index